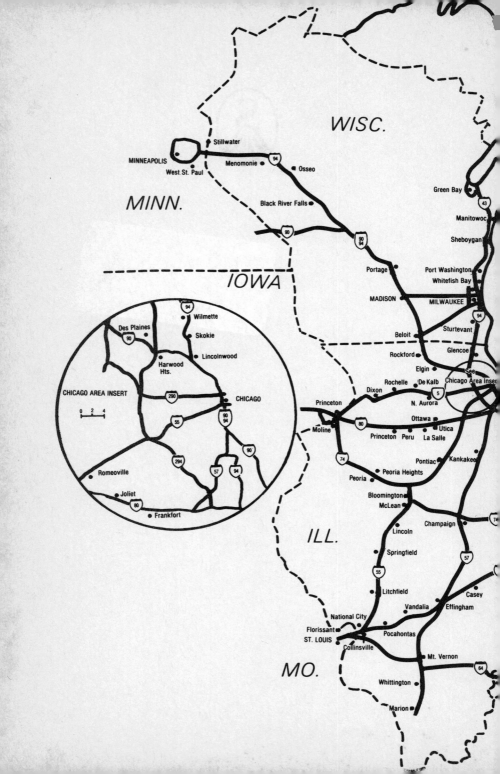

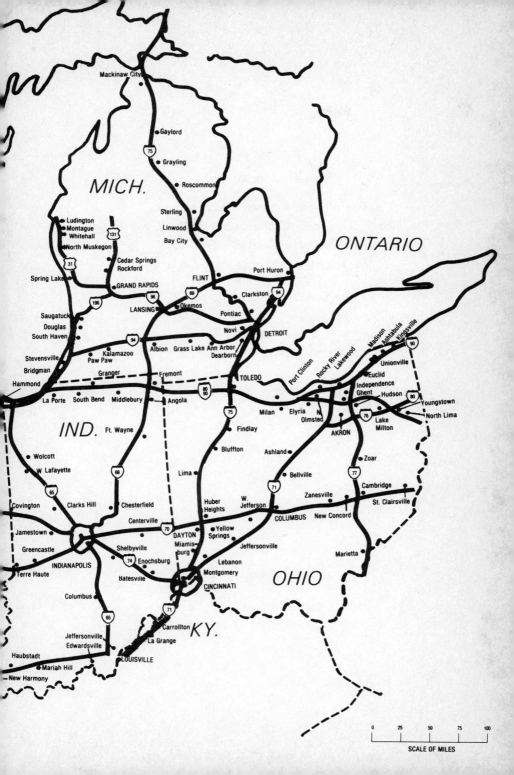

THE INTERSTATE
GOURMET

Midwest

Neal O. Weiner and David Schwartz

SUMMIT BOOKS

NEW YORK

The reader should be aware that the restaurant business is unpredictable. Restaurants change their menus, prices and hours; some even change their names or addresses. While we have made every effort to update this book over the past year, we would be most grateful to hear about any changes you have encountered in your travels so that we may keep future editions up to date.

Copyright © 1986 by The Interstate Gourmet, Inc.
All rights reserved
including the right of reproduction
in whole or in part in any form
Published by SUMMIT BOOKS
A Division of Simon & Schuster, Inc.
Simon & Schuster Building
1230 Avenue of the Americas
New York, New York 10020

SUMMIT BOOKS and colophon are trademarks of Simon & Schuster, Inc.
Designed by Eve Kirch
Illustrations: Kristin Funkhauser
Maps: Mary Lou Brozena
Manufactured in the United States of America

Library of Congress Cataloging in Publication Data
Weiner, Neal O.
    The interstate gourmet—Midwest.
    Includes index.
    1. Restaurants, lunch rooms, etc.—Middle West—Directories. I. Schwartz,
David M.   II. Title.
TX907.W4374   1985   647'.9577   85-25073
ISBN 0-671-52335-X

ACKNOWLEDGMENTS

As always with efforts like this, there are more people to thank than it makes sense to mention. Most special appreciation must go, however, to Merna Holloway and Mary Lou Brozena, who shared the journey and lightened the load in every way.

After them come Frank Bocknick, Bernie and Judy Cantor, Glenn Cantor and Inge Eriks, Frank and Pat Johnson, Leo and Helen Kretzner, Joe McCraith, Kae and Sue Moore, Mary Piscotty, Joe and Mary Romanick, Rosalee and Jim Schneck, and Bob and Laura Stein.

But without leads from those who knew the local area there would be no *Interstate Gourmet* at all. For them we must thank: Molly Abrams, Paula Bivens, Mary Lou Brown, Robert Brown, Leona Carlson, Jan Careaux, Doral Chenoweth, Liz Cook, Pat Coy, Jacque Dickenshield, James Diefenbeck, Valerie Gager, Robin Garr, Marge Hanley, Wayne Hearn, Ann Heller, Gloria Hizer, Dick Houston, Kathy Kelly, Jerry Klein, Dan Kraft, Elizabeth Meegan, Karen Moyars, Karen Palmer, Carol Richardson, Carol Rugg, Virginia Shafer, Ken Shapiro, Sam Shapiro, Sheila Smith, Jane Snow, Jim Stingl, Karen Tancil, Mary Wade, Carol Wait, Sue Wallis, Barney Wolf, and Linda Wolfa.

CONTENTS

Contents

INTRODUCTION

Does a roadside meal *have* to be an exercise in misery? If it can't be a memorable culinary event, couldn't it at least be a window on local life or a sampler of regional cooking? Or at the very least, couldn't the restaurant be pleasant enough to make you feel like you're not still hurtling along at 55 mph while you eat your meal?

Fifty years ago a well-traveled salesman who made good eating a personal mission came to the aid of his fellow motorists. Duncan Hines published a guide to the best roadside restaurants in the land. Though he later sold his name to a cake-mix company, Hines' fame was based on this attempt to solve the where-to-eat-on-the-road dilemma.

Highways are now wider and faster, and the quality of American restaurants has soared. But the highway restaurant problem is worse now than it was in the thirties. Then you could see what you were driving through. With luck you could end up in a local establishment of some sort. Now freeways give us the impression that fast-food chains are the traveler's only option; worse yet, turnpike service-area restaurants make high-school cafeteria food seem exquisite by comparison. And for the privilege of eating this plastic chow in plastic surroundings, the victim discovers the modern meaning of "highway robbery." Clearly the time has come for an updated version of Hines' efforts.

We had to chart a new course—the U.S. highway system had given way to the interstate system of the sixties. So we explored the network of freeways from one end of the country to the other, wandering a mile or two (occasionally more) from the exit ramps

11

to sniff out restaurants with appealing food, agreeable prices, and local color—places that would make for a relaxing break from the interstate grind. And we wrote down careful, stop-sign-by-stop-sign directions so our readers could find them with ease.

There's no limit to what can be found just beyond the great green interstate signs: hole-in-the-wall ethnic eateries where the emphasis falls decidedly on the food, not the decor; barbecue shacks whose hickory-smoked aromas greet you long before you open the car door; little breakfast nooks that make their French toast from challah and serve the eggs the very day they are laid; a small-town family restaurant where the Austrian owner demonstrates the making of strudel right out in the middle of the dining room; Irish pubs and Jewish delis; Cincinnati chili parlors, Michigan pastie shops, and Chicago-style pizzerias; bakeries, ice creameries, purveyors of old-fashioned chicken dinners, and the avant-garde creators of the New American Cuisine.

It may sound like an unlikely crowd, this cross-cultural pastiche of roadside restaurants. And the truth is that all these places have but two things in common: The first is that we liked them, and this for any of many possible reasons; and the second is that they are all relatively accessible from the interstate. Although for a few very special restaurants we would stretch our preferred 5-minute limit to 10, the majority of our selections can be reached in less time than it takes to negotiate the restroom line at a turnpike service area in midsummer.

Here's what we came up with in our journeys through the Midwest. We like to think it would have done Duncan Hines proud.

Wisconsin

MADER'S, *Exit 1R, Milwaukee*

Once upon a time Mader's was the kind of down-to-earth, intimate restaurant we love to recommend, but that was when big steins of Milwaukee's favorite beverage sold for 3 cents each, two for a nickel. Now, the restaurant's "castleized" interior is home to $1,000,000 worth of medieval armor, and dinners are $11–$16. Pschorr Brau beer comes by the glass, stein, baby boot, regular boot, king's boot, quarter-barrel, or half-barrel for somewhere between $1 and $145.

In short, Mader's has the reputation of being *the* Milwaukee restaurant. It's been around since 1902, and though success and innumerable awards have certainly changed its character, it's still the place that visiting celebrities get taken.

We tend to be hard on places like this, but there is simply no denying that the restaurant's reputation is deserved. Everything we tasted was somewhere between very good and excellent, from a yellow split-pea soup with a deep smoky flavor, to superb buttered noodles and a mellowed, deepened version of sauerkraut. The Wiener schnitzel itself was less interesting than its accompaniments, we thought, but still very good. Next time we'll get the roast pork shank, which is a Mader's specialty, or the sauerbraten with raisins and almonds. Bavarian-style cooking seems to be what Mader's does best.

Luncheons are $4.75 to $8.25, ranging from salads to wurst platters to a sirloin sandwich. Mostly, though, it's the likes of goulash, pork loin with apple-raisin dressing, or tenderloin tips à la Deutsch.

An added benefit to a visit here is that much of what is left of Old Milwaukee seems to be in the urban preservation area that surrounds Mader's. There's a 105-year-old sausage factory right across the street, for example, and the old Pabst Brewery is only 7 blocks away.

HOURS   Mon. 11 am–9 pm; Tues.–Sat. 11:30 am–11:30 pm; Sun. 10:30 am–9 pm.

SPECS   1037 N. 3rd St.; (414) 271-3377; major cards; full bar.

DIRECTIONS   **Northbound:** Take Exit 1R. Go through the little underpass and then 3 blocks to 3rd St. Turn left onto 3rd and go 2 blocks. It's on the left.

Southbound: Take Exit 1R (Wells St.). Bear left on the ramp following signs for Wells St. At the end of the ramp go straight onto Wells and go 6 blocks to 3rd St. Turn left onto 3rd and go 3 blocks. **Mader's** is on the left.

     Easy to get to even though downtown. Parking may be a problem. If you've got the bread, let the valet take care of it.

SOLLY'S, *Exits 3C & 4A, Milwaukee*

     If you're heading north you will pass within a block and a half of 1982's "best hamburger in Milwaukee," according to *Milwaukee* magazine. If you're southbound it's still less than a mile, so consider a quick, cheap, and delicious stop at this clean, pleasantly plastic, purely local restaurant. The waitress will shout the order back to the grill man, who works in clear sight of everyone to produce greasy but great, supersimple burgers garnished only by fried onions and served on a good hard roll with lots of butter. At $1.25, it's a real treat—a welcome relief from the more trendy "8 ounces of pure sirloin of beef, charbroiled to perfection, on a Kaiser roll beneath blue cheese and bacon—$3.95."

     It is a joy to see them doing one thing well; doing it simply, cheaply, and without pretension. Which is not meant to say that Solly's 25 other sandwiches are not good, or that there's no point in trying one of the 6 dinner plates at $3.80–$5.25. It's just that we were so happy with what we got, we lost all desire to explore further.

     Take a seat at the counter and give this humble eatery a try. If you're like us, you'll fall in love.

HOURS   Tues.–Sat. 10 am–9 pm. Closed Sun. & Mon.

SPECS   4629 W. Port Washington Rd.; (414) 332-8808; no cards; no liquor.

DIRECTIONS   Northbound: Take Exit 4A (Hampton). Bear right at the end of the ramp onto Port Washington Rd. The restaurant is 1 block, on the right.

Southbound: Take Exit 3C (Capital Drive) and exit in 1½ blocks for Port Washington Rd. Turn left onto Port Washington, go 0.8 mile, and it's on the left.

JACK PRANDL'S WHITEFISH BAY INN,
Exit 5A, Whitefish Bay

There's something warm, wonderful, and timeless about Jack Prandl's. Perhaps it's the homey way the old-fashioned radiators stick out without apologies—an insouciance characteristic of institutions so well established they know they have nothing to prove and are therefore left free to be their own excellent selves.

We liked this place, and even without knowing that it's been here since 1915, you can feel its solidity in the familylike warmth that runs through the people who work here. The helpful waitress explained in detail the making of Prandl's famous German pancake (fry it, bake it so that the edges lift up, use lots of butter, confectioner's sugar, and lemon), a dish that is remarkably light and simply superb, serving either as dinner for one or dessert for four ($6.95).

We also tasted some excellent corned beef here—sweetly spicy, and very, very tender. The ribs, too, were a wonderful combination of spices, seemingly both mellowed and sharpened by a deep smoky flavor. Broiled whitefish is a Jack Prandl specialty, but we preferred the broiled catfish, which may be out of place in this part of the country, but tasted wonderful anyway.

We concluded that whatever you order at Prandl's you're going to get more than your money's worth. Dinners are $9.25–$12.95, luncheons from $5.85–$7.25. A few sandwiches are available at $4–$8 during dinner hours, $3–$6.95 at lunch.

If you aren't going to have that German pancake for your main dish, we really don't want you to forego it as dessert. But we must tell you about Prandl's Schaum torte, which is a hardened meringue shell filled with ice cream and strawberries —as good a dessert as you'll come across anywhere, and there's perfectly brewed coffee to make the meal's end a moment of sheer perfection.

HOURS Mon.–Thurs. 11:30 am–2:30 pm & 5–9 pm; Fri. & Sat. 11:30 am–2:30 pm & 5–11 pm. Closed Sun. & major holidays.

SPECS 1319 E. Henry Clay St.; (414) 964-3800; major cards; full bar; children's menu.

DIRECTIONS **Northbound:** Take Exit 5A for Silver Spring Drive. Turn left at the light and go 1 block to Silver Spring Drive. ■ Turn right onto Silver Spring and go 1 mile to Lake Drive. Turn right onto Lake and go 0.5 mile to Henry Clay. Turn left onto Henry Clay, and the place is 2 blocks, on the right.

Southbound: Take Exit 5A for Silver Spring Drive. Turn right at the end of the ramp onto Silver Spring, then as above from ■.

SMITH BROS. FISH SHANTY RESTAURANT
and others, *Exit 24, Port Washington*

We've come across many a seafood restaurant that sells its own fresh fish, and even a few perched at the water's edge that occasionally pull out a trout or a catfish to supplement the regular offerings. But Smith Bros. is the only one we've visited with its own fishing fleet! Or is it the other way around? It seems that the Smith family of Port Washington have been commercial fishermen on the Great Lakes ever since Gilbert Smith headed west in 1848!

That makes for a 137-year-old family business. The restaurant is a comparative newcomer—merely 50 years old, but still old enough to have long ago outgrown the seven stools and single deep-fryer with which it began. Part of the large place is comfortably old and can boast some wonderful paintings of fishing scenes. Things get a bit hokey toward the wall of windows with the view of Lake Michigan, but not so much as to become annoying.

History and decor should not obscure the fact that the broiled whitefish, for which the restaurant is famous, is very, very good ($6.95 for lunch, $9.25 for dinner). It was, in fact, the best version of this regional specialty we found, mildly seasoned with a judicious use of paprika. Use the lemon, but skip the tartar sauce, which overpowers the fish's delicate flavor.

As good as the whitefish was the smoked chub ($5.45). The Smith Bros. smoke their own and make all those delicacies that you probably associate with Jewish delis and assumed were made in Brooklyn.

What we tried here was better than anything we ever got back East. Since the appetizer version of the chub is only $2.75, you can taste what may well be the world's best example of this delicacy for very little money indeed. (And for not much time, either, since the store next to the restaurant sells all kinds of smoked fish to go.)

Quality at the restaurant is uneven. Soups were very good, salads better than average, and the famous lemon pie was only "eh," as were the scallops. Stick to the whitefish and the chub, however, and we promise you happiness. Dinners are $8.75–$14.45, lunches $4.95–$9.95. A fried fish noon buffet is available weekdays at $4.75. Sandwiches are $2.50–$3.25.

Though Smith Bros. is a true family operation, do not expect family intimacy. Aside from the fleet, the restaurant, and the store, the Smiths own a Best Western Motel right opposite the restaurant, two more restaurants in Los Angeles, and at least one retail outlet in Milwaukee. "Progress" to be sure, but then 137 years is a long time.

Port Washington is a lovely little town and a delightful rest for the traveler. If the Smith Bros. is too pricey, consider **Bernie's Fine Meats** across the street (local cheese and his own sausages) and **Harry's** restaurant (not very special), 1 block up.

HOURS Daily 11:30 am–9 pm. Closed Thanksgiving, Christmas.

SPECS 100 N. Franklin Ave.; (414) 284-5592; major cards; full bar.

DIRECTIONS From Exit 24 turn right if northbound and left if southbound onto Route 3. Follow Route 3 for 3 miles to Port Washington. The restaurant is right at Lake Michigan at the end of the road in the center of town.

SCHULZ'S RESTAURANT
GOSSE'S, *Exit 53, Sheboygan*

Sheboygan is a working man's town, and the restaurants we turned up there are working men's eateries that make no sacrifice of quality. In fact, we doubt you'll find a better "brat" anywhere than you can buy for $1.25 at **Schulz's,** and we know that nowhere will you find a better version of the 90-cent "torte" than the one at Gosse's.

"Brat" means a bratwurst sandwich. Usually it's the familiar-looking sausage laid between two halves of a roll, but at Schulz's it's a hamburgerish-looking patty with seasonings and a wonderful flavor that's all its own. Charbroil it, put it on a good hard roll, top it with a pat of butter, add a bit of raw onion, and you've got yourself a true gem of American ethnic regional cooking.

There's also good reason to try some of the smoky, hearty, split-pea soup at Schulz's. It comes with lots of ham and costs but 60 cents a cup. There are lots of other inexpensive sandwiches in this very plain eatery with two walls of painted cinder block and one of tacky paneling, but why mess around with perfection?

Do not, however, order the apple pie at Schulz's. It was honest apple pie, and it is made, as all such pies should be, by a little old lady who lives nearby. But just half a mile down the road is what has got to be one of the all-time great American desserts.

Forget any associations, legal or culinary, that you might have for the word "torte." The Sheboygan torte probably arose from the Sacher torte and other fancy-sounding items of Viennese baking, but by now it is absolutely *sui generis.* The one you'll find just down the road at **Gosse's** is a 3-x-3-x-2-inch-tall near-cube, the first stratum of which is ¼ inch of light and tasty graham cracker crumbs. Next comes 1½ inches of egg white, incredibly, almost divinely, light, and in it are suspended delicate little poppy seeds. Whipped cream occupies the next ½ inch, and finally a scant ¹⁄₁₆ inch of pure coconut covers the visible surface.

This torte, or whatever you call it, was truly delicious—so light you hardly realized you were eating, yet so full of flavor it felt like a cascade of fireworks in the mouth. Don't miss it, even if you're already late. Brats too at Gosse's, but come for the torte.

HOURS   **Schulz's:** Mon.–Thurs. 11 am–11 pm; Fri.–Sat. 11 am–12:30 am. Closed Sun., major holidays, and 1 week in August and 1 in April
Gosse's: Mon.–Sat. 5 am–7 pm; Sun. 7 am–5 pm. Closed major holidays.

SPECS   **Schulz's:** 1644 Calumet Drive; (414) 452-1880; no cards; no liquor.
Gosse's: 1637 Gelle Ave. (corner of Calumet); (414) 458-1147; no cards; no liquor.

DIRECTIONS   From Exit 53 go east on Route 23 for almost 2 miles to the light at Business 42. Turn left and follow Business 42 for ½ mile through a jog to the right. **Schulz's** is on the left. **Gosse's** is 0.4 mile straight ahead on Business 42 (Calumet Drive), on the right, on the corner.

THE PENGUIN DRIVE-IN, *Exit 76, Manitowoc*

This is a real, honest-to-God drive-in left over from the days when it wasn't all that unusual to see a huge penguin atop a tiny roadside eatery—a bit of Los Angeles architecture on the shores of Lake Michigan.

The hamburger was really very good (the secret is to smother it in butter, which seems to be a Wisconsin trademark—see **Sol-**

ly's, p. 14). The fried chicken was *very* fried, and the famous custard is just okay ice cream.

Eat outside in the semicircle of cars or come in to the counter and the not-so-badly paneled dining area.

HOURS   Mon.–Thurs. 6 am–midnight; Fri. & Sat. 6 am–1 am; Sun. 6:30 am–midnight.

DIRECTIONS   From Exit 76 turn right if northbound and left if southbound. Go 1 very quick mile. It's on the left.

BEERNTSEN'S CONFECTIONERY, *Exit 76, Manitowoc*

The Midwest must have some deep and abiding affection for its ancient candy store/ice cream parlors. We stumbled across no less than four of them in our midwestern travels, while four times as many miles brought us exactly none in the rest of the country.

Of the four, Beerntsen's was surely the most beautiful. Up front its dark and venerable wooden fixtures display a miniature wonderland of hand-dipped chocolates, and kids, anxious to get every bit of goodness their quarters will buy, still come in and hesitatingly ask how much tax there is on 24 cents' worth of polar stars.

The homemade ice cream comes from the fountain, which is also at the front of the store. And good, tasty, honest ice cream it is—not that trendy, expensive stuff overloaded with butterfat and named after cookies. You can also get homemade chili, about 20 simple sandwiches (80 cents–$1.60) and a dozen lunches with names like "beans and wieners," "au gratin potatoes and bacon," or "chicken stew" ($1.30). Dessert might be a Wisconsin beauty, a Kewpie doll special, a turtle, or maybe even something as simple as a hot fudge sundae ($1.20–$1.50). Egg shakes, milk shakes, malted milks, lime freezes, and phosphates—all that you might want is here, at a price that is right.

The fun really begins, however, when you pass through the mahogany archway into the back of the store. There you are greeted by three rows of old walnut booths, the tables of which boast veneer inlays. The ceiling soars to 25 feet, mirrors abound, and there are fine little antique lights and coat hooks.

Beerntsen's is, in short, a delightful step back in time—beautiful to look at, good to the taste, and lots of fun.

HOURS Daily 10 am–10 pm. Closed Christmas, Easter, New Year's.

SPECS 108 N. 8th St.; (414) 684-9616; no cards; no liquor.

DIRECTIONS From Exit 76 turn right if northbound and left if southbound onto Route 151 toward Manitowoc. Go 1.8 miles to light at 26th St. Turn left and then right again with traffic, and then go 1.2 miles to 8th St. Turn left onto 8th. The confectionery is 5 blocks, on the left.

BUDDHA'S SAUSAGE, *Exit 110, Green Bay*

It was the name that first attracted us—we didn't know he ate that sort of thing—and the colorful sign—a hand-painted version of a bearded butcher with his arm raised above his head like a waiter carrying an invisible tray.

Idiosyncrasy leads to excellence, we suspect, and so we checked it out and found the shop a delightful jumble of reasonably priced, deliciously spiced delicatessen goodies. The ham sausage was absolutely stupendous; the summer sausage and beer salami only a little less good.

They don't make sandwiches here, but 50 cents will buy you all you need in the meat department. Then walk across the street to a little bakery and for another 12 cents buy yourself a good hard roll. There's soda back at Buddha's. The people are friendly and will be glad to help a traveler in search of a tasty bargain.

HOURS Mon.–Fri. 8 am–6 pm; Sat. 8 am–3 pm. Closed Sun.

SPECS 1734 Main St.; (414) 468-5423; no cards; beer only.

DIRECTIONS From Exit 110 (Mason St.) turn left if northbound, right if southbound, onto Route V (Mason St.). Go 1.7 very fast miles and then bear right onto Main. Go 0.6 mile on Main. The shop is on the left.

JOHN NERO'S RESTAURANT, *Exit 119B, Green Bay*

* *Untried but likely*

For 35 years John Nero wanted to build a restaurant that would look onto the lovely limestone quarry in which he swam as a boy. Now he's done it, creating, in his words, "a little bit of Door County in Green Bay." The pleasant, up-to-date design of the restaurant uses natural woods and earthy colors to enhance the view—nothing all that remarkable, but in good taste and a far cry from anything that perches by the roadside.

For 30 years John's was located in a nearby shopping center where it earned a reputation for good, straight American food at reasonable prices. Natural ingredients set the tone, most everything was from scratch, and complete dinners went from $4.20–$5.95, including soup, salad, potato, vegetable, croissant, beverage, and dessert. The soups and rolls are said to be especially good, but it is for his pies that John is known all over Green Bay.

How deserved the reputation is we cannot say. The new restaurant had not quite opened when we came through, and the old one had already been closed down. But if pride of ownership is any index of quality (and we think it is), then we doubt you'll go far wrong at Nero's.

HOURS Mon.–Sat. 6 am–10 pm; Sun. 8 am–2 pm. Closed major holidays and a week in May.

SPECS 2130 Velp Ave.; (414) 434-3400; AE; no liquor; children's menu.

DIRECTIONS From Exit 119B (US 41 South) go south on US 41 ½ mile to Velp Ave. Exit. Turn right onto Velp and go ¼ mile. **Nero's** is on the right.

Missouri
Illinois

Missouri

CUNETO HOUSE OF PASTA
LOU BOCCARDI'S, *Exit for I-44, St. Louis*

We heard from more than one authority that **Cuneto** was the best restaurant in the Hill section of St. Louis, the town's old Italian neighborhood where trattorias are about as common as mailboxes. To judge from the lines, that advice was good. Too good, it seemed, since the wait can be anywhere from 20 minutes to 2 hours (dinners $5–$9.25, lunches $3.25–$4.50).

So over we went to **Lou Boccardi's** right across the street and found a charming little restaurant gaily decorated with murals that we can only describe as Italian-American folk art. The diminutive rooms had a childlike quality that makes you happy despite yourself, and for that alone we'd recommend a stop. The murals may have to be your chief pleasure here—the toasted ravioli were only "eh"; the cannelloni were better, but not memorable. We did love the house dressing, however, an anchovy-based affair that had a lot of character without getting pushy. (Dinners $3.25–$7.95, pizza $3.95–$5.25, sandwiches $3.55–$5.)

HOURS **Cuneto:** Mon–Thurs. 11 am–2 pm & 5–10:30 pm; Fri. 11 am–2 pm & 5pm–midnight; Sat. 5 pm–midnight. Closed Sun. & major holidays.
Lou's: Mon.–Thurs. 11 am–12:30 am; Fri. & Sat. 11 am–1:30 am; Sun. 3–11 pm. Closed major holidays.

SPECS   **Cuneto:** 5453 Magnolia Ave.; (314) 781-1135; major cards; full bar.
Lou's: 5424 Magnolia Ave.; (314) 647-1151; V, MC; full bar.

DIRECTIONS   Take I-44 west from I-55 for 2.6 miles to Exit 287 (Kingshighway). Turn left onto Kingshighway and go 0.4 mile to Southwest; turn right onto Southwest. Go 5 blocks to the intersection with Magnolia. **Lou's** is on the left; **Cuneto** is on the right.

AMIGHETTI'S BAKERY, *I-44 Exit, St. Louis*

Once upon a time Louis Amighetti ran a tiny little bakery. Then his only problem was how to produce enough good, crusty Italian bread. If he had had it his way, that would still be the case, but his wife, Marge, had other ideas. In 1961 she started selling sandwiches through a window that looks directly onto the street. She had the imagination to flavor the sandwiches with a garlicky mayonnaise dressing, and soon the bakery was a St. Louis institution.

Pizza soon followed. Not just ordinary pizzas, mind you, but also a rolled version that sports alternating spirals of bread and red sauce ($1 per slice, $7 for the loaf).

Success. Now there's a new and very pleasant dining area, a separate Italian ice cream parlor with excellent homemade *gelato,* and even a little patio for fast-lunching *al fresco.*

The sandwiches are modestly priced, and they are indeed good, as was the pizza—not the best we've ever come across, but good enough. What we liked best of all was Marge Amighetti herself, whose infectious energy and effusive warmth permeated everything and almost demanded that everyone have a good time.

"My customers' smiles are my best payment," she says. If it's true, she is a very rich lady.

HOURS   Tues.–Fri. 9 am–7 pm; Sat. 9 am–6 pm. Closed Sun., Mon., major holidays, and 2 weeks after Labor Day.

SPECS   Wilson and Marconi Aves.; (314) 776-2855; no cards; beer & wine.

DIRECTIONS Take I-44 West for 2.6 miles to Exit 287 for Kingshighway. Turn left onto Kingshighway and go 0.4 mile to Southwest. Turn right onto Southwest and go 1 long block to Marconi. Turn right, and go 3 blocks to Wilson. It's on the corner, on the right.

Illinois

THE STOCKYARDS INN
SCOVILLE'S CAFE, *Exit 2, National City*

We figured that there just had to be good steaks at the East St. Louis stockyards. The country's largest cattle exchange just had to have a restaurant that serves the very best of what passes through its pens.

We were right about the restaurant (actually there are two of them) and right about the steaks (they were very good indeed). But we were wrong about most everything else—starting with the location. The yards are in National City, not East St. Louis. Nor do they constitute the largest cattle exchange—more hogs pass through than steers. What's more, there's no slaughtering done here. The steaks come from the same wholesalers who supply the other restaurants in St. Louis.

We were not wrong about the flavor, however. Wherever they come from, the steaks are excellent at both **Scoville's** and the **Inn,** but in ways appropriate to the very different character of the two restaurants.

The **Inn** has two personalities, one of them a frowsy, funky cafeteria whose main concern is to breakfast the farmers who must wait around all morning to see what prices their livestock fetch. For them it's biscuits and gravy and inexpensive lunches. For the businessmen, the packing company agents, and the commodity brokers there's the Red Room, where steaks at $7.95, steak sandwiches at $4.85, and $3.95 barbecued pork are what it's all about, plus roast beef dinner ($4.50), pork chops ($4.95), and even a few interlopers "from Neptune's realm," as the menu says ($4.50–$5.25). Our excellent fillet was served to us in a room that was sort of macho-plush—a bare floor, Formica tables, red wallpaper, and red upholstered chairs with a substantial array of oil paintings on the walls. A place meant for business deals.

Scoville's Café is essentially a truck stop. At least its primary clientele seems to be the men who haul the huge semis laden with 3 stories of squealing porkers. If so, it's got to be the most historical truck stop in America. The 111-year-old hotel that houses Scoville's was once a fashionable dance hall. Now its grand ballroom is painted that dismal shade of green, and the café's U-shaped counter huddles down at one end of the cavernous room like a mouse in Grand Central Station. Here $5.25 got us a grilled club steak that was good, but not super, with mashed potatoes that did not come out of a box. There are 20 sandwiches from $1–$2 and lots of daily specials at about $3.50. Burgers go for $1.10. Very good cornbread.

In all these eateries the food is very good for the price you pay, and though they display clear class differences, all of them are hearty, masculine places with lots of character and all the local color you could ask for—more color, maybe, than you want. It is not a pretty sight to see how the animals are treated here, to hear their squeals or smell their droppings. But it's a lesson in realities. If you're curious but don't want to face it all squarely, come after the noon hour. By that time most of the animals have been shipped out, though enough are left to give you the general idea.

HOURS   **Inn:** Cafeteria: Mon.–Fri. 5:30 am–9:30 pm. Restaurant: Mon.–Fri. 11:30 am–2 pm. Closed weekends.
Scoville's: Mon.–Thurs. 24 hours; Fri. until 4 pm; Sat. 6 am–1 pm; Sun. 2 pm–midnight

SPECS   **Inn:** (618) 274-6416; major cards; full bar.
Scoville's: (618) 271-3716; no cards; full bar.

DIRECTIONS   Take Exit 2 for Route 3 North (St. Clair Ave.) and go north on Route 3 for 0.2 mile. You'll be led straight to the stockyards. **Scoville's** is right near the entrance. For the **Inn,** continue about 100 yards into the yards and turn right. It's at the end of the road.

EL DORADO RESTAURANT, *Exit 11, Collinsville*

There really is a good Mexican restaurant in Collinsville, Illinois—a restaurant so good, in fact, that it need make no apologies to its immediate progenitors in southern California, and maybe not even to its distant ancestors south of the border.

The essential story can be told in a few brief clauses: They make their own light and tasty chips; the rice was superbly seasoned with capers; the beans were very, very good; and the pork simmered in hot chili sauce was wonderfully rich and delicious, more flavorful than it was explosive. "Carnitas" they call it, and it is the house specialty at $8.50. Most dishes, however, are in the $3–$5 range, which makes the El Dorado about as good and cheap as a restaurant can be.

In such eateries you pay for the food, not the looks. From the outside the architect appears to have started on a miniature cathedral, decided instead on a Taco Bell, and then reverted to the original plan by adding a nominal second story for the glory of God. It's too silly to be pretentious, and it matches to a T the sparsely furnished Tex-Mex interior.

Our only complaint about the El Dorado was the water. It was awful, but its undrinkability only added an unplanned note of authenticity. There was plenty of Dos Equis instead.

HOURS Sun.–Thurs. 11 am–11 pm, Fri. & Sat. 11 am–1 am. Closed major holidays.

SPECS 1701 Collinsville Rd.; (217) 344-6435; no cards; full bar.

DIRECTIONS From Exit 11 turn right onto Route 157 and go 1.4 miles to the light. Turn right and go 0.2 mile, and it's on the left.

ARISTON CAFÉ, *Exit 52, Litchfield*

For 50 years the Ariston has been perched by old Route 66 serving solid American food to travelers who appreciate a bit of class.

Although *ariston* means "best" in Greek (as in *aristo*cracy) there's nothing especially upper class about the brick building that houses the café—it looks like an old airplane hangar, and the ancient neon sign out front has a down-home, 1930-ish look about it. Aside from an endless soup and salad bar and a few Mexican dishes, the menu is as pedestrian as any diner's, and the prices are within reach of the traveling proletariat—burgers for $1.35, dinners from $4.25–$6.75.

Class here comes from the small touches—white tablecloths, for example, and a fresh yellow flower on every table; napkins folded to resemble flames, and milk glass chandeliers. These gestures, which we much appreciated, mix with the old wood of the booths and the venerable red-padded chairs to make a pleasing blend of funk and formality that is sure to bring relief to the travel-weary soul. For many people this is *the* famous old stop between St. Louis and Chicago.

It was at the Ariston that we met a pair of journalists from National Public Radio who were doing a story on old Route 66. They loved it as much as we did, and so will you, unless you're a food snob. What we sampled was fair to good—better than chain restaurant food, to be sure, and certainly good enough for a highway stop, but nothing very special.

HOURS Mon. & Wed.–Fri. 11 am–11 pm; Sat. 7 am–11 pm; Sun. 7 am–10 pm.

SPECS Route 16 & Route 66; (217) 324-2023; V, MC; full bar.

DIRECTIONS **Northbound:** From Exit 52 go right ½ mile to second light. It's on the right.

Southbound: From Exit 52 go left 0.9 mile to second light. It's on the right.

THE ROSE
CASA GONZALES, *Exit 94, Springfield*

We include these two new suburban restaurants only so you'll be able to find a convenient lunch in the Springfield area. They're just 3 blocks from the exit, and while neither is really our kind of place, each does all right in its own way.

The Rose is a classy-looking but still informal version of the all-too-familiar natural wood–Victoriana look, with your basic QRS menu—quiche, Reuben, and spinach salad. Soup and half a sandwich are $3.95, and a ½-pound hamburger is $4.45. Dinners are $7–$11.

Casa Gonzales from the outside is a sort of Hacienda del Taco, with an interior done up to look like a garden patio. The Americanized Mexican food is only fair to good. Lunch specials are from $2.25 and dinners are mostly $3–$5.

> **HOURS** **The Rose:** Mon.–Sat. 11 am–3 pm & 5–11 pm; Sun. 10:30 am–10 pm.
> **Casa Gonzales:** Sun.–Thurs. 11 am–11 pm; Fri. & Sat. 11 am–midnight.

> **SPECS** **The Rose:** 2830 Stevenson Drive; (217) 529-6623; V, MC, AE; full bar.
> **Casa Gonzales:** 2840 Stevenson Drive; (217) 529-5759; M. V; full bar.

DIRECTIONS Go 0.3 mile west from Exit 94. Both places are on the left, right next to each other.

SOUTHERN AIR, *Exit 98, Springfield*

If you're looking for a really good dinner between St. Louis and Chicago, we think you'll do no better than at the Southern Air Supper Club. It's not a bargain ($12–$16), and the menu is pretty much straight American stuff (exceptions allowed for chicken Cordon Bleu and "fillet parmesan"), but what they do they seem to do very well here, from the superb barbecued ribs that they smoke themselves to the excellent coffee that is ground in the restaurant.

29

Ribs are really the Southern Air's specialty ($12.95 as dinner, $4.95 as an appetizer). The flavor of hickory smoke penetrates deeply into the tender meat, and the sauce is redolent with lovely spices. Vegetables are not ignored—the broccoli in hollandaise was excellent and the rice pilaf had been interestingly prepared in a seasoned chicken broth (order it instead of the baked potato). Even the French pastries ($1.95) scored well—light, memorable, and not oversweet.

As for looks, the Southern Air is a huge red farmhouse from the 1850s, done up inside with a sort of overstuffed 1890s look. Not garish or offensive, mind you, but the white tablecloths, oil paintings, heavy wallpaper, and gilted chairs make for an atmosphere of luxury without elegance.

If the ribs are good, who cares? And the people are very friendly.

HOURS   Mon.–Fri. 5–11 pm; Sat. 5 pm–midnight; Sun. 10:30 am–2 pm & 5–10 pm.

SPECS   3045 Clear Lake Ave.; (217) 522-6951; AE, CB, DC; full bar.

DIRECTIONS   From Exit 98 go 0.6 mile west toward Springfield (easy driving). On the right.

LINCOLN DEPOT, *Exits 123 & 133, Lincoln*

We have seen in our day many a train station turned restaurant that claims to be the town's best eatery. The decor is usually Victorian, the prices are not cheap, and the boast is, unfortunately, often true.

So it is in Lincoln, where the decoration is more tastefully carried out than is the very uninspired cooking, so far as we could judge from an $11.25 breakfast buffet.

Perhaps it's unfair to judge a place from its buffets. Sitting around in steam tables does little for food, and its preparation *en masse* ought to be confined to schools and hospitals. But the manager boasted of this affair, so we figure it's fair game.

Hamburgers and fancy sandwiches are $2.25 to $3.25; soup and salad, $3.25. Dinners are mostly steak and seafood augmented by a few chicken dishes, $5.45–$11.25. And it *was* the best in town.

HOURS Mon.–Sat. 11 am–2 pm & 5–10 pm; Sun. 10 am–9:30 pm.

SPECS 101 Chicago St.; (217) 735-4433; major cards; full bar; children's menu.

DIRECTIONS It's far, but by reversing the directions you can lose almost no time at all. (Southbound leaves town by reversing northbound directions and vice versa).

Northbound: Take Exit 123 for Business 55. Go 3.7 miles to the light at 5th St. Turn right and follow the traffic for 1.1 miles to Broadway. Turn right, go 1 block, and the depot is on the corner, on the right.

Southbound: Take Exit 133 (Business 55). Turn left onto Business 55 and go 1.7 miles to the Holiday Inn. Bear left at the inn and go straight ahead 1.8 miles to Broadway (you'll be traveling on Regent St. which will change its name to Kickapoo St.). Turn right on Broadway, go 1 block and it's on the corner, on the left.

GEM CONEY ISLAND RESTAURANT,
Exits 123 & 133, Lincoln

Since 1919 the Gem has been purveyor of foot-long hot dogs to Lincoln, Illinois, a town honest Abe did the legal work for, and the first city to bear his name.

No one knows exactly when or why a small lunchroom in the middle of the prairie got named for the seaside playground in Brooklyn, but as if to legitimatize it, there's a wall-sized photo mural of the sea that looks as if it's about to roll in on the restaurant's floor and sweep before it the orange vinyl booths, the counter, and the cheap Tiffany-style lamps.

The place has character that transcends decor. Order one egg, you get two; order two, you get three. And so on. It's the kind of small-town restaurant where everyone knows everyone and more energy goes into the joking than the cooking.

A red hot is $1.05. For $2.60 you can get a cold pork loin sandwich; $1.80 buys a sandwich of country sausage. Homemade soups are 80 cents and 6 humble dinners run between $4 and $5.

HOURS   Mon.–Sat. 5:30 am–2:30 pm. Closed Sun. & major holidays.

SPECS   414 Pulaski St.; (217) 732-3296; no cards; no liquor.

DIRECTIONS   Far, but if you leave by reversing the directions you did not come in on (northbound reverses southbound directions, etc.) you will lose very little time.

Northbound: Take Exit 123 for Business 55. Go 3.7 miles to the light at 5th St. Turn right and follow traffic for 1 mile to Pulaski St. Turn right, go 1½ blocks, and it's on the left.

Southbound: Take Exit 133 (Business 55). Turn left onto Business 55 and go 1.7 miles to the Holiday Inn. Bear left at the Inn and go straight ahead for 1.8 miles on Regent St. (which becomes Kickapoo) to Pulaski St. Turn right on Pulaski, go ½ block, and it's on the right.

DIXIE TRUCKER'S HOME, *Exit 145, McLean*

Ask any gearjammer for the best truck stop between Chicago and St. Louis, and you're almost sure to be told about the Dixie. It took us a while, but we think we finally figured out why.

It wasn't the food, which was about the same as any other truck stop (canned vegetables in an okay soup, gummy cherry pie, and an exactly-what-you'd-expect hamburger for $1.40). And it certainly wasn't the dining room (about as plain and bare as a bone chewed clean by a pack of dogs). There *is* a lot of trucker's gear for sale here, and the truckers' cult is maintained by segregating the drivers into their own dining room. But that can be found at dozens of truck stops around the country. What made the Dixie special?

In the parking lot we saw a Mercury Marquis from Texas driven by an overdressed woman with a prissy little lap dog. The next spot was taken by a pale young couple in an old gas guzzler loaded to the gills with household items—Chicago-bound from Arkansas. Then came a Mercedes, and then a baby blue, sunbleached bus from Arizona, its faded letters announcing a traveling gospel team; there was a black couple traveling with four children and a couple of pet chickens; a BMW; and a dusty farmer in his pickup truck.

It was night. The stars and the vast expanse of the land reminded us that this is America, that we were on old Route 66, and that at this spot more than any other you can feel the romance of the American road—southerners moving north to Chicago, easterners headed west to LA, and all of them thrown democratically together at the Dixie for no other reason than that it is open 24 hours, and because its lights offer comfort out here on the lonely prairie.

HOURS   Daily 24 hours.

SPECS   (309) 874-2323; major cards; no liquor.

DIRECTIONS   Right at Exit 145. Can't be missed.

BOB JOHNSON'S RESTAURANT, *Exit 157, Bloomington*

"You might try Bob Johnson's glorified truck stop," we were told when we asked where to get a good cheap meal near I-55. "It's open 24 hours, and a lotta people love that place."

The people who love it turned out to be a lotta guys with short hair, big bellies, string neckties, and socks that matched their shirts instead of their pants. They didn't seem to mind at all the brightly, not unpleasantly plastic look of things, or the slightly artificial taste to the otherwise quite good and gooey country-style ribs. We got three of those ribs and two pieces of quite good fried chicken for $6.95, accompanied by half a good baked apple, an acceptable blueberry muffin, a poor example of garlic bread, and an undistinguished bread pudding.

Chicken is the specialty. You'll realize that as soon as you see the sign, which, in huge letters formed from light bulbs, reads simply: CHICKEN DINNERS. It's $4.85 for the cheapest version (five wings), with chicken fried steak at $4.25 and pork chops at $5.95. Eggs, potatoes, muffin, and unlimited coffee go for $2.55. If you carefully scrutinize the menu's small print, you will find hamburgers for $1.75.

HOURS Daily 24 hours.

SPECS US 150 and I-55 Business; (309) 663-8481; no cards; no liquor.

DIRECTIONS **Northbound:** Take the exit for I-55 Business. Go 3.4 miles on I-55 Business to the light at Morrisey. It's on the right.

Southbound: Take the Exit 157 for I-74 East, and then almost immediately take the Exit 134 for I-55 Business. Go 3.4 miles on I-55 Business to the light at Morrisey. It's on the right.

THE CUT ABOVE, *Exit 160A, Bloomington*

You go down to reach the Cut Above—down into the brick-vaulted, rathskellery cellar of a downtown building, there to find what many consider the best food in Bloomington.

The menu is a mixed bag of American and continental food ($7–$13 for dinner, $4–$7 for lunch), but the emphasis falls clearly on the side of class. The waiters wear tuxes, the tables are beautifully set, and the presentation of the food is exquisite. None of which stopped the farmer in his bib overalls from pulling up a chair and ordering his prime rib well done, or got the sincere and unpretentious waiter to pronounce the French correctly.

The Cut Above is a mixed bag, as we said, and if you're hot and sweaty from the drive you needn't feel odd about ordering from a black-tied waiter. They'll be glad to have you, and it's delightfully cool down in those cellars.

The food was good. We took the waiter's advice and ordered the house specialty—swordfish Kiev at $13. It had been deep-fried for just an instant to seal in the juice, then baked to produce an excellent light-tasting dish. The vegetables were good, but not as good as the fish; the bread was just okay. If that doesn't sound good enough for $13, then get the lunchtime hamburger with fries for $3.25, or perhaps the Carolina Beauty at $4.25—an English muffin stuffed with turkey, bacon, asparagus, and sauce Mornay, garnished with peach and cranberry sauce.

HOURS   Lunch: Mon.–Fri. 11:30 am–2 pm; Dinner: Mon.–Thurs. 5:30–9:30 pm; Fri. & Sat. 5:30–10:30 pm; Sun. 10:30 am–2 pm. Closed major holidays & last 2 weeks of Feb.

SPECS   612 N. Main St.; (309) 829-3379; V, MC, AE; full bar.

DIRECTIONS   From Exit 160A go east on Route 9 (Market St.) for 1.8 miles to Main St. Turn left and go 1½ blocks. It's on the left. A parking lot is ½ block south on Main.

PENNY'S PLACE, *Exits 197 & 201, Pontiac*

"Gourmet? You're in the wrong place, honey. Everything here's fried!" And so it was, but well fried, we thought, in this cute, clean, local, and utterly unpretentious little bar and restaurant. The chairs are of tubular steel, the tablecloths of matching vinyl; the bar is old wood—unspectacular in any way, but nice, as was the food.

Dinners only, from $3.25 for fried chicken to $10.65 for 16-ounce T-bone. In between are catfish and pike ($5.45), frog legs ($7.65), pork chops ($6.20), and about 10 others. Nightly specials get as cheap as $2.50; sandwiches are 80 cents to $2.25.

A perfect stop for "just folks" dining.

HOURS   Sun.–Thurs. 4:30–10 pm; Fri. & Sat. 4:30–11 pm. Closed major holidays.

SPECS   624 W. Howard; (815) 842-1309; no cards; full bar.

DIRECTIONS   **Northbound:** From Exit 197 turn right onto Route 116 and follow it for 2 miles to **Penny's,** on the right. There is a jog left at 1.3 miles and right again at 1.8 miles.

Southbound: From Exit 201 turn left at the end of the ramp toward Pontiac and go 2.6 miles to a stop sign. Turn right and go 0.4 mile to another stop sign. Turn left, 0.2 mile, and it's on the right.

WHITE FENCE FARM, *Exits 267 & 269, Romeoville*

We'd heard good things about the White Fence Farm, but almost passed it up after seeing it ballyhooed on Chicago TV. Our first look at the place only reenforced our suspicions. It was a huge commercial operation that had obviously grown from modest beginnings in a real farm to a tourist-trap success story.

Not our kind of thing at all, we thought. Then we spotted 70-year-old Doris Hastert in a bright yellow outfit bicycling across the football-field parking lot from her home out back. Nice of the owners to house the employees, we thought, but soon we learned that this was indeed the owner herself, or at least one half of the couple that has owned the White Fence Farm since 1954.

Her energy, honesty, and enthusiasm captivated us, so in we went to taste the fried chicken on which this local empire was built—fried chicken that is first pressure cooked, and then quickly deep-fried to produce a morsel that is as juicy *and* as crispy as chicken comes. It was terrific, as were the light corn fritters. With an array of good relishes like pickled beets and kidney beans, half a chicken costs $6.35. Have it by itself to go and it's just $2.45 (45 cents for half a dozen fritters).

You can have steaks here ($10–$12), french-fried shrimp ($6.35), and what the menu mysteriously calls "sautéed Alaskan fish" ($7.25). But chicken is what the restaurant is about—chicken, that is, and antique cars like Clark Gable's 1928 Packard or John Wayne's 1931 model. The decor is about what you'd expect, except in the South Room, which is the original dining area and is devoid of kitsch.

You may have to wait as much as a full hour on Sunday, a half hour at peak dinner hours on Saturday.

HOURS Tues.–Sat. 5–9 pm; Sun. noon–8 pm. Closed Mon., Thanksgiving, Christmas, & all of Jan. & Feb.

SPECS Joliet Rd.; (312) 739-1720; major cards; full bar; children's menu.

DIRECTIONS **Northbound:** Take Exit 267 (Route 53) and turn right at the light onto Route 53. Go 3 lights (1.5 miles) and turn left onto Joliet Rd. Go 1 long block, and it's on the left.

Southbound: Take Exit 269 and just go with the flow of traffic. You'll be on Joliet Rd. headed in the right direction. Go 1.6 miles, and it's on the right.

TOSCANO, *Damon Avenue Exit, Chicago*

Toscano's is one of several restaurants in an old Italian neighborhood that has steadfastly resisted both urban blight and upscale gentrification. The bakery, drugstore, and restaurants are still here, unself-consciously going about their business just as they've been doing since the day the city decided to raise the street half a story and thereby turned the local first floors into basements.

Toscano's admittedly has some spiffy-looking awnings out front, but don't be fooled. Inside it's a plain trattoria—bare tables, bentwood chairs, old tin ceiling, and a slatey-looking vinyl floor. We couldn't have asked for more (or less) and were delighted to find one wall decorated with a huge black-and-white photograph of the restaurant and its rugged-looking patrons from the days of Al Capone and Elliot Ness. Anywhere else it would have been a cheap shot, but at Toscano's it seemed authentic.

We don't know whether Capone ever dined here, but we do know that if you do you'll get excellent, crusty Italian bread and light, fluffy gnocchi that are as good as the menu promises ($4.75 a la carte, $6.50 with soup, salad, beverage, and dessert). The meat sauce was truly homemade—light but distinctively tasty, accented by a gentle tang.

HOURS Tues.–Thurs. 11 am–10 pm; Fri. & Sat. 11 am–midnight; Sun. noon–10 pm. Closed Mon., Christmas, Easter, New Year's.

SPECS 2439 S. Oakley St.; (312) 376-4841; AE, DC; full bar; children's menu.

DIRECTIONS Take Damon Ave. Exit. Northbound turn left, and southbound turn right onto Damon. Go 0.8 mile to Blue Island Ave. Turn left and go 0.4 mile to Oakley St. Turn right, and it's 1½ blocks, on the right.

Illinois

PIERSON's, *Exit 53, Marion*

We weren't in the mood for so formal a lunch as turbot alman-dine ($3.80), a spinach salad ($3.50), or even a trio of stuffed croissants ($3.50). Instead we just sipped at a lovely, spicy gazpa-cho soup ($1.95) and nibbled at an appetizer of baked Brie with almonds, fresh fruit, and a loaf of toasted bread ($5.50).

Not exactly what we expected from the middle of southern Illinois farm country, and Pierson's looks weren't exactly Ma and Pa Kettle either—subtle, tastefully arrayed tones of plum and gray, formally set tables, etched glasswork scattered discreetly about. All of which confirmed our theory that in such restaurants as Pierson's all thought of the road is soon forgotten.

This happens readily if you're dining on chicken breast Dijon-aise ($8.95), lemon sole ($11.95), an 8-ounce fillet ($12.95), or barbecued shrimp for $17.95. The menu is obviously a synthesis of local and international tastes, a point made clear by the least expensive dinner item—liver and onions in sherry sauce for $6.95.

Fear not. Though the place obviously means to stress class, it's not so spiffy that a local bridge club couldn't meet there and play out a few rubbers after lunch. The lounge is as comfortable as your living room, but if sofas and a fireplace just don't appeal to you, try the attached coffee shop that offers delicious Danish and muffins for 75 cents, pies, subs ($2.25), and the same great soups that are served in the restaurant proper.

HOURS   Restaurant: Mon.–Thurs. 11 am–2 pm & 5:30–10 pm; Fri. & Sat. 11 am–2 pm & 5:30–11 pm. Coffee Shop: Mon–Fri. 7:30 am–5 pm; Sat. 7:30 am–noon. Closed Sun. & major holidays.

SPECS   103 N. Market St.; (618) 993-6209; V, MC; full bar.

DIRECTIONS From Exit 53 turn right if northbound and left if southbound. Go 1.7 miles to the Marion town square. **Pierson's** is at the north end of the square to your left as you enter it.

BURTON'S CAFÉ, *Exit 77, Whittington*

For almost 50 years Burton's has been the classically perfect highway stop—great home cooking, low prices, friendly people, and a location just 1 minute from the highway.

These virtues are wrapped up in a sweet and pure little white box of a building, the modest sign of which proclaims just HOME COOKED MEALS. And that is exactly what we found within this ten-stool establishment: terrific cornbread and bean soup for $1.25, and a fine bacon-wrapped chopped sirloin with fries and a salad ($3.75). Most unforgettable, however, was the wide array of country pies for which Burton's is famous. We tried the "white" pie—whipped cream and pecans atop a base of light vanilla custard—and found it delicious in that American pie way.

Fifteen sandwiches run $1–$1.90; full meals were advertised southern style as a meat and three vegetables, and there were sweet potatoes among the veggies. No grits, however.

Burton's was full of local people who were quite happily noisy at 1:30 pm, a sure sign of excellence, which our taste buds confirmed empirically.

HOURS Mon.–Sat. 6 am–8 pm. Closed Sun., major holidays, & Dec. 25–Jan. 1.

SPECS Route 37; (618) 629-2515; no cards; no liquor.

DIRECTIONS From Exit 77 turn right if northbound and left if southbound. Go 0.4 mile to Route 37 and turn left, then go 0.7 mile. It's on the right.

CINDI'S CAFÉ AND CATERING, *Exit 95, Mt. Vernon*

We don't know where else south of Chicago and north of New Orleans you could find a happier combination of good food, low prices, sophisticated looks, and downhome friendliness than

39

at Cindi's Café. The chic black-and-white awnings announce to the street that it is no ordinary small-town eatery, and lingering doubts are put to rest the moment you enter—bare white walls and a black tin ceiling, black-and-white checked tablecloths, just a few plants and antiques for accents. Decidedly classy, but as soon as you talk to folks you realize that the place is as warm and friendly as any diner.

Certainly the menu is humble enough: 7 sandwiches, from the basic hot dog at $1.25 to roast beef on a croissant with horse-radish sauce or Dijon mustard ($2.50). Cindi smokes her own pork to make the barbecue sandwich, and there's an Italian beef sandwich on a hard roll ($1.95 each). Breakfast is two eggs for $1.30, $2.25 with a pair of sausage patties, biscuits, and hash browns. And that's the whole menu—except for salads, soups, and a daily plate lunch that changes to take advantage of what looks best at the market.

Everything we tasted at Cindi's demonstrated the determination to do a few simple things well—fresh, natural ingredients, imaginative preparation, attention to detail. It's a real pleasure to find such a restaurant, and apparently Mt. Vernon appreciates what it has. No one was sure at first how a lunchroom without hamburgers would go over here, but Cindi's been turning a profit since the very first week she opened her doors.

HOURS Mon.–Sat. 5 am–3 pm. Closed Sun. & major holidays.

SPECS 222 S. 9th St.; (618) 242-6221; no cards; no liquor.

DIRECTIONS Take Exit 95 (Route 15) and go 2.7 miles into Mt. Vernon. Turn right on the far side of the town square at 9th St. **Cindi's** is ½ block, on the left.

KING'S BARBACOA, *Exit 95, Mt. Vernon*

Why should the very best barbecue sauce we've ever come across be in Mt. Vernon, Illinois, and not some more exotic place like Jackson, Georgia, or Murphysboro, Tennessee? We can't explain it, and we aren't even sure it's true—memory can be deceptive, especially when you're wandering around southern Illinois in 100° heat looking for a culinary discovery. But we do know this: Whatever your motives and whatever the temperature, if you're a fan of ribs you're going to love King's Barbacoa.

They go for $12 a slab, and the sauce comes hot or mild. The hot is not hot enough to obscure the wonderfully rich flavor of the meat, but it's potent enough to keep you tasting the meal for an hour after dessert. Half a slab is $6; a quarter slab is $3.50, nonchalantly served with two pieces of Wonder Bread and a toothpick. If you haven't $3.50, at least try the pork sandwich for $1.75 or the smoked, baked beans for 65 cents.

Whoever invented the recipe is a genius, and just as should be the case with genius, it is completely unself-conscious. The management seemed hardly interested in its own doings at this tiny, four-stool, five-table, carpeted, paneled, drop-ceilinged shack, the principal decoration of which is a TV tuned to soap operas and game shows. Which is not to say people weren't friendly enough. It's just that when you know you're good and your ambitions are not that great, you can sit back and be comfortable in the knowledge that the world will come to you even if you're a mile from the center of town.

HOURS Mon. & Wed.–Sat. 10 am–8 pm; Tues. 10 am–7 pm. Closed Sun. & major holidays.

SPECS 918 Gilbert St.; (618) 242-9853; no cards; no liquor.

DIRECTIONS   From Exit 95 go 2.7 miles to Mt. Vernon on Route 15. Turn right at the light at 10th St. Go 1.1 miles on 10th to Gilbert (look for a hand-painted sign of a tall man pointing to the left). Turn left and go ½ block, on the left.

THELMA'S
TRAILWAYS, *Exits 160 & 162, Effingham*

See pp. 76–77 for descriptions of these two restaurants, the former a pretentious but "nice" place, the other a decent enough roadside eatery.

DIRECTIONS   In the vicinity of Effingham, I-57 and I-70 run together, so that you will go exactly right if you follow the directions on pp. 77 and 78.

THE GREAT IMPASTA, *Exit 235A, Champaign*

The pastabilities are endless at this marvelous Italian restaurant/snackerie/deli/wine bar. It's worth an even longer detour than the 5 minutes it will take to get here. See description on p. 118.

DIRECTIONS   Exit 235A of I-57 sends you into town on I-72 East, which ends in 2 miles at Mattis Ave. Continue straight (you're on University Ave. now) and exactly 1.6 miles from the light at Mattis, turn left onto Randolph. Two short blocks brings you to Church. Make a right onto Church and the restaurant is on your left, across from Robeson's Department Store. Free parking for **Impasta** customers is in Robeson's lot, the next block on Church.

YESTERYEAR, *Exit 312, Kankakee*

First, let's get two things straight: This is no neocolonial inn. Nor is it a pseudo-Victorian eating and drinking emporium either. Actually, it's one of the most extraordinary buildings ever converted to a restaurant, Frank Lloyd Wright's masterful Bradley House.

Why then Yesteryear? The secret is known only by the restaurant's original owners. Perhaps they confused Frank Lloyd Wright with McKim, Mead, and White. The egregious stylistic errors extend beyond the restaurant's name, unfortunately: Garish velveteen wallpaper and Old Master's–style paintings line the walls and frilly Williamsburg-style outfits garb the waitresses. But Yesteryear is now in the well-intentioned hands of John and Rose Murray who are hellbent on undoing the unhandiwork of their predecessors.

Even flawed, Wright's building is magnificent. Our lunch was similar: marvelous overall, with a few areas begging for improvement. Our rum rolls and poppy seed buns, for instance, would have been winners if we'd eaten them a day earlier. But the huge chicken salad was gorgeous, mounded on a bed of leaf lettuce, artfully arranged with a cornucopia of wedged and cross-sectioned vegetables, deftly herbed and creamed to the right consistency ($6.25). Also a delight was the Reuben sandwich ($3.95), stuffed with thick slices of good corned beef, sided by real shoestring french fries; if the rye bread had been better than supermarket grade, we could really rave. But we found nothing to complain about in the dessert department: coconut cream pie, baked here, was tops, as was the velvety cheesecake brought down from Eli's in Chicago.

Dinners are *haute* in both cuisine and price: Chicken breast with apricot mustard sauce is near the bottom of the menu at $9.95, while veal Oscar, at $13.50, is more typical. Sunday's $12.95 brunch is said to be spectacular, but as a highway stop it would probably slow your momentum considerably.

HOURS Mon.–Sat. 11 am–10 pm; Sun. 11 am–8 pm.

SPECS Harrison Ave. (at the river); (815) 939-3131; major cards; full bar; children's portions.

DIRECTIONS From Exit 312, turn left if northbound, right if southbound onto IL 17 (Court St.) into Kankakee. In about 1 mile, turn left on Greenwood. Go ½ mile on Greenwood to Eagle. Make a right onto Eagle, and go 2 blocks until it ends. Make a left here on Harrison, and **Yesteryear** is on your right.

I-64

Illinois
Indiana
Kentucky

Illinois

THE STOCKYARDS INN
SCOVILLE'S CAFÉ, *Exit 2, National City*

Just east of St. Louis I-64 runs together with I-55 and I-70. See pp. 25–26 under I-55 for descriptions of two very beefy restaurants in the St. Louis stockyards.

EL DORADO RESTAURANT, *Exit 11, Collinsville*

Just east of St. Louis I-64 runs together with I-55 and I-70. See pp. 26–27 under I-55 for a very good Mexican restaurant.

CINDI'S CAFÉ AND CATERING
KING'S BARBACOA, *Exit 95, Mt. Vernon*

I-64 and I-57 run together in the vicinity of Mt. Vernon. See pp. 39–41 for descriptions of a terrific barbecue shack and a very good lunchroom that's sort of earthy-chic.

DIRECTIONS   Same for either highway.

Indiana

THE RED GERANIUM, *Exit 4, New Harmony*

We are not going to tell you that the food at the Red Geranium was wonderful (our veal Cordon Bleu was dry and dull, the green beans in the casserole were canned). Nor will we claim that it is cheap (dinners are $8.95–$15, lunches $4.50–$7.50, sandwiches $2–$3) or convenient (the town is 6 miles from the interstate). The restaurant *is* a very pleasing mixture of formality and country life, and it *is* in a handsome 19th-century building, but that alone would not justify the trip. What makes it worth it is New Harmony itself, a beautiful old town that seems to have a very special, even a spiritual, feel to it, and a uniquely beautiful, contemporary version of a Shaker hotel.

The story begins early in the last century when a German religious sect first founded the town. Then came British Socialist Robert Owen, who attempted to set up a utopian community here. Both efforts were doomed to the historical dustbin, but after such a start it was impossible for New Harmony to be just another town on the banks of the Wabash. You can see the difference in the small but handsome buildings on Main Street and in the grand old trees that shade them, but the real story of modern New Harmony revolves around Jane Owen, who is married to one of Robert Owen's descendants and who has used her formidable resources to revive the spirit of New Harmony.

It was she who studied religion with Paul Tillich, one of the most renowned of 20th-century theologians, and it was she who interested him in New Harmony. Tillich is buried here in a garden-shrine studded with quotations from his works. The restaurant and the hotel are actually parts of the shrine, all conceived and financed by Jane Owen to honor her teacher. She has created a place where spiritual values can take precedence over all else. There is also a very lovely open-air church that looks out over a tranquil Indiana farm, and a museum for the arts.

We know of nothing in the world quite like New Harmony. There is a very special spirit here that transcends the efforts of thoughtless employees to botch things up or pretentious ones to make them stuffy. So far as the food goes, there are other restaurants in town, and we were later told that the quality at The Red

Geranium is very uneven. Stick to steaks and the lettuce salad and you may just do very well indeed. In any case, we promise you that you will nowhere find a more lovely motel at anything like the nightly price of about $35.

HOURS Tues. 11 am–10 pm; Fri. & Sat. 11 am–11 pm; Sun. 11 am–8 pm. Closed Mon. & Christmas Day.

SPECS North St.; (812) 682-4431; major cards; full bar.

DIRECTIONS Just head for New Harmony from Exit 4. The town is very small and you'll find everything quite easily.

LAKEVIEW TRUCK STOP, *Exit 25B, Haubstadt*

Though it is not as awful to look at as the typical truck stop, there is really nothing to recommend about the Lakeview but its hours and the food—good homemade vegetable soup, excellent homemade cornbread, tender cuts of roast beef in real pan gravy, and mashed potatoes that were instant but didn't taste it.

Prices are modest, to say the least (sandwiches $1–$2.80; half a dozen dinners from $3.80–$5.80). The clientele was about evenly split between truckers, polyester-suited businessmen, and wholesome-looking couples.

HOURS Daily 24 hours.

SPECS US 41 & Route 68; (812) 768-6167; V, MC; no liquor.

DIRECTIONS Go north on US 41 for 1.5 miles from Exit 25B. It's on the left.

OLD LOG INN, *Exit 25B, Haubstadt*

Eat where Abraham Lincoln did, in a genuine log cabin that was once a stagecoach stop and is now the Evansville area's most popular fried chicken emporium. There's a lovely old room from 1825, currently done up in red-checked tablecloths, wood stoves, and lots of kitsch that somehow fails to detract seriously from the building's charm.

For $6.95 you get family-style service that offers either half a very good fried chicken, ham, or roast beef as a main course with perfectly acceptable mashed potatoes, gravy, peas, corn, slaw, rolls and butter. A quarter bird can be had a la carte for just $2.65, and there are lots of sandwiches for less than $2.

A "fun" stop, officially recognized as the oldest restaurant in Indiana.

HOURS   Tues.–Sat. 4–10:30 pm. Closed Sun., Mon., major holidays, & 3 weeks in January.

SPECS   Route 2; (812) 867-3216; no cards; full bar; children's menu.

DIRECTIONS   From Exit 25B go ½ mile north on US 41 to a sign for the restaurant on the right. Turn right and go 1 mile. It's on the left.

LA CANTINA, *Exit 63, Mariah Hill*

Who would have thought that Mariah Hill, Indiana, would be home to a terrific Mexican restaurant that produced the best plate of nachos we've ever tasted? How La Cantina got here is a long story, but the essential point is that everything is made with the careful, personal touch of Orie Burkam, and served up in the kind of wonderfully funky atmosphere that gets created when a great cook sets out on a shoestring to prove that she can do in a restaurant what she did at home.

The nachos were $2.40. An excellent beef enchilada goes for just $2.85, and a taco is $1.20. Burritos ($4.65 and up) plus tostadas ($2.25 and up) complete the very basic menu—so don't come looking for chicken mole or anything other than the hearty Mexican standbys beautifully put together from the very best ingredients. Hamburgers and a few American dishes are available.

La Cantina has quite understandably taken the area by storm, and after 5 years the owners are about to open another place in nearby Tell City. Which is really just as well: We may end up with La Cantinas from coast to coast, but so long as there is only one, the lines are pretty long on weekends.

Do check out the lounge. It's got an old wooden bar that would be the pride and joy of any big-city quicherie, but here it is just an old store fixture that fits right in. The walls of the lounge are papered in dollar bills that bear their donors' signatures. No one knew how or why that tradition got started, but we like to think it's a token of the customers' appreciation.

HOURS   Mon.–Sat. 4:30–10 pm; Sun. 3–9 pm. Closed major holidays.

SPECS   Main St.; (812) 937-4247; V, MC, AE; full bar.

DIRECTIONS   From Exit 63 go south on Route 162 for 2.5 miles to the stop sign at Route 62. Turn right and go 2.5 miles to a sign for the restaurant on the left at the outskirts of Mariah Hill (there's a gas station on the right). Turn left, go ½ block, and **La Cantina** is on the right.

POLLY'S FREEZE, *Exit 118, Edwardsville*

Three things distinguish Polly's from any old run-of-the-road ice cream stand/snack bar, and any one of them makes Polly's worth the stop. The 1950s-vintage sign—a neon parrot, its head cocked back toward the highway—is a classic, worthy of inclusion in any museum of Americana. The parklike surroundings are infinitely more pleasant than the asphalt sea most drive-ups provide. And the food—soft ice cream and simple sandwiches— while certainly not high urban chic, shows real effort.

A few years ago, under increasing pressure to shuck their independence and sign up with one of the national chains, Paul and Donna Eisert (Donna's mother Polly started the stand in 1952) switched their ice cream mix to that used by Dairy Queen. Three weeks and hundreds of complaints later, they were back to their old formula. If they couldn't go it on their own, they decided, they wouldn't go it at all.

Judging by the large crowd and carnival atmosphere we found on a warm Saturday night in July, they seem to be going it just fine. Try the peanut butter milk shake, a concoction the Eiserts devised themselves from real peanut butter thinned to a butterscotch consistency ($1). With a barbecue-topped hot dog (75 cents) or an abundantly appointed "Pollyburger" ($1.35), that's serious snacking out, southern Indiana style.

HOURS Open from last week of March through first week of October only. Summer: Sun.–Thurs. 10:30 am–10:30 pm; Fri. & Sat. 10:30 am–11 pm. In fall and spring, close a half hour earlier during the week; same hours on weekends.

SPECS (812) 945-6911; no cards; no liquor.

DIRECTIONS From Exit 118, turn right if eastbound, left if westbound, onto IN 62 West toward Edwardsville. In ¾ mile, it's on the right.

Kentucky

THE SEELBACH CAFÉ, *Exit 4, Louisville*

The Seelbach Hotel is the grand old dame of Louisville—a hotel from the days when luxury was taken seriously and the wealthy didn't hesitate to flaunt it. This was where the Great Gatsby stayed when he brought Daisy down from Chicago. In the Seelbach's lobby you can see seven kinds of marble, and in its cellars you can see an entire room beautifully tiled in Rookwood pottery.

The place is, in short, magnificent—a gem. A small-scale version of the very best of pre–World War I opulence. It is hard to believe that for decades all this slid into neglect and disrepair, its marble hidden by cheap paneling and its brass tarnished beyond recognition. But with the revival of downtown Louisville, millions were poured into The Seelbach, and now it looks once again like its former self—except that the clientele are now more Yuppie than Gatsby.

Though a meal in The Seelbach Café is not cheap, it is possible to experience all this with only minor damage to your pocketbook and without a necktie or even a jacket. Sandwiches are no bargain at $5–$6, but entrees start at $5.25 for a frittata with braised vegetables and go to $11 for an 8-ounce sirloin. You can get the stew of the day for just $6.75, and there are pasta dishes like fettuccine primavera for about $7. Watch out for dessert—a slice of locally renowned Seelbach pie goes for $3.50, more common pastries for just $1.75.

Some of what we tried here was really excellent, like the cream of mushroom soup redolent with fresh mushroom aromas. The sautéed squash and cauliflower were very good, and so was the ever-so-slightly-too-garlicky trout in lemon butter and capers. We were disappointed though by fried potatoes that were discernibly mushy and frozen, and we wondered about a place like this trying to get away with a thing like that.

We should not dwell overmuch on that one sin. In general, the food was very good. And as a total experience the Seelbach can't be beat.

HOURS Mon.–Thurs. 6:30 am–10:30 pm; Fri. & Sat. 6:30 am–midnight; Sun. 6:30 am–11:30 pm.

SPECS 500 Fourth Ave.; (800) 626-2032 & (502) 585-3200; major cards; full bar.

DIRECTIONS **Eastbound:** Take Exit 4 for 9th St. Go straight at the light at the end of the ramp for 3 blocks to Muhammad Ali Blvd. Turn left and go 6 blocks. It's on the right.

Westbound: Take exit 5B for 3rd St. Go 5 blocks to Muhammad Ali and turn right. Go 1 block.

The hotel has valet parking if you have trouble finding a spot on the street (we had no trouble at 7 pm). It's $2 for 2 hours before 5 pm. After 5 pm it's a $3 flat rate.

BRISTOL BAR & GRILLE, *Exits 4 & 5B, Louisville*

Cheers for Louisville! Instead of sinking millions into one of those gargantuan eating malls cloned after Boston's Quincy Marketplace or Baltimore's Harborplace, the River City has decided to put its money where its water is. The result is a masterpiece of urban landscaping, the Riverfront Belvedere, spread out over several city blocks between the broad Ohio and the soaring black-glass-shrouded Kentucky Center for the Arts.

A stroll through the Belvedere is not only a refreshing break from the interstate grind, but also a tonic exercise likely to result in a healthy appetite. We have just the place to sate it. The Bristol Bar & Grille, right inside the Kentucky Arts Center, is where Louisville's snappy set turns out for *au courant* cuisine served in sharp, chic surroundings. It may be trendy, but it's not clichéd; further, the prices are surprisingly manageable and the food is up to the decor.

Choose between light and serious: omelets; crêpes; gourmet burgers and sandwiches; or the likes of poulet Alexandria, pork Dijonnais, and green fettuccine with white clam sauce. Our juicy Bristolburger sang out with flavor (the blue cheese topping added its own choice notes to the chorus, $3.65). Mishi mulfoot, an ingenious mixture of spicy ground lamb with sour cream and capers rolled into cabbage leaves could easily have commanded more than its $5.25 dinnertime price tag. For dessert, we couldn't pass up Derby pie, a Louisville variation on pecan pie that utilizes walnuts, chocolate bits, bourbon, and who knows what other (top secret) ingredients.

HOURS   During Arts Center's season (mid-September–mid-June): Daily 11 am–10 pm or later, depending on when the theater lets out. Summer: Mon.–Thurs. 11 am–10 pm; Fri. 11 am–midnight; Sat. 5:30 pm–midnight; closed Sun.

SPECS   Kentucky Center for the Arts, Main between 5th and 6th; (502) 583-3342; V, MC, AE; full bar.

DIRECTIONS   Eastbound: From Exit 4 (9th St.) turn left at the light onto Market St. and go 5 blocks to 4th St. Turn left onto 4th and go 1 block to Main. Turn left onto Main; look for parking on either side of the street. The Kentucky Arts Center is between 5th and 6th; the restaurant is just inside the main entrance.

Westbound: Use Exit 5B, stay in the left lane and go straight to second light (Main St.). Make a right onto Main and go 2 blocks; the Kentucky Arts Center is on the right; look for parking on either side of Main. The restaurant is just inside the main entrance of the Arts Center.

BRISTOL BAR & GRILLE, *Exit 8, Louisville*

If the thought of downtown traffic and parking daunts you, the Bristol has another location (actually the original) in a residential neighborhood. Same good food, same reasonable prices, similar snappy decor, even better hours.

HOURS Mon.–Thurs. 11:30 am–2 am; Fri. 11:30 am–4 am; Sun. 10 am–midnight.

SPECS 1321 Bardstown Rd.; (502) 456-1702; V, MC, AE; full bar.

DIRECTIONS From Exit 8, turn right if eastbound, left if westbound. In 0.1 mile, go straight through the light at Lexington and you'll be on Business US 60 (Grinstead Drive). Keep following signs for Business 60 (not to be confused with Alternate 60) for a total of 1.2 miles, at which point turn left onto US 31E/US 150 (Bardstown Rd). In 0.4 mile, it's on the left, just after Rosewood Ave.

BICO MATTEI, *Exit 10, Louisville*

Not only marathon runners are loading carbohydrates these days: pasta bars—caloric Nirvanas for marathoners and gourmands alike—are sprinting into popularity in the big cities. Bico Mattei is Louisville's first, and from the early heats it appears to be a winner.

Located in the bare bones dining room of a private airport terminal building, Bico puts its emphasis on the food. There are chicken and fish dishes and various pasta dinners, but you'll be missing the mark if you choose any of them over the pasta and salad bar option. The deal is thus: For $5.95 you can order unlimited quantities of homemade pasta (7 varieties), access 6 sauces on the steam table, and help yourself to copious fruit and salads on the salad bar. You will not go away wanting.

A few slight deficiencies hardly interfered with the fun we had here. All right, so cream of broccoli sauce doesn't improve with age on a steam table—neither white clam nor primavera nor sausage sauces seemed to have suffered. And, highlighted by an abundance of fresh (ripe, even) fruit, the salad bar was a pleasure; don't miss the beguiling smoky ham and pasta salad.

HOURS   Mon.–Thurs. 5–9 pm; Fri. & Sat. 5–10 pm; Sun. 4:30–8:30 pm.

SPECS   Bowman Field Terminal, Taylorsville Rd.; (502) 458-0555; V, MC, AE; wine only.

DIRECTIONS   From Exit 10, turn right if eastbound, left if westbound; go ½ mile (no traffic, no lights) to the stop sign at Dutchman's Lane. Turn right, and go another quick ½ mile to the light at Taylorsville Rd. Make another right, and in 0.4 mile pull into the parking lot of Bowman Field Administration Building.

Kentucky
Indiana

Kentucky

LEE'S RESTAURANT, *Exit 131A, Louisville*

Here in a modern office building on the outskirts of Louisville is a little restaurant with a split personality: American up front, Korean in back. We suggest you head for the rear.

If you've never been educated in the ways of Korean cuisine, this is a wonderful place to start. Not only is the food superb, but the charming waitresses take the time to explain the marinated side salads, collectively called kimchee, that are placed in front of every diner. There are turnips with carrots, for instance, spinach with bean sprouts, and Chinese cabbage, all of them effusing a delicate nutlike fragrance.

But before you even get to the kimchee, we suggest fried mandoo as an appetizer. Similar to won tons, these irresistible meat-filled dumplings are dipped in a white vinegar–soy sauce blend that the waitress mixes before you. Eight of them come for $2.30.

For main courses, you won't be disappointed (no matter how Americanized your taste buds) with bool-ko-ki, ultra-thin slices of charbroiled beef served with a peppery soy-based sauce ($5.50). Or, for a slightly more exotic approach, opt for the mild-flavored chop-chae, translucent bean thread noodles intertwined with assorted vegetables (all fresh) and slivers of beef ($4.85).

The serene though not overly atmospheric Korean dining room is open only for dinner; at other times of day, you must content yourself with the bare bones American-style lunchroom.

Although the menu there doesn't stray far from hash browns, eggs over easy, and tuna salad sandwiches, tell your server you'd prefer bee-bim-bop or gal-bee-jim, and your wish will be her command.

HOURS Mon.–Sat. 7 am–3 pm (cafeteria) and 4–10 pm (dining room). Closed Sun. & Christmas.

SPECS Watterson Building, 1941 Bishop Lane; (502) 456-9714; V, MC; no liquor.

DIRECTIONS Exit 131A puts you on I-264 East. Go about 2 miles to Exit 15A (Newburg Rd. South). The first light, which comes up immediately, is Bishop Lane, and if you could turn left you'd be there, but a left turn is Verboten. So, continue to the first permitted left and go around the block with 3 consecutive left turns. It's in the first floor of the Watterson Building.

BICO MATTEI, *Exit 131, Louisville*

Ever tried a pasta bar? You might not want to miss it. Read about one on pp. 52–53.

DIRECTIONS Use Exit 131 to enter the Watterson Expressway East (I-264). In about 3 miles, take Exit 17B onto Taylorsville Rd. North. Go ¾ mile; the restaurant is in Bowman Field Administration Building, on right.

BRISTOL BAR AND GRILLE, *Exit 137, Louisville*

It's only moments out of your way to this worthy restaurant; choose either of two locations. Read descriptions on pp. 50–52.

DIRECTIONS Exit 137 of I-65 puts you on I-64. For the Kentucky Arts Center location of the Bristol Bar and Grille, head west on I-64, and immediately take Exit 5B. Use Westbound directions given on p. 51. For the Bardstown Rd. location, head east on I-64 to Exit 8 and use directions given on p. 52.

Indiana

ROCKY'S SUB PUB, *Exit 1, Jeffersonville*

For some super whole-wheat pizza (without that dense whole-wheat taste) in cozy, woody (but not slick) surroundings, try Rocky's Sub Pub and get a glimpse of Ohio River barge traffic on the side. Rocky's is across the street from the riverfront plant of the Jeffboat Company, largest inland barge manufacturer in the world, and a block away from the Howard Steamboat Museum.

But Rocky's stands alone on its merits. Owner John Fondrisi, a Long Islander by birth and taste bud, has brought a bite of the Big Apple to southern Indiana—wide, thin-crusted, ebulliently sauced New York–style pizza. The high-gluten crust (properly tossed on the maker's fists) is just right, in both white and whole-wheat versions, and the well-herbed sauce is outstanding; we recommend spicy Italian sausage as a topping. Pizza prices run from $4.95 for a plain small to $12.70 for a loaded large.

It's not all pizza at Rocky's. The subs are hits too, on your choice of homemade white, rye, or whole-wheat bread ($3.25–$4.75). There's a full complement of Italian dinner entrees and barbecued ribs. We realize the Midwest is rib crazed, but still, we had to ask John how he explains ribs with french fries and coleslaw on his otherwise ethnically consistent menu.

His answer was irrefutable: "Da Rock can't eat Italian food every night."

Expect a formidable line between 6 and 10 pm on Friday and Saturday nights.

HOURS Mon.–Thurs. 11 am–11 pm; Fri. & Sat. 11 am–1 am; Sun. 3–11 pm.

SPECS 1207 E. Market St.; (812) 282–3844; V, MC, AE; beer & wine.

DIRECTIONS From Exit 1, follow signs for IN 62 East/Jeffersonville. Turn right at the light onto Spring St. (don't take the sharp right onto an unmarked street). Go 0.7 mile to Market St. Make a left onto Market, and go 1 mile to the restaurant, on the left.

THE LEFT BANK, *Exit 68, Columbus*

Southwestern Indiana may be corn country, but you wouldn't know it inside The Left Bank, where a young urbane crowd gathers for up-to-date offerings in stylish surroundings. Though encumbered somewhat by the clichés of modern restaurant design, there is much here that is refreshingly original, inspired by *Architectural Digest* perhaps but certainly not by the average Hoosier eatery.

Sit in the lounge or the dining room; each has its own menu. We went barside, and enjoyed a cup of homemade cream of mushroom soup (99 cents), an abundantly provisioned chicken-walnut salad with an enticing dill dressing ($4.25), and a respectable portion of lasagne ($3.99, with garlic bread). Other than that, expect the same kinds of sandwiches, salads, and appetizers that are making it big in the suburbs.

Over on the dining-room side, where the feasting gets a little more serious, you'll be looking at $10 steak and seafood entrees. Oysters Rockefeller is the biggie when it comes to appetizers ($4.99) and prime rib wins the greatest number of fans in the red meat department.

HOURS Mon.–Thurs. 11 am–11 pm; Fri. & Sat. 11 am–midnight; Sun. 4–10:30 pm.

SPECS 418 4th St.; (812) 379-2376; all cards; full bar.

DIRECTIONS From Exit 68, Take IN 46 East toward Columbus. Stay on 46 East through its various curves, including a 90° turn to the left that occurs in about 2 miles (continuing straight at this point would put you on IN 7, but don't do it). Two blocks after making this 90° turn, turn right onto 4th St. (just after Sears). The restaurant is on the left, in the middle of the second block.

SHAPIRO'S DELI, *Exit 110B, Indianapolis*

Read about this first-rate Jewish deli/cafeteria on pp. 83–84.

DIRECTIONS Exit 110B puts you on I-70 West. Almost immediately, take Exit 79B (McCarty) and follow the directions given.

THE CANARY CAFÉ, *Exit 83A, Indianapolis*

Tucked into a triangle of downtown traffic is a winning breakfast and lunch spot that's as cheery as any we've found. Once we met The Canary Café's smiling owner, Cynthia Tabbert, whose warm and affable manner exuded unaffected hospitality, we understood how the restaurant got its charm. And once we talked with Cynthia we also learned how The Canary Café got its good tastes.

The eggs she serves, for instance, come from her own Barred Rock hens, raised just to keep the restaurant's breakfasters in good stead. Proudly, Cynthia opened a recycled egg carton to reveal a dozen behemoth brown beauties. These find their way into 4 different kinds of omelets, including the house specialty, a delicious cream cheese–bacon–tomato version, as well as a tasty Mexican omelet with avocado, Monterey Jack cheese, and picante salsa. All omelets come with honest home fries, and are priced around $3. You can also have your eggs cooked up as French toast made from Cynthia's home-baked challah and served with real Vermont maple syrup.

At lunchtime, Cynthia serves sandwiches (including a veggie special), full-meal salads, homemade soups, German potato salad, chili, and whatever else she feels like putting together that day (all prices are under $3, some under $2). But save room for dessert, especially if you're lucky enough to be in Indiana during the October persimmon season. Then, Cynthia makes that most delectable of Hoosier specialties, persimmon pudding, and she's especially proud of her own invention, persimmon cream pie. Once you've experienced the zestful tastes and undertastes harbored by these versatile wild fruits, you'll never want to settle for the comparatively flavorless grocery-store persimmons cultivated in California.

HOURS   Mon.–Fri. 7 am–3 pm; Sat. 8 am–2 pm; Sun. 10 am–2 pm.

SPECS   620 N. Delaware St.; (317) 635-6168; no cards; no liquor.

DIRECTIONS   **Note: For access to The Canary Café,** I-65 through traffic should not take the I-465 loop around Indianapolis. Stay on I-65; it's just as fast anyway.

Northbound: From I-65 Exit 113, turn left at light onto Pennsylvania Ave. Go to third traffic light and turn left onto North St. Go 1 block to Delaware Ave. Turn left onto Delaware and go 1 block to restaurant on the left. Parking area in front.

Southbound: From I-65 Exit 111, turn right at first light onto Michigan St. Go 5 traffic lights (about ½ mile) to Delaware. Turn right onto Delaware and go 2 blocks to restaurant on the left. Parking area in front.

SAM'S HICKORY BAR-B-Q, *Exit 121, Indianapolis*

You know it's real barbecue the moment you open your car door outside this recycled Burger Chef. And you'll savor the pungent hickory smoke before the succulent meat even hits your tongue. This is the barbecue lover's barbecue, as good as any we've ever tasted. Anywhere.

"Saint" Sam Johnson, who has garnered a following of devout loyalists in just 3 years, says the secret is more in the sauces than the wood. The gospel according to Sam maintains that it's essential to have two sauces, one that's sugarless for basting (sugar would caramelize and then burn), and one that's tomato-based for slathering across the meat just before it's served. Another necessity is long, slow cooking—4 hours minimum, says Sam.

Whatever his secrets, we adored his results. Thick, juicy, unbelievably tender swatches of rib meat just fell off the bones, and the sauce remaining after all the meat was gone found its way onto slices of bread. Best tasting Wonder Bread we've ever had!

Barbecue plates, including beans, slaw, or potato salad and a small drink go for around $3.50. Choose between beef, pork, chicken, or mutton. Or, forget about all the amenities, and opt for straight ribs. Twelve dollars buys a whole slab; fractions thereof are priced proportionally.

HOURS　Mon.–Thurs. 11:30 am–10 pm; Fri. & Sat. 11:30 am–1 am. Closed Sun.

SPECS　5604 N. Michigan Rd. (Northwestern Ave.); (317) 255-2637; no cards; no liquor.

DIRECTIONS　From Exit 121 of I-65, turn left if northbound, right if southbound, and go ½ mile to the second light (Georgetown Rd.). Turn left onto Georgetown and go 1.3 miles to second light (56th St.). Turn right onto 56th, and go 2.3 miles (3 lights) to Michigan Rd. Turn right and **Sam's** is on the right.

Note: If you are on the north leg of I-465, use Exit 27. Turn right if eastbound, left if westbound, onto Michigan Rd. In 4.9 miles, **Sam's** is just beyond the light at Kessler Rd., on the right.

CLARKS HILL FISH & STEAK, *IN 28 Exit, Clarks Hill*

Arriving in town via a disorienting and circuitous route, we pulled up beside a touch football game and asked the whereabouts of Clarks Hill Fish & Steak. Six of the hustlingest linebackers that Purdue University's football coach will try to enroll in 1995 dashed toward our car, shouting, pointing, and gesturing in unison. The restaurant's location ascertained, we solicited a menu suggestion. "Fish!" came the six voices as one.

Their obvious pride was as well placed as the field-goal kick we observed in our rearview mirror. Clarks Hill Fish & Steak is no run-of-the-suburbs steak and seafood house. With varnished wood booths, floral wallpaper, and a wonderful neon-rimmed clock that says "1950s" as loudly as it says "7:45," this is a strictly local establishment that exudes the kind of unself-conscious charm and warmth that comes only with time and care.

"Fish!" as we discovered, means just one thing. Oh, you *can* get smelts or perch, breaded shrimp or scallops, but "Fish!" means catfish, and catfish it was. Farm-fresh catfish, breaded in cornmeal and fried. Three 10-inchers (along with two side dishes including excellent "sugar slaw" and crisp fresh broccoli) over-lapped the plate. They were the very definition of succulence in fish—white, flaky, ever so moist. The cost for such pleasure is $6.50 ($1 less as a Wednesday night special).

Of course you can defy the wisdom of our budding football stars and order from the steak side of the CHF&S persona—anything from a breaded tenderloin sandwich ($1.50) to a 20-ounce sirloin ($13), with burgers, pork chops, fried chicken, and such in between. You can even nod to the '80s with potato skins or breaded mushrooms. All those things are very good, we have heard, but it would take a 1,000-pound winch to pry us away from our "Fish!"

HOURS　Mon.–Thurs. 4–9 pm; Fri. & Sat. 4–10 pm. Closed Sun.

SPECS　(317) 523-2424; no cards; beer & wine.

DIRECTIONS　From exit marked IN 28/Attica/Frankfort, head west toward Attica. In about 2½ miles, turn right on US 52, and in ½ mile turn left with IN 28. Go ¾ mile and turn left toward Clarks Hill. In ½ mile turn right (no sign, but first turn past the RR tracks). Go ¼ mile into town. The restaurant is on the left, in a white building just beyond the stop sign.

PARTHENON RESTAURANT, *West Lafayette*

Souvlaki, moussaka, and dolmades are no longer Greek to the students of Purdue University. Jacovas Jacovou has taken care of that part of their education. Jacovou managed restaurants in Chicago's Greektown for over 10 years before he brought his talents to West Lafayette. Tucked into a small shopping center on the edge of campus, the Parthenon keeps company with Taco Bell, Arby's, and a few others of their ilk, but this restaurant is a world apart.

To be sure, it's fast food Greek style, and as such it can't compete in quality with the denizens of Halstead St. in Chicago or Monroe Ave. in Detroit. But for a highway stop in central Indiana, it's a charm. Taped Greek music and latticework arbors soften the dining room's hard surfaces and there's an altogether pleasant deck with sun umbrellas.

No matter where you sit after placing your order at the front counter, we suggest you feast on the Parthenon's Olympian-portioned combination platter consisting of dolmades (stuffed grape leaves), moussaka, pastitsio (Greek lasagne), tiropite (cheese pie), egg lemon soup, gyros, rice, and pita bread. Any shortcomings in quality (the soup was dull and pasty, the twice-warmed rice pallid) were compensated for by the enormous quantity of food bought for $6.90. Furthermore, the opportunity to taste so many different Greek dishes in one sitting is enlightening. We especially enjoyed the much-better-than-average gyros, made on the premises to Jacovou's own formula of beef, lamb, and spices. Of course, smaller appetites can be satisfied too, and for smaller cost (all the items are available individually), but the combination described will feed two easily.

HOURS   Sun.–Thurs. 11 am–11 pm; Fri. & Sat. 11 am–1 am.

SPECS   Chauncy Hill Shops, 135 S. Chauncy Ave., West Lafayette; (317) 743-5551; no cards; beer & wine.

DIRECTIONS   From exit marked IN 43/West Lafayette/Brookston (northernmost of the Lafayette exits), turn toward West Lafayette on IN 43 South. Go about 5½ fast-moving miles until the road ends at a T, and turn right. In 0.2 mile, turn left on Chauncy Ave., and you're looking at it, in the Chauncy Hill Shops.

CURVE-IN CAFÉ, *Wolcott*

You can get fried chicken any day the Curve-In is open, but on Thursdays the preparation of this humble dish is raised to an art. Here, run-of-the-week chicken is simply frozen and deep-fried, but on "Chicken Day," Bev Dyer does chicken right, starting with fresh whole birds that she cuts up, breads, and pan-fries over a slow, slow fire. The result is genuine Hoosier fried chicken—smooth and elegantly tender meat encased in a soft, buttery, slightly nutty jacket of breading. If there's any better—on either side of the Mason-Dixon Line—we'd like to know where.

Two large pieces of this gorgeous poultry come with (instant) mashed potatoes, a vegetable, and coffee for all of $2.80. But don't wait until 5 minutes before closing or they'll be out—not many of the farmers around Wolcott go home for lunch on Thursdays.

Other specials—beef and noodles, roast pork and dressing, Lake Erie perch, chicken-fried steak—also have their days of honor in this ingenuously charming, scrupulously clean roadside café. All the regular breakfast and lunch fixings also appear; like everything else served here, they carry time-warp prices. And if you want to learn something of midwestern farm life, just keep your ears open.

HOURS   Mon.–Fri. 5:30 am–2 pm; Sat. 5:30 am–10:30 am. Closed Sun. & holidays.

SPECS   (219) 279-2225; no cards; no liquor.

DIRECTIONS   From exit labeled US 24/US 231/Remington, turn right if northbound, left if southbound (away from Remington). Go 3¾ miles; it's on the right.

Note: The exit to use is the one marked as above; this is the southern of two Remington exits; both are marked for US 231, but this is the only one for US 24. And don't take the exit labeled US 231/Wolcott/Chalmers, either. It's confusing, we realize, and we are puzzled indeed as to why the highway engineers weren't smart enough to use exit numbers.

*Indiana
Michigan*

Indiana

HO MING, *Exit 0, Indianapolis*

Some of the best—certainly the hottest—Szechuan Chinese cooking we found in the Midwest came out of Ho Ming's kitchen. Prices are low, portions are generous, access from I-69 (or the northern leg of I-465) is a snap, but there's one hitch: Ho Ming has no place to sit. It's a take-out.

Actually, when we visited, there were chairs around two tables in the shop, and nobody shooed us out when we occupied them, but the seating arrangement looked like it was giving way to an Oriental gift shop.

About that Szechuan food: We urge you to be conservative in assessing the fire-retardant powers of your lips and tongue. Having been forewarned, we went for medium and still had to fan our open mouths for 15 minutes afterwards. Fortunately, the food wasn't only hot, it was delicious too: fresh, brightly colored green and red peppers, crisp peanuts, and succulent little morsels of sautéed poultry constitute the dish unceremoniously called "Szechuan chicken." (A quart, costing $4.89, is enough for two.)

Beer is the only appropriate libation to cool such scorching fare, and the Ale Emporium next door makes that possible.

The owner of Ho Ming, who came to Indianapolis from Taiwan to teach Chinese language but ended up teaching Chinese cooking, also makes fine spring rolls and a delicious appetizer of red bean sprouts. Still a cooking teacher at heart, he has no secret sauces or arcane formulas. In fact, he has written a book, *Chinese Cooking As Easy As 1-2-3*, in which he tells all. It's available at the shop for $7.95.

HOURS Mon.–Thurs. 11 am–7:30 pm; Fri. & Sat. 11 am–8:30 pm. Closed Sun.

SPECS Castle Creek Plaza, 8613 Allisonville Rd.; (317) 849-7377; no cards; no liquor.

DIRECTIONS From Exit 0 (that's right!), get in the right lane and take I-465 West for ¾ mile to the first exit, Exit 35 (Allisonville Rd.). Head north (sign toward Nobleville) and turn right at the first light, then left into Castle Creek Plaza.

Note: From the north leg of I-465, use Exit 35 and follow the directions above.

ALL-STAR PIZZA, *Exit 34, Chesterfield*

Twenty-three hundred people live in the little town of Chesterfield, Indiana, and every year when spring fever strikes, 700 of them cure it by practicing the national pastime on some kind of organized team. "Everybody in this town is a baseball nut!" says Barb Geiger, owner of All-Star Pizza. "I mean everybody. Even me!"

There's not much doubt about that, and a casual glance around her restaurant, a recycled Shell station, will confirm it. In addition to comfortable corduroy booths and tasteful trimmings (all hand done by Barb and her local boosters), there's baseball

memorabilia of both the small-town and big-league varieties—
caps from more than thirty of Chesterfield's sundry teams next
to the Dodgers jerseys once worn by Carl Erskine and Duke
Snider.

From what we could see in the umpire's box, Barb's pizza
scores. It might not sweep the World Series of pizza, but for
central Indiana it's definitely major-league material. You've got
your choice of thick or thin crust and 4 sizes from 5 to 16 inches.
The crust is nicely done, the sauce gutsy, and most of the toppings quite tasty. The menu states, "Nothing is frozen or
canned," a play that we'll have to call in error, having detected
processed mushrooms, but the excellent fresh sausage sparked
with whole aniseed is a real slugger.

Although we stuck with pizza, the lineup has other stars,
including broasted chicken that comes with homemade biscuits
and real (for a change!) potatoes, rare roast beef stacked high on
French bread, and nice chewy breadsticks.

In the 2 years since Barb showed the people of Chesterfield
how good a real pizza can taste, she has sent two chain pizzerias
to the showers. One hung up the towel completely and the other
switched its sport to Mexican. Of course, we're cheering for Barb
and for all the other small-time entrepreneurs willing to play
hardball with quality against the big-name megabucks chains.

HOURS   Sun.–Thurs. 11 am–10 pm; Fri. & Sat. 11 am–midnight.
Closed Christmas only.

SPECS   209 E. Main St.; (317) 378-0273; no cards; beer only.

DIRECTIONS   From Exit 34, follow signs for IN 32 and turn west
toward Anderson. The restaurant is about 1 mile down, on the left.

BLUE MOUNTAIN COFFEE COMPANY CAFÉ,
Exit 105A, Fort Wayne

The renovation craze has hit Fort Wayne, and "The Landing,"
site of a canal that once connected Indianapolis with Detroit, is
where it struck. By the time you read this there will probably be

half a dozen new restaurants there, but they will have a tall standard to match in the Blue Mountain Coffee Company Café.

It *is* a coffee shop; it's also a trend-conscious quicherie and a health-conscious natural foods–type restaurant where all the ingredients are fresh and cooked to order. Sit in the venerable woody ambiance of a 1914 paper factory, or under sun umbrellas on the sidewalk. Either way, it's a charming place, made more so by a delightful and inexpensive menu.

For under $4 there are bounteous entrée salads—pasta, spinach, seafood, Greek, etc. Our Bombay chicken salad came as a sandwich on excellent home-baked whole-wheat bread ($3.25). A delicately spiced quiche jardiniere ($2.65) was accompanied by wonderful pumpkin muffins. There are sandwiches both old- and new-fashioned, pizza bagels, and chili served with a kaiser roll. You may have trouble choosing between 15 herb and black teas and almost as many coffees, but if you're inclined toward cheesecake you won't be hard pressed to pick a dessert—the version offered here will stand up to most any competitor.

HOURS   Mon.–Thurs. 11 am–midnight; Fri. & Sat. 11 am–1 am. Closed Sundays, but that may soon change (call to check); closed on Sun. & Mon. of major holiday weekends.

SPECS   122 W. Columbia ("The Landing"); (219) 426-1142; V, MC, AE; beer & wine.

DIRECTIONS   Exit 105A puts you on Illinois Rd. In about 2 fast miles, turn left at the T onto Jefferson. Go 0.9 mile and bear left onto W. Main (Lindenwood Cemetery on the left). After 0.4 mile, Main runs into Leesburg. Turn right in order to stay on Main, and 1½ mile later, turn left on Calhoun (1 block past Harrison). Go 1 block on Calhoun and The Landing is on your left. The restaurant is midway down the block, on the left. Park anywhere in the vicinity.

AZTECA, *Exit 109A, Fort Wayne*

How nice to find a family-run Mexican restaurant in an old wood-frame house, a place with real character (not to mention excellent food), whose decor doesn't look like a clone of the last thirteen sombrero joints you've seen.

Don't miss the chicken burritos topped with almond sauce. Okay, maybe it isn't what you'd find on the streets of Guadalajara, but you won't find anything half as good at Chi-Chi's (or its dozens of imitators). For $3.95 you'll get a gigantic plate-filled portion doused in a sauce so divine you'll want to pour it into a cup and drink it. The chunky ranchero sauce that tops the enchiladas is also special, made from tomatoes, onions, and white wine; three of these enchiladas (try chorizo) with soup, beans, rice, and beverage run $6.15 ($3.25 for two at lunch).

Mike and Juanita Rey, who have been presiding over events at Azteca for the past 11 years, have developed such rapport with their customers that they've all taken to vacationing together in Acapulco. If you come looking for one of those gigantic burritos in January, you may go hungry.

HOURS   Mon.–Thurs. 10 am–11 pm; Fri. 10 am–1 am; Sat. noon–1 am; Sun. noon–10 pm. Closed major holiday weekends & the third week of Jan.

SPECS   535 E. State Blvd.; (219) 482-2172; major cards; full bar.

DIRECTIONS   Exit 109A puts you on Goshen. Go about 2½ miles until Goshen ends at State. Turn left onto State and go 0.9 mile to the restaurant, on the left, shortly after crossing the St. Joseph River.

CAPTAIN'S CABIN, *Exit 148, Angola*

We have to give a mixed report on this lovely log restaurant gracing the shore of Crooked Lake. Certainly we can't fault the setting or the lodgelike ambience—they provide as refreshing a diversion from interstate monotony as one could hope for in northeast Indiana. But the Captain's Cabin provided one of our more forgettable seafood dishes, and an unforgettable anecdote associated with it.

Inquiring of the hostess whether what's called whitefish on the menu was Great Lakes whitefish or orange roughy—a pale New Zealand fish also known as "whitefish"—we were brusquely answered by the rhetorical question, "How should I know?" Asking, "Do you know where it comes from?" we were treated to "Out of a box." Then, perhaps because we seemed incredulous, she attempted to assuage our doubts: "We've been serving it for 22 years and it's excellent."

Which it wasn't, and neither were the instant mashed potatoes that accompanied it, a crime we found inexcusable in so upscale a dinner house (most items priced $10 and up.)

But in the least expensive item on the menu—and the one least suggestive of the restaurant's waterfront location—we found perfection. The fried chicken was marvelous, and it cost a mere $5.95 for four full pieces. We'd heard about Indiana-style fried chicken, but hadn't found anything extraordinary until we stopped here. This was our first chance to discern Hoosier-fried from southern-fried. The Indiana version is the result of long, slow pan-frying, a process that cooks the meat through but retains all its luscious juices. The soft batter is not doughy, but it isn't crisp either, and it adheres to the meat, adding its mildly spiced flavor to that of the chicken, rather than seeming like a separate entity.

We also appreciated the cheese-and-cracker plate that reached us the moment we sat down, the baked potato dolloped with scallion-and-chive-sparked sour cream, and the insulated quart pot of coffee that was set on our table after dinner. All were included in the dinner price.

Stick with the chicken, enjoy the view, and you'll be glad you took the crooked road to Crooked Lake.

HOURS   Summer (week after Mother's Day through Labor Day): Mon.–Thurs. 5–9:30 pm; Fri. & Sat. 5–10:30 or 11 pm; closed Sun. Winter: Wed. 5–8:30 pm; Fri. & Sat. 5–9:30 pm; closed Sun.–Tues. & Thurs. In summer, reservations helpful on weekends.

SPECS   184 Crooked Lake Rd.; (219) 665-5663; no cards; full bar.

DIRECTIONS   From Exit 148, turn left if southbound, right if northbound. Go about ½ mile to the first crossroad and turn left (sign for Crooked Lake). In 1½ miles, turn left at the stop sign onto Highway 100N. In 0.9 mile, turn right at the stop sign onto Highway 290W. In 0.6 mile, the road turns 90° to the left; stay on it and you'll see the restaurant 0.2 mile farther, on the right. There, there, it isn't so bad.

Michigan

PADDY McGEE'S, *I-75 Interchange, Flint*

The food isn't as Irish as the name, but it sure is good. See pp. 146–147.

DIRECTIONS At the I-75 interchange, enter I-75 North for about 1 mile to Exit 118. Then follow directions given on p. 147.

ANGELO'S CONEY ISLAND,
Northern terminus of I-69, Flint

For short-order fare, Angelo's is at the top of its class. See pp. 145–146.

DIRECTIONS When I-69 ends in downtown Flint, continue straight on M-21 to I-475 North, which you should take to Exit 8B. Then follow northbound directions given on p. 145.

Missouri
Illinois
Indiana
Ohio

Missouri

ABOUT ST. LOUIS

If you take I-270 around St. Louis you may save some time, but you'll miss the best eats. If you insist, however, we found a good pasta and pizza place for you out in the northern suburbs. It's **The Pasta House Co.,** in Florissant, Missouri, included here at the end of the I-70 entries for St. Louis.

CROWN CANDY KITCHEN,
Exit 248 & St. Louis Street Exit, St. Louis

George Karandzieff's father started this neighborhood candy store in 1913, back when the dairies would outfit your soda shop for free with walnut booths and Tiffany lamps if only you'd carry their ice cream. George grew up in the apartment over the store and stuck it out while the neighborhood around him declined. His reward came when the nostalgia craze propelled the Crown to citywide recognition, and now the place is packed at lunchtime with downtown folks who enjoy his corned beef sandwiches and malted milks.

The Crown is cheerful, bright, bustling, noisy, and *very, very* friendly. The clientele may be more prosperous than the neighborhood, but the prices aren't—sandwiches from $1.25–$2.35, sundaes are $1.65, malts and Newberrys for 10 cents less (you'll just have to visit if you want to find out what a Newberry is). George's sons make the ice cream right here, and if the corned beef on rye wasn't perfection for the species (it came with lettuce!), it was really very good.

This was not the most beautiful soda shop we found in the Midwest. In fact, its wooden fixtures have actually been painted, and there's really nothing left that is picturesque. What the Crown does have though is love, enthusiasm, cheerfulness, and the kind of spirit that gets generated when people who like each other work together for 20 years.

You'll like it! We promise.

HOURS Mon.–Sat. 10:30 am–10 pm; Sun. noon–10 pm. Closed major holidays.

SPECS 1401 St. Louis St.; (314) 621-9713; no cards; no liquor.

DIRECTIONS **Westbound:** Take Exit 248B/Branch Street. In the exit ramp bear left following signs for Natural Bridge. Go under the interstate and then immediately turn left. Go 4 blocks to St. Louis. Turn right, go 1 block, and it's on the corner, on the right.

Eastbound: Exit at St. Louis St. Go 3 blocks west. It's on the corner, on the right.

LACLEDE'S LANDING RESTAURANTS,
Cole Street & Memorial Drive Exits, St. Louis

Laclede's Landing is an urban gentrification project that has turned about 10 square blocks of old St. Louis into a veritable beehive of trendy restaurants. You name it, it's here, from clams and oysters in a restaurant that looks like an East Coast diner, through fast food from at least five nationalities, to all the fettuccine alfredo, quiche, or spinach salad you could want.

We counted at least twenty restaurants. No way we were going to check them all out, so this one we leave to your spirit of adventure. If you need more inducements, know that all this is right on the levee of the Mississippi, and it will take you less than a minute to reach it from I-70.

DIRECTIONS   Eastbound: Take the Cole St. Exit and get into the lane that is as far to the right as possible. From the end of the ramp go straight ahead for 3 lights and turn left onto Laclede's Landing Blvd. You're there. Park where you can and walk. **Note:** If you turn too sharply to the left you will end up on the Martin Luther King Bridge bound for Illinois. You got into the right hand lane so that you could make the gentlest possible left turn. All traffic must turn left here.

Westbound: Take the exit for Memorial Drive/Arch. Follow signs for Laclede's Landing, which is north of the arch.

AMIGHETTI'S BAKERY
LOU BOCCARDI'S
CUNETO HOUSE OF PASTA, *I-55 Exit, St. Louis*

Travelers on I-70 may want to take the extra time to learn about the Italian restaurants in The Hill section of St. Louis. See pp. 23–25 for details.

DIRECTIONS   To get there from I-70 wait until you are near the arch, just west of the bridge over the Mississippi. Then follow signs for I-55 South. Go south on I-55 for about a mile and then turn onto I-44. From there follow directions on pp. 24–25.

THE PASTA HOUSE CO., *I-270, Exit 27, Florissant*

We thought that pasta with asparagus and mushrooms in cream sauce would be a pretty severe test for a local pizza and pasta chain that decks itself out in a cheap version of Tiffany lamps and butcher-block tables. Frankly, we weren't expecting much, and so we were delightfully surprised by the not subtle and not exquisite but nonetheless hearty, full-flavored, and inexpensive dish ($5; $3 for a half order). We sincerely doubt you'll do much better without going into St. Louis, so this is the best bet for those determined to avoid downtown. The spumoni, however, was only so-so, and the Muzak was what you'd expect.

There are about two dozen other pasta dishes, half with red sauces and half with white, ranging from $3.55 to $6.50. All can be gotten in half orders. Pizzas are $4.50/$5.50, and sandwiches are $3.25–$3.95.

HOURS   Mon.–Thurs. 11 am–12 midnight; Fri. 11 am–1 am; Sat. 2 pm–1 am; Sun. 4 pm–10 pm.

SPECS   1788 N. Florissant Rd.; (314) 837-1500; V, MC, AE; full bar; children's menu.

DIRECTIONS   From Exit 27 of I-270 go 2 miles north on N. Florissant Rd. to Lindberg. Cross Lindberg, and it's on the right, in a little shopping plaza.

Illinois

THE STOCKYARDS INN
SCOVILLE'S CAFE, *Exit 2, National City*

Just east of St. Louis I-70 and I-55 run together. See pp. 25–26 under I-55 for two very beefy restaurants in the St. Louis stockyards. Directions are on p. 26.

EL DORADO RESTAURANT, *Exit 11, Collinsville*

Just east of St. Louis I-70 and I-55 run together. See pp. 26–27 for a description of a very good Mexican restaurant just a little over a mile from the road.

THE POWHATAN MOTEL AND RESTAURANT,
Exit 36, Pocahontas

We listened here to farmers talking about the rain that came in from Brownsville but missed Pocahontas. We checked out the display of bowling trophies on the pie cooler and considered buying a license plate that read HAPPINESS IS YELLING BINGO. We also ate a good, honest barbecued beef sandwich for which we'll make no apologies ($2.95) and noticed that the American fries were real while the mashed potatoes were not.

Dinners are $4.95–$6.75; burgers are $2.95 with salad and fries. The place is clean, light, plastic, inoffensive, and new— quite innocent of anything like style or decoration.

HOURS   Daily 24 hours. Closed Christmas.

SPECS   (618) 669-2233; no cards; full bar.

DIRECTIONS   Eastbound turn right and westbound left at Exit 36. Go ¼ mile, on the right.

THE TOWNE HOUSE, *Exit 61, Vandalia*

We're pretty sure that you'll do no better hereabouts than at The Towne House, which, despite its orthography, put up for us a terrific taco salad—black olives, red onions, cherry tomatoes, red cabbage, and shredded American cheese over standard greens and spicy ground beef, topped with sour cream, guacamole, and salsa. All of this was stuffed to overflowing into a crispy 6-inch shell, and though it was neither authentic nor superb, we'd be happy to come back and try it again anytime.

We didn't expect that from Vandalia, nor a menu with bouil-

75

labaisse and a nightly international special. It's all the doing of owner Bill Braden, who's been all over the country on the horse-racing circuit and now has come back to teach Vandalia what he learned about eating.

Bill is learning too—that you can only step out so far ahead of your audience. The bouillabaisse has already bitten the dust, but lots of good sandwiches, like Italian beef and Reubens, remain at lunchtime ($1.95–$3.95) and at night there's chicken cordon bleu ($8.50) right next to breaded, fried catfish ($7.95). The taco salad is $5.95, and you can get away with just $4.95 for liver 'n' onions or spaghetti.

Expect no grand decor. Attempts have been made to nicen things up by placing brown tablecloths over red, but the tubular steel chairs and the indoor mansard roofs make it clear that this is still a country place without serious pretensions.

The waitresses were *very* helpful, and everything about the place seemed to show that it is really trying.

HOURS   Mon.–Sat. 11 am–midnight; Sun. 10 am–2 pm.

SPECS   401 W. Gallatin; (618) 283-1812; V; full bar.

DIRECTIONS   From Exit 61 turn right if eastbound and left if westbound. Go about 1.2 miles to the light at Gallatin. Turn right, go 1 block, and it's on the right.

THELMA'S, *Exit 160, Effingham*

Thelma's is, by all accounts, the "really nice" restaurant in Effingham, and it's got a handful of stars from the *Mobil Guide* to prove it. So we thought we'd check it out even though it's attached to one of those Ramada Inns where the lobby is done up like a brothel to satisfy an impoverished conception of luxury.

We decided that the *Mobil Guide* must award its stars for wallpaper, which, we grant, was here used very imaginatively. And, of course, everything looked very "nice." But the pork chops were flavorless and dry, and the deep-dish apple pie was only okay, even though it was touted as a house specialty. The rice was the best thing we tasted, but it was marred by dried-out grains that found their way onto the plate.

Dinners are $4.95–$12.95; lunches from $2.95 for a pita sandwich to $6.95 for a Louisiana shrimp bowl.

HOURS   Daily 6 am–10 pm.

SPECS   N. Keller Drive; (217) 342-2131; major cards; full bar.

DIRECTIONS   Just north of the Exit 160 ramp, in the Ramada Inn. Can't be missed.

TRAILWAYS, *Exit 162, Effingham*

So far as we could tell, Trailways is *the* place in Effingham. It's close to the exit, it's cheap, and all that we tried there was good or better.

From the outside, Trailways is barn-siding styled so as to give it a vaguely western look, a look that would be more convincing were it not plunked down between a Shell station and the Lincoln Lodge Motel. Inside, there's one section that is inoffensively plain and plasticky, and a dining area that is a bit classier but certainly without pretensions.

We liked it just fine, beginning with its friendly, smiling waitresses, proceeding on to its fine, light, tasty pancakes and fresh eggs. We talked them into letting us sample the fried chicken house specialty at breakfast and can report a savory concatenation of spices and a batter that was not overwhelming—a good deal at $3.55 for three pieces and three vegetables.

The daily lunch specials are modestly priced in the vicinity of $2.35, and you can get a catfish dinner for $3.95. Absolutely the most you can spend is $7.25 for a 10-ounce rib eye. Hamburgers are $1.35.

We can't think of a reason to go looking anywhere else, unless maybe you've got to entertain a client, in which case, see Thelma's above.

HOURS   Sun.–Thurs. 6:30 am–9:30 pm; Fri. & Sat. 6:30 am–10 pm. Closed Christmas & 10 days in early January.

SPECS   (217) 342-2680; no cards; no liquor.

DIRECTIONS   Turn right from Exit 162. It's just north of the exit, on the right.

RICHARDS FARMHOUSE RESTAURANT,
Exit 129, Casey

We've seen plenty of barn restaurants in suburbia, and even a few in true urbia. But this is the first one we've come upon in a genuinely agricultural area, and it's the first we've seen that really works. Gary Richards grew up on the farm that included this handsome 1930s specimen of rural architecture, and in it he raised a few hogs for 4-H shows and such. Later the barn fell idle. After marrying Diane, Gary began casting about for a use for the neglected building.

Although the conversion of an old barn to a new restaurant probably wouldn't have raised any eyebrows in the suburbs, rural America considered it the cat's meow (the pig's squeal?). In 1977, its first year of operation, Richards Farmhouse Restaurant was the subject of feature articles in *Farm Wife News*, the *Prairie Farmer*, and other magazines. Real farmers found it a sincere tribute to their vocation and their way of life.

Fortunately, Richards Farmhouse Restaurant is a farmhouse restaurant in more than just decor. The cooking here is country style, and it is very, very good. Knowing full well that southern Illinois is hog country, Gary and Diane specialize in pork. The dish they have made famous is the 1-pound pork chop. This behemoth arrives standing upright, cloaked in a tangy red barbecue sauce, cooked through and through, but sweet and succulent just the same. The $11.95 dinnertime price tag includes the soup and salad bar, and a dandy one it is, complete with fresh loaves of white and whole-wheat bread just waiting to be cut and slathered with zesty apple butter or strawberry preserves fruity enough to be baked in a pie.

Richards also has giant fresh tenderloin sandwiches ($4.95), ham steaks ($8.95), ribs (weekends only), and—straying from swine but almost as popular hereabouts—farm-raised catfish ($7.95). For dessert, we draw your attention to peanut butter pie, a smooth and creamy southern specialty that seems right at home here in southern Illinois.

HOURS   Lunch: Sun.–Fri. 11 am–1:30 pm. Dinner: Sun.–Thurs. 5–8:30 pm; Fri. & Sat. 5–9:30 pm. No lunch Sat. Closed major holidays.

SPECS   (217) 932-5300; V, MC; full bar; children's menu.

DIRECTIONS   From Exit 129, turn left if westbound, right if eastbound, onto IL 49 South. In 1 mile turn left at the stop sign onto US 40. Go exactly 0.6 mile to the first crossroad and turn left. You'll see it, on the right.

Indiana

RICHARDS TOWN HOUSE RESTAURANT,
Exit 7, Terre Haute

When Gary and Diane Richards found their Farmhouse Restaurant (see above) so well received, they decided to go to town. Wisely, the Richards didn't try to put their townhouse in an ersatz barn, but housed it instead in a fine old lushly appointed brick home. It's a lovely place, with marble-hearthed fireplaces and all the trappings of class, but we think the Richardses got a little carried away with their newfound status as townsfolk. They could have done without the 40-foot gold canopy that runs out to the sidewalk; the waiters in bow ties and cutaways might also have been toned down, especially their practice of hoisting trays into the heave-ho position—even when they're carrying just one little dish 10 feet!

Still, between the chuckles, we enjoyed our lunch. A lovely sweet-and-sour salad dressing started things off right, and the quiche that followed was tasty, if unorthodox—an abundance of finely chopped vegetables made it denser, less of a custard than usual. (Unfortunately, the accompanying croissant was a total disaster.) Other lunch possibilities include chicken crêpes, fresh tenderloin sandwiches, taco salad, and a spicy beef sandwich. Most items run $4–$6.

At dinnertime, prices and menu offerings go uptown—sole amandine, for instance, steak Diane, or charbroiled swordfish ($10–$13). And while Richards Townhouse does not echo the Farmhouse's menu, the cult of the giant pork chop is continued and here it reaches its ultimate expression: They don't merely serve the 1-pound cut of meat, they make it into a Broadway production. Each chop is numbered and its recipient is asked to "preserve this exclusive experience in the annals of time by signing our register."

The meat itself may not be overdone, but the act surely is.

HOURS   Lunch: Mon.–Fri. 11 am–2 pm. Dinner: Mon.–Thurs. 5–9 pm; Fri. & Sat. 5–10 pm. Closed Sun.

SPECS   1000 S. 6th St.; (812) 232-4879; major cards; full bar.

DIRECTIONS   From Exit 7, turn left if eastbound, right if westbound, onto US 40 North (3rd St.). Go about 1½ miles to the light at Farrington (unmarked, but it's 1 light after Washington). Turn right onto Farrington to 6th St. It's on the corner.

THE BRIARPATCH
THE BAKERY, *Exit 11, Terre Haute*

Once upon a time, Mrs. Loyd ("only one *l*, it's Welsh") was a nursery-school teacher who raised 150 varieties of herbs in a Colonial-style garden for pleasure (but not a bit of profit). She considered selling her herbs but never did she even dream of opening a public eatery. "If someone had given me the money to open a shiny new restaurant in the middle of town," she declares with a never-waning twinkle in her eye, "I wouldn't have been the least bit interested."

No, Mrs. Loyd was quite satisfied being "The Herb Lady of Terre Haute." She appeared on television once a month to discuss herb gardening and cookery. Being naturally sociable, she invited the TV audience to her 30-acre homestead on the edge of town, and she promised them tea and herb cookies if they wanted to stay. They came, they stayed, and they returned with families, friends, garden clubs, and whatnot. And soon Mrs. Loyd found herself swept into the restaurant business, preparing and serving gorgeous herb-sparked salads, richly appointed quiches, marvelous crêpes, and fluffy omelets, in a tastefully refurbished vinegar barn beside her garden. And then, with the same gentle vengeance that she brought to her gardening and her cooking, she took up baking to supply the restaurant. It, too, expanded beyond her reasonable expectations, and to stem the tide of enthusiastic pastry seekers she opened a full-scale bakery nearby.

So, for the residents of Terre Haute, the story of The Briarpatch is a happy tale of culinary pleasure. But for the interstate traveler it is more problematic: Mrs. Loyd has (so far) resisted all temptation to expand her dining room beyond thirty seats, and it is usually impossible to occupy one of them without reserving it first. Normally, that would disqualify her restaurant from inclusion in a book like this, but we couldn't resist telling you about The Briarpatch, especially considering that it is found in a region of the country noted much more for growing food than for cooking it. If you can phone Mrs. Loyd in advance, you won't regret the effort. Ask to sit in the glass-enclosed garden room and you'll be doubly happy.

But even if such planning is impossible, you can at least have coffee and dessert (or Continental breakfast) at The Bakery, where sweet rolls, cookies, coffee cakes, pastry, and breads come out of the oven 7 days a week.

HOURS   **The Briarpatch:** Lunch: Tues.–Sat. seatings at 11:30 am
and 1 pm; Dinner: Fri. & Sat. only, 6–8:30 pm.
The Bakery: Mon.–Sat. 7 am–6:30 pm; Sun. 8 am–noon.

SPECS   **The Briarpatch:** 2000 S. Fruitridge Ave.; (812) 232-6283; no cards; wine only.
The Bakery: 2410 College Ave.; (812) 235-2531.

DIRECTIONS   The Briarpatch: From Exit 11, turn right onto IN 46 North for a few hundred yards to the first possible left turn onto (unmarked) Margaret Ave. Go 1.4 miles to Fruitridge. Turn right on Fruitridge, and go 1.2 miles to the restaurant, on the right, 0.2 mile past the stop sign at Hulman. Look for a maroon mailbox on the left, across from the restaurant's long driveway.

The Bakery: Continue 0.3 mile past **The Briarpatch** to the first left, a small unmarked country lane. Go 1 mile to the light at 25th St. **The Bakery** is ½ block past the light, on the right.

TORR'S RESTAURANT, *Exit 41, Greencastle*

To be perfectly honest about it, we didn't expect we'd be writing about Torr's when we first saw it. For one thing, it looks on the outside like just about every other vaguely Colonial steakhouse, and inside the decor is plushly pretentious, like a clubby basement barroom. And the menu—well, we practically fell asleep reading it.

But something surprising happened: The food was good. Here we found our best grilled pork tenderloin in a state that prides itself on that dish. The fresh meat was thick and juicy, nicely browned on the outside, sandwiched into a decent bun with frilly leaf lettuce and generous slices of bright red tomato ($2.25). We also had fluffy, tender, batter-dipped onion rings that clearly were not out of a freezer bag ($1.65). A tostada from the Tex-Mex side of the menu didn't inspire us to shout *"Ole!"* but it could have held its own in the ring against most Hoosier-style Mexicana we found. For dessert, homemade strawberry pie was clearly the way to go, and with it we went. There was no dearth of fresh strawberries, bound together with a nice light syrup, and topped with real whipped cream.

Not everything here is fresh and homemade, but if you pick and choose (consult your waitress—ours was most candid), you're likely to do very well, especially with the meats, all of them selected and hand cut by Terry Torr, whose father opened this restaurant 24 years ago. The decor has changed since then, but not the reputation for quality food.

HOURS Tues.–Sat. 11 am–midnight; Sun. 11 am–10 pm. Closed Mon.

SPECS US 40 at US 231; (317) 653-2666; V, MC, AE, D; full bar; children's portions.

DIRECTIONS It's 3½ miles north of Exit 41, at the junction with US 40, on the left.

SHAPIRO'S DELI, *Exit 79B, Indianapolis*

There's a hand-lettered sign behind the cash register at Shapiro's Deli in the south end of Indianapolis:

> COOK GOOD
> SERVE GENEROUSLY
> PRICE MODESTLY
> PEOPLE WILL COME

And they have, since 1905 when Louis Shapiro opened Indianapolis' only Kosher deli/grocery in order to serve the city's growing Jewish community on the south side. The Jewish population has migrated north since then, but Shapiro's is still a thriving Indianapolis institution run by Louis' son Max, now 80 years old.

We arrived prepared to allow for "Indiana Kosher," but left knowing allowances weren't needed. Our brisket sandwich, for example, was absolutely first rate—2½ inches thick, juicy, tasty, and served on fresh-baked rye bread that would have been admired in New York's lower East Side. The hard rolls were also excellent, and Shapiro's corned beef was as good and authentic as the brisket. All the meats here have been cooked on the premises; in sandwiches, they are well worth their $2.95 price tags.

We were also happily satisfied with Shapiro's stuffed cabbage ($3.95). While somewhat short of Grandma Schwartz's unmatchable standard, the matzoh-ball soup and chopped liver were highly respectable; potato latkes were thick and tasty, but a little too greasy to tempt us to fill our plate (55 cents apiece).

Shapiro's is in a single, spacious, no-nonsense room that has expanded to four times the size it was when young Max was the floor sweeper and salami sold for 29 cents a pound. In addition to the main cafeteria, there's also a deli counter where you can stock up on carry-out orders. With a loaf of that good rye and some sliced tongue or perhaps a few smoked golden whitefish, you'll feast in high Jewish style all the way to Chicago. Just make sure to grab a fistful of napkins on your way out the door.

HOURS   Daily 6:30 am–8:30 pm. Closed major holidays.

SPECS   808 S. Meridian; (317) 631-4041; no cards; no liquor; children's portions.

DIRECTIONS   **Eastbound:** From Exit 79B, go straight, following signs for McCarty St. Turn left at the first light. **Shapiro's** parking lot is in the first block, on the left. The restaurant is through the lot and across the street.

Westbound: From Exit 79B (McCarty), turn left at the light and in ½ block you'll see **Shapiro's** parking lot on the left; the restaurant is through the lot and across the street.

THE CANARY CAFÉ, *Exit 83A, Indianapolis*

On pp. 58–59 you can read about this adorable little breakfast and lunch nook. It's easily reached from I-70.

DIRECTIONS   **Westbound:** From Exit 83A, turn right at the first light onto Michigan. Go 5 lights (about ½ mile) and turn right onto Delaware. In 2 blocks, the restaurant is on the left. The parking area is in front.

Eastbound: At the I-65 interchange, enter I-65 North (toward Chicago). Within a mile, take Exit 113 and turn left at the light onto Pennsylvania. Go to the third traffic light and turn left onto North St. One block brings you to Delaware; go left on Delaware and in 1 block the restaurant is on the left. Parking area is in front.

JODY'S RESTAURANT, *Exit 145, Centerville*

Jody's may be the only business in Centerville that doesn't sell antiques. Not in the market for an oak washstand or a Governor Winthrop chair, we were happy to take a seat in this comely lunchroom that has lost none of its charm in 50 years. In fact, based on the faded picture postcards sold at the front counter, Jody's seems to have improved with age. Recent redecorating has yielded a stenciled look, cozy corner seats, and a skylight framed by plants.

But don't get the impression that this is a stylish bricks-plants-and-oak café. It's still the same neighborhood restaurant it always was. And the pork tenderloin sandwiches, a Hoosier specialty, are as good—and as big—as ever. The breaded slice of meat came out of the fryer practically greaseless; it overlapped the bun by an inch all around. This came for $2.80 with french fries and a fragrant herbed vinegar coleslaw.

Although there are a few concessions to modern taste (french-fried zucchini and potato skins, for instance), the regular selections on Jody's menu lean heavily toward sandwich platters of the old-fashioned kind. Featured items change from day to day, but they're not likely to stray far from fresh roast pork, chicken and dumplings, or ham with beans and cornbread ($4.95, with three sides). Another old-fashioned winner is the apple dumpling, a most comforting and delicious dessert ($1.35) that has been a favorite here since the restaurant opened 30 years ago.

We asked Jody's manager if the restaurant had any particular specialty. Her emphatic answer used only two words: "Home cooking!" From what we could taste, it was the truth.

HOURS   Sun.–Wed., & Fri. & Sat. 6 am–8 pm. Closed Thursdays; also closed Christmas week & some holidays (open for most).

SPECS   Main St. & US 40; (317) 855-5277; no cards; no liquor; children's portions.

DIRECTIONS   From Exit 145, turn right if eastbound, left if westbound. Go 2¾ miles into Centerville. The restaurant is at the traffic light, on the right.

Ohio

MYUNG SUNG RESTAURANT, *Exit 38, Huber Heights*

Myung Sung means "Bright Star" in Chinese, and if you've a penchant for adventuresome Oriental eating, this extremely pleasant restaurant may well be the bright star in your journey. Oh, there are Mandarin and Cantonese dishes of the Moo Goo Gai Pan variety, all right, but we suggest you address yourself to the Korean specialties.

If you're willing to venture into Korean cuisine but want to play it safe, opt for bool-ko-ki, marinated beef barbecue that is basically familiar but flavored exotically enough to keep you guessing. Like all the Korean entrees, it comes with three kinds of kimchee (pickled vegetables served as side dishes). Slightly more daring is bool-kal-bi, a best-seller among Myung Sung's Korean patrons; it's similar to bool-ko-ki, but ribs are used and sliced so artistically as to be hardly recognizable (also $8.75). And if you've a proclivity for spicy foods, tell us if you've ever had anything hotter than yuk kae jung ($5.95), a full-meal soup of beef with Korean greens (including ferns) and the sizzlingest peppers on either side of the Pacific, ground and fermented all winter. Another soup, much easier on the palate, is naeng myun ($5.95), a cold broth with delicious, chewy buckwheat noodles.

Should you be traveling in a caravan, request seating in one of the three tatami rooms where guests sit on cushions and eat off a low table; parties of six or more are needed to occupy these secluded and serene chambers. But no matter where you sit, and whatever you order, you'll be charmed to receive the obligatory fortune cookie amidst an artful array of fresh fruit slices. It's that kind of place.

HOURS   Mon.–Thurs. 11 am–10 pm; Fri. & Sat. 11 am–11 pm; Sun. noon–9 pm.

SPECS   5186 Brandt Pike; (513) 233-7764; V, MC; full bar.

DIRECTIONS   From Exit 38, turn right if eastbound, left if westbound, onto OH 201 South. In 3 miles, it's on the left; big sign.

YOUNG'S JERSEY DAIRY, *Exit 52A, Yellow Springs*

The students of Antioch College in Yellow Springs are nationally known for their flagrant individualism, but you would be hard pressed to find one who is not a devoted fan of Young's Dairy about 6 miles up the road in the little town of Hustead. A western Ohio institution since the '50s, Young's is a working farm and a 24-hour dairy bar.

Jersey cows, whose milk is famed for its quality but not quantity, are shunned by most dairymen as uneconomical. Not the Youngs, whose herd is 100 percent Jersey. These small, brown-backed bovines can be seen, heard, and, yes, whiffed from the picnic tables in front of the dairy. The raw ingredient they produce is sold in every form possible inside the dairy bar. Of course, the most popular one is ice cream, guaranteed to be 14 percent butterfat, available in 15 or so flavors as a calf shake (2 scoops plus whole Jersey milk), cow shake (4 scoops), or diet-dashing bull shake (5 scoops). Our strawberry cow shake contained walnut-sized nuggets of firm, fresh strawberries ($1.99).

It's not all ice cream here (though you might get the wrong impression in a quick glance). There are freshly baked doughnuts, breads and pastries, egg breakfasts, homemade biscuits, hamburgers, sandwiches, and chili, all at most reasonable prices (i.e., 55 cents for grilled cheese).

As we left (another shake in hand), we got to musing about how students select their colleges, and in the end we concluded that Antioch might not be a bad choice at all.

HOURS   Daily, 24 hours.

SPECS   6880 Springfield-Xenia Rd., Hustead; (513) 325-0629; no cards; no liquor.

DIRECTIONS   From Exit 52A, take Route 68 South for 5¼ miles. It's on the left. No traffic or lights, so it's just 5 or 6 minutes from the highway.

HENRY AND MIRIAM'S RESTAURANT,
Exit 80, West Jefferson

There's a sign outside Henry and Miriam's Restaurant: YOU CAN'T BEAT OUR PRICES OR OUR QUALITY. Seeing it, the trusting motorist may salivate while contemplating a plate of appetizing home-cooked food. But underneath that sign, another one shatters the image: CUSTOM EXHAUST PIPE BENDING DONE HERE.

Henry and Miriam's Restaurant, a wing off the west end of Henry's Sohio Service Station, is a relic from an earlier age, from before the days when service station restaurants had the grimy ring of "truck stop" about them. Henry's is decidedly *not* a truck stop—not in its clientele, not in its lodgelike pine-paneled decor, and certainly not in its cooking.

With the exception of powdered mashed potatoes and a few mushy canned vegetables, the food at Henry's is home cooked and good. Navy bean soup was delicious, highlighted by nice chunks of ham (85 cents). Two grilled pork chops were juicy, and perfectly cooked, and they came with french fries, tossed salad, bread, and coffee for just $3.75.

But a slice of pie will be the highlight of any stop at Henry and Miriam's. A display case on the wall flaunts the ribbons that the owners' neighbor, pie-baker-extraordinaire Madge Knox, has copped at the Ohio State Fair's annual pie-baking competition. It's a lean year when Madge walks away with fewer than a dozen awards. Sour cherry is her most consistent blue-ribbon winner, but we arrived before the cherries did. However, we had no trouble consoling ourselves with slices of Madge's rhubarb-strawberry and apple pies, both of them winners in our contest.

HOURS   Mon.–Sat. 6:30 am–8 pm. Closed Sun.

SPECS   6275 US 40, between towns of West Jefferson & Lafayette; (614) 879-9321; no cards; no liquor.

DIRECTIONS From Exit 80, turn right if eastbound, left if westbound, onto OH 29 for 2¼ miles to the flashing light at US 40. Turn right and in ½ mile, it's on the left, adjacent to the Sohio station.

COURT OF SMALL CLAMS,
Exits 100A & 100B, Columbus

Uptown, tony, Yuppie, trendy—all the adjectives of tasteful urbane extravagance apply to this chic food and spirits emporium. It's a theme restaurant, all right, but the legal theme isn't one that's been overworked, and it *is* across the street from the County Courthouse and the Ohio Supreme Court. Menus are served up in the form of a subpoena, and dishes wear names like Jury Pick-erel and No Confession Breast of Chicken.

Gimmicks aside, it's a gorgeous place. The downstairs lounge is truly elegant in a Victorian manner; upstairs, there are well-placed touches of fine modern design.

What's nice is that you can pick your menu as you decide where to sit. In the lounge, fish and meat entrees as well as salads and sandwiches are available all day for a surprisingly reasonable $4.50 or $5. Prices climb as you ascend the steps, where luncheon entrees average $7 and most dinners are twice that. What you're paying for, besides the atmosphere, is the ultimate in today's notion of rustic luxury: mesquite-broiled fish. The fish is brought in fresh from both coasts and the Great Lakes, the mesquite from Mexico. If you've not yet discovered what happens to seafood when it meets smoking mesquite branches, this is as good a place to learn as any you're likely to find in land-locked America. Swordfish was our choice, but it could have been tuna, salmon, red snapper, or half a dozen others. Dinner entrées include soup or salad and are garnished with redskin potatoes and fresh vegetables. Satisfied as we were, we thought it rather nervy that they charged $1.25 extra for a baked potato. But if you're pinching pennies, you'd best stay downstairs, where the mesquite broiling is just a faint aroma in the background.

HOURS Downstairs: Mon.–Thurs. 11 am–10 pm; Fri. & Sat. 11 am–midnight; Sun. 5–10 pm. Upstairs: Mon.–Thurs. 11 am–2 pm and

6–10 pm; Fri. 11 am–2 pm and 6 pm–midnight; Sat. 6 pm–midnight; Sun. 5–10 pm. Closed Christmas day only.

SPECS 350 S. High St. (at Mound); (614) 464-1919; V, MC, AE; full bar.

DIRECTIONS **Eastbound:** From Exit 100A, turn left at the second light onto S. High, go 2 blocks and the restaurant is on the right, at the corner of S. High and Mound.

Westbound: From Exit 100B, go straight, following signs for 23 South; don't bear right onto 4th St. Go 3 lights and turn right onto S. High St. Go 1 block to the restaurant, on the right, at the corner of S. High and Mound.

LINDEY'S, *Exits 100A & 100B, Columbus*

This is an outstanding restaurant situated in one of the nicest urban renovations we've seen. See pp. 103–104. I-70 and I-71 run concurrently here, so it's equally accessible from either.

DIRECTIONS **Eastbound:** Exit 100A puts you on Livingston. Turn right at the fourth light (Mohawk) and in 2 blocks it's on your right at the corner of Beck.

Westbound: From Exit 100B, follow the signs for 23 South (*don't* bear right onto 4th St.) At the second light turn left onto 3rd St. and cross over the interstate. Be sure to get into the center lane or you'll be forced back onto the highway. Immediately after crossing the highway, turn left and then right at the first light onto Mohawk. In 2 blocks the restaurant is on your right, at the corner of Beck.

TOM'S ICE CREAM BOWL, *Exit 153A, Zanesville*

For "serious" restaurants, we found Zanesville to be Zerosville, but eventually we were led to this gleaming 1950-vintage dairy bar that doubles as a candy store and lunch counter. In Tom's, Zanesvillians have something to be proud of, an endangered species of classic American eatery alive and thriving.

The kitchen specials are basic but honest: fresh ground chuck in the hamburgers, for instance, and only 90 cents at that, but don't expect mushroom or zucchini toppings. The Virginia ham sandwich (all of $1.15) was slightly sweet and delicious; the homemade vegetable soup was decent (75 cents). Of course, these and a few others of their ilk are mere preludes to the main act—Tom's made-on-the-premises ice cream, served in its many permutations and variations. There are only 13 or 14 flavors, however, and among them you will not find piña colada or Macadamia nut, but the old standbys come off ever so smooth and creamy.

If a limited menu will do, Tom's is just the place to chase away those mid-Ohio interstate blues.

HOURS   Sun. & Tues.–Thurs. 11 am–10 pm; Fri. & Sat. 11 am–11 pm. Closed Mon. & week of July 4th.

SPECS   532 McIntire Ave.; (614) 452-5267; no cards; no liquor.

DIRECTIONS   Eastbound: From Exit 153A, turn left at the stop sign and left again at the light onto State St. Cross over the highway and turn right at the second set of lights onto McIntire. In 0.4 mile, it's on the right.

Westbound: From Exit 153A, turn right onto State St. and right again at the first light onto McIntire. In 0.4 mile, it's on the right.

INN-TOWN RESTAURANT, *Exit 169, New Concord*

Here's a corner restaurant in what was once an Oldsmobile showroom. The food is a mixed bag, so we will guide you directly to the mouth-watering pork tenderloin, hand cut into thick slices by owner Pat Clapper, whose "secret recipe" breading had a delightful nuttiness. As a complete dinner it's $3.45, in a sandwich just $2.10. Pat also makes pies and doughnuts, and when time allows she roasts her own beef, but many of the other menu items are prepackaged convenience items, so it's best to quiz the waitress.

While hardly what we'd call cozy, the place is clean and cheerful in a linoleum sort of way. However, one vestige of the old car dealership still in effect is garage-style rest-room facilities that we found to be less than adequate, so you might want to plan accordingly.

HOURS   Mon.–Sat. 6 am–8 pm; Sun. 7 am–3 pm. Closed major holidays.

SPECS   W. Main St.; (614) 826-4716; no cards; no liquor.

DIRECTIONS   From Exit 169, head north on OH 83 to the junction of US 40; it's on the corner.

THE CONEY ISLAND, *Exit 178, Cambridge*

In midwestern lingo, a hot dog is called a "Coney Island" if it's topped with chili and onions. Presumably, it's named for New York City's now-defunct beachside amusement park. But there, it's called a hot dog! Clearly, The Coney Island in Cambridge, Ohio, specializes in hot dogs (er, "conies"). In genuine midwestern fashion, they come topped with mustard, onions, and chili. Not bad, and only 55 cents.

This is a clean and comfortable downtown eatery with a few Victorian touches that seem more accidental than stylish. Aside from franks, it serves basic American fare—sandwiches, fresh ground hamburgers, meat and potatoes dinners, etc., all at low, low prices ($2.75 for a roast beef dinner or $1 for tuna salad, for example). Not everything is homemade—respectable, homemade coleslaw shares the plate with instant mashed potatoes.

But we weren't disappointed at all with The Coney Island's pies: tender, flaky crusts holding sizable morsels of obviously fresh fruit, not oversweetened or lost in glutinous syrup, but slightly tart and bursting with flavor. The peach pie we enjoyed here goes down in the annals as the gold medalist in its class.

For the pies and the prices, The Coney Island is a real find; for most anything else, it'll do just fine.

HOURS   Sat. & Mon.–Thurs. 6 am–7 pm; Fri. 6 am–9 pm. Closed Sun.

SPECS   630 Wheeling Ave.; (614) 432-3878; no cards; full bar.

DIRECTIONS   From Exit 178, head north on OH 209 about 2 miles until you're facing the courthouse and must turn onto Wheeling Ave. Turn left, and in 1½ blocks it's on the left.

STONE CRAB INN, *Exit 218, St. Clairsville*

We should say from the start that this is not our kind of place. It's a suburbanized roadhouse done up in nautical mishmash with a little stained glass here, a touch of Bavarian there, a few fake Tiffanies, and a name that's out and out wrong: there's nary a stone crab on the menu or in the kitchen. Those Florida critters are so perishable that they almost never leave their native territory. But the blue crabs served here, both hard-shelled and soft, are flown in fresh from Baltimore. You can find them converted into almost every conceivable crab concoction. All of those we tried were first-rate.

The spicy, chunky crab soup was a joy to sniff and slurp ($1.45 a bowl). Crab cakes were heavy with backfin meat and light on breading; you can get them in a sandwich for $4.45, or as a dinner entree for $9.95. Of course, there are whole crabs, too, doused with peppery Old Bay seasoning as at any real Maryland crab feast (prices vary); soft-shell crabs are properly sautéed in butter ($9.75). All the other fish and shellfish are also fresh (prices from $3.50), but we didn't try any of it, preferring to stick with crabs while they were available; in the off-season, they don't appear on the menu at all. To us that's a sign that even if the Stone Crab Inn is misnamed and badly decorated, someone in the kitchen is doing things right.

HOURS   Mon.–Thurs. 11 am–midnight; Fri. & Sat. 11 am–1 am; Sun. noon–11 pm.

SPECS   Mall Road; (614) 695-2500; major credit cards; full liquor license.

DIRECTIONS   Restaurant is 0.4 mile south of Exit 218, on Mall Road, on the left.

Kentucky

SOOS INN, *Exit 22, La Grange*

This unencouraging roadhouse looks like a former tavern that got left high and (literally) dry when the county banned booze; we were delighted to find a surprising reuse of the building as a Hungarian restaurant.

Unfortunately, we didn't time our visit to partake in *toltott kaposzta* (stuffed cabbage rolls) or *fokhagymas rostelyos* (marinated, paprika-doused strip steak). The Sunday brunch buffet we found was mostly American, except for chicken paprikash. Given the inherent liability of steam-table fare (and our arrival at meal's end), we can only say it ranged from sad (doughy fried clams) to amiable (the paprikash) to wonderful (homemade spaetzle). An accompanying salad bar also yielded mixed results, the high points of which were fresh spinach from the owner's garden and a heavenly sour cream–based cucumber salad.

This all-you-can-eat Sunday affair may have provided more food for $5.95 than items off the regular dinner menu, but we would rather have had a shot at the true Hungarian dishes provided through the week by Budapest-born Steve Soos. His goulash soup and zesty Hungarian fried chicken were recommended to us with great vigor. Lunch prices run $3–$4; dinners are mostly $6.50–$7.95.

HOURS Lunch: Tues.–Fri. 11 am–2 pm. Dinner: Thurs.–Sat. 5–10 pm. Sun. brunch: 11 am–2:30 pm. Closed Mon.

SPECS   617 Jefferson St.; (502) 222–1568; V, MC; no liquor (dry county); children's menu.

DIRECTIONS   From Exit 22, turn right if southbound, left if northbound onto KY 53. Go about ½ mile to the junction of KY 146 (blinking light); turn left and in ½ mile it's on your left.

CARROLLTON INN, *Exit 44, Carrollton*

Carrollton has all the makings of a spiffily restored little riverfront town, except that nobody has ever bothered to restore it. Which is fine with us. We found its historical roots and riverfront charm plainly visible and, in their own way, more authentic than a preservation project would have allowed.

Brightest star of Carrollton's old buildings is the Carrollton Inn, a venerable brick hotel since the 1880s (although a public restaurant only since the mid-1980s). In two dining rooms, wallpaper and furnishings convey a sense of history without affecting an overly atmospheric ambiance. We liked it.

The food fit the decor: well-done with a touch of class here and there, but not overambitious. We liked that, too. The Inn's "chicken and ham au gratin" is a variation on Louisville's famous "Hot Brown," but here chicken fills in for turkey and salt-cured ham upstages the city ham usually used in that dish. The Carrollton's version made a satisfying lunch for $4.95, including a so-so salad bar. The entire menu is available all day, so you can opt for a pork barbecue sandwich ($1.95) at breakfast or Kentucky ham with two eggs and red-eye gravy ($3.95) as a late-night snack. Prime rib is the biggie on weekends ($9.50), but you can get cornmeal-coated southern-fried catfish any day of the week. At weekday lunches, pile your rye bread high at the deli bar for just $2.95, and help yourself to seconds.

HOURS   Mon.–Wed. 6 am–10 pm; Thurs. & Fri. 6 am–11 pm; Sat. 7 am–11 pm; Sun. 8 am–10 pm. In winter, may close at 9 pm, Sun.–Tues. Closed Christmas.

SPECS   3rd & Main Sts.; (502) 732-6905; V, MC, AE; beer & wine.

DIRECTIONS   From Exit 44, turn right and go 3½ miles on KY 227 North. At the traffic light, turn left onto US 42. Go 1 mile to 3rd St. (sign for the inn). Turn right on 3rd, and go 1 block to the inn, on the left.

Ohio

ARNOLD'S, *Exits 1B & 1D, Cincinnati*

Arnold's is a vintage bar and grill, Cincinnati's oldest, as warm and pubby as anything found in Boston or New York—or London or Dublin, for that matter. Sit at one of the booths, its wood darkened with age and polished to a sheen by more than a century's worth of backsides. Or, settle down in the truly European-style courtyard. There's Guinness and Hudepol on tap, and live acoustical folk music many nights.

The grub is good too, most of it light sandwich and salad fare ($2.50–$5). Our club sandwich ($3.75), spread with avocado mayonnaise on darn good rye, was satisfying in all respects. And our peanut butter chocolate cheesecake ($1.50)—a Reese's cup elevated to serious dessert status—was one of the postmeal highlights of our trip.

Cincinnati is a city of wonderful restaurants, but if your appetite is light and your penchant for classic pubs strong, you couldn't do any better than Arnold's.

HOURS   Tues.–Fri. 11 am–9:30 pm; Sat. 5:30–10:30 pm. Closed Sun. & Mon.

SPECS   210 E. 8th St.; (513) 421-6234; no cards; full bar.

DIRECTIONS Northbound: From Exit 1D, follow signs for Main St. Once on Main, go 5 blocks to 8th and it's ½ block to your right. However, 8th goes one way the wrong way, so you'll have to go around the block, or park and walk over to it.

Southbound: From Exit 1B, stay on Elm St. to 7th. Turn right on 7th and go 4 blocks to Main. Turn left on Main and go 1 block to 8th. **Arnold's** is ½ block to your right; drive around the block or park and walk over.

IZZY'S, *Exit 1B, Cincinnati*

You don't have to schlep all the way to Manhattan for a *real* Jewish deli. Read about this one on pp. 125–126.

DIRECTIONS Northbound: On the bridge over the Ohio River bear left for I-75 North (not I-71, which you can return to after eating). Use Exit 1G, following the signs for Linn St. Turn right at the light onto Linn St. Northbound. In 1 block turn right onto W. 8th St. and follow signs for 7th St. At the third light, turn left onto Elm. Go 1½ blocks to **Izzy's,** on the left. It's actually quite quick and easy, even if it doesn't read that way.

Southbound: From Exit 1B, follow the Elm St. signs until you reach 8th St. **Izzy's** is on the left.

CAMP WASHINGTON CHILI,
I-75 Interchange, Cincinnati

You'd be missing out on the Cincinnati experience if you went without a bowl of this city's claim to culinary fame. It's a quick 3-mile detour on I-75 to the chili parlor we liked best. See pp. 126–128.

DIRECTIONS Northbound: Coming over the bridge into Cincinnati follow the signs for I-75 North (not I-71, which you can easily return to after eating). At Exit 3, turn right onto Hopple St., and in 1 block it's on the right at the corner of Colerain.

Southbound: From the I-75 interchange, take I-75 North for 3 miles to Exit 3. Don't follow I-71/I-75 South over the bridge into Kentucky; you can do that after eating. From I-75 Exit 3, turn right onto Hopple St., and in 1 block **Camp Washington Chili** is on the right, at the corner of Colerain.

ALPHA RESTAURANT, *Exit 3, Cincinnati*

Whether you're in the mood for smoked chopped chicken livers, escargots Florentine, or a thick and juicy steak, you'll find it at the Alpha. See pp. 128–129.

DIRECTIONS **Northbound:** Coming over the bridge into Cincinnati, follow the signs for I-75 North (not I-71, which you can easily return to after eating). At Exit 3, turn left onto Hopple, cross the bridge, and go more or less straight (don't turn onto US 52/27) for 1 mile to the light at Clifton. Turn right onto Clifton, and go for ½ mile to the T at McMillan. Turn left here, and the **Alpha** is on the left at the end of the first block.

Southbound: From Exit 3 of I-71 turn right onto William Howard Taft Rd. for about 2 miles (Taft will become Calhoun, but don't worry) until it ends at a T. Go left for 1 short block and then left again onto McMillan. The **Alpha** is on the left at the end of the first block.

MONTGOMERY INN, *Exit 14, Montgomery*

The Montgomery Inn's logo shows a gloating Ted Gregory sporting a pointy crown. Underneath, the restaurant's nickname explains: "Ribs King." Owner Gregory, according a framed letter from the U.S. Pork Producer's Association, is the nation's number one restaurant purchaser of ribs. Customers at his single restaurant gobble up 170 *tons* of the meaty bones each year.

Among those customers are members of the Cincinnati Reds baseball team, Cincinnati Bengals football stars, Ohio State University sports heroes, famous jockeys from Lexington and Louisville, local TV and radio announcers, and miscellaneous personalities including the likes of Billy Carter. Bob Hope is said to order umpteen hundred pounds of the Montgomery Inn's famous ribs for his annual bash in Palm Springs. And the stories go on.

Each of Gregory's famous fans has left at least an autographed picture on the wall; some have left caps or jerseys or other paraphernalia. So loyal is Gregory to his hometown sports teams that when Pete Rose was traded, the restaurant owner banned the Cincinnati Reds management from his establishment for life. We don't know if he's rescinded the order now that Rose is back as player-manager.

Of course, the ribs taste just as good to ordinary mortals as they do to national heroes, and we have now joined the roster of diehard Ted Gregory fans. Of Hellenic heritage himself, Gregory gives his baby pork loin back ribs a slightly Greek flavor, imparted by carefully measured doses of cinnamon, nutmeg, and other spices in the sauce. You can get beef instead of pork if you prefer; both are fab, but the pork had a sweet crunchiness we preferred just slightly. Can't decide? Go half and half.

It's also possible to mix your bones with chicken, duckling, or fried shrimp. Don't dismiss the latter as inappropriate in this carnivore's den: the shrimp comes with an unbeatable hot mustard and plum sauce. No matter how you juggle the possibilities, expect to spend between $8 and $9 for your dinner, which will include tossed salad and another Ted Gregory specialty, Saratoga chips. These amount to homemade potato chips—real spuds sliced ever so thin and deep-fried. Once you've had them, you'll lose all interest in the store-bought wafers.

For light appetites there are barbecue sandwiches and burgers in the $2.75–$3.50 range, but if you go that route, you'll be eating in the minor leagues.

HOURS Mon.–Thurs. 11 am–11:30 pm; Fri. 11 am–12:30 am; Sat. 4 pm–12:30 am; Sun. 4–9:30 pm. Closed Sundays in summer. Reservations extremely helpful at dinnertime.

SPECS 9440 Montgomery Rd.; (513) 791-3482; V, MC; full bar.

DIRECTIONS From Exit 14, take Cross County Highway East. Stay in the left lane and in about ¾ mile enter Montgomery Rd. North. The restaurant is on the right, in about ¼ mile. Parking is in the rear.

THE GOLDEN LAMB, *Exit 32, Lebanon*

Somehow, it would seem un-American to dislike this place, and we're not going to be called traitors. True, they lay it on pretty thick, greeting you at the door with a sign listing all the presidents and other noteworthies in whose plate prints you are about to follow. They also carry the mutton theme rather to excess, from paintings, etchings, and samplers to weather vanes, sheep banks, and a full-fleeced Lamb Shop downstairs. And the food wasn't as great as the reputation, but for the most part it was quite good. For a change of pace from the interstate and the "get there" mentality it imparts, a leisurely stop in this venerable hostlery (Ohio's oldest) will be far more invigorating than a hundred Saturday nights at Ye Olde Theme Restaurante.

We came for lunch and enjoyed a chicken salad sandwich on a croissant, with fruit salad on the side ($5.75). Not bad, especially the almond-sparked chicken, but what were those canned grapefruit and orange slices doing next to real strawberries and blueberries? No complaints about the richly flavored diced lamb and eggplant, however, sided by sautéed zucchini nicely herbed with basil ($5.35). Dinner rolls, in the classic puffy format, were excellent.

Dinner entrees will run you about $11—traditional American stuff, of course, and always one or two lamb dishes along with the likes of roast duckling, scrod fillet, and chicken breast on wild rice. It may not be the most imaginative meal of your trip, but if your own imagination is fed by keeping company, across time, with folks like Henry Clay and Mark Twain and President McKinley, you won't leave hungry.

HOURS Lunch: Mon.–Sat. 11 am–3 pm. Dinner: Mon.–Thurs. 5–9 pm; Fri. & Sat. until 10 pm; Sun. 8–10 am and noon–8 pm. Reservations recommended at peak lunch and dinner hours.

SPECS 27 S. Broadway; (513) 932-5062; all cards; full bar.

DIRECTIONS From Exit 32, turn left if northbound, right if southbound, toward Lebanon. You are on OH 123, which becomes Main St. Just go straight and in 3½ miles the **Lamb** is on the right at the corner of Broadway. Lots of parking.

VILLAGE ICE CREAM PARLOR, *Exit 32, Lebanon*

If The Golden Lamb is too busy, or too dressy, or too expensive, or you'd just rather eat where the locals eat than where the presidents ate, head across the street to the Village Ice Cream Parlor. Only 15 years old instead of 150-plus, it's too new to be authentic anything—it's not even an authentic ice cream parlor although it isn't a bad imitation. (Too bad about the red-flocked wallpaper and Olan Mills–style portraits.)

Mainly, though, you're going to come here for simple, well-prepared food at prices that befit its modesty. The daily soup-and-sandwich special did us just fine for just $2.50: homemade cream of tomato soup and a very respectable ham sandwich spread with pimento-flecked cheese on lovely Vienna bread. There are hamburgers, low-cal salad specials, and, for a whopping $3.25, dinner specials such as chicken cordon bleu or Hungarian goulash.

It would take willpower to get out the door without something cold and creamy in hand. The ice cream is, in fact, quite decent and it comes in a frosted cup, but it's unlikely to muscle its way to the pinnacle of Cincinnati ice cream parlors so long as Graeters and Aglamesis Brothers are still around, competing to be the cream of the cone.

HOURS   Mon.–Sat. 7 am–9 pm; Sun. 9 am–9 pm.

SPECS   22 S. Broadway; (513) 932-6918; no cards; no liquor.

DIRECTIONS   As for **The Golden Lamb,** above, but turn right on Broadway, and it's in the first block, on your right.

HOME RESTAURANT, *Exit 69, Jeffersonville*

Behind two arched windows on Jeffersonville's Main St. is a plain and simple farm-town lunchroom whose name appropriately describes about half of its cooking. In our fried chicken dinner special, for instance, the two large pieces of poultry were obviously fresh and breaded to order but the sides of mashed potatoes and "scalloped" corn fell woefully far from the home-cooked mark. Oh well, the chicken alone was probably worth what we paid ($2.75). And we got to take in some good-natured banter among area farmers trading fish stories, tornado tales, and other exaggerata.

As at many small-town midwestern eateries, the last course is likely to be the best—if you order pie. All the Home Restaurant's pies—apple, peach, rhubarb, etc.—are freshly baked from real fruit, and they're a treat for eyes and tongue alike.

Prices are uniformly low and the rest of the menu is as American as the pie.

HOURS Mon.–Fri. 6 am–8 pm; Sat. 6:30 am–8 pm; Sun. 7 am–2 pm.

SPECS 10 S. Main St.; (614) 426-9653; no cards; no liquor.

DIRECTIONS From Exit 69, turn left if northbound, right if southbound, onto OH 41 North/734 West. In 1¼ miles, it's on the right, next to the post office.

LINDEY'S, *Exits 100A & 100B, Columbus*

Columbus, the capital of Ohio and home of monstrous Ohio State University, has a less celebrated distinction. At the south end of town is German Village, the nation's largest urban restoration financed entirely by private funds. We expected to find a Teutonic Disneyland but were impressed by a cobblestoned 12-block area whose planners had exercised tasteful restraint in keeping the German theme at the level of historical appreciation.

Restaurants are in keeping with the neighborhood. Instead of featuring pasted-on half timbers and dirndl-clad waitresses, the places we saw had genuine character and charm that came from within. Lindey's was our favorite. Its age-darkened wainscoting and plaster walls breathe with a richly historied ambiance that was shattered only a little when we learned that the restaurant has been around only 3 years (the building, of course, is much older). With linen tablecloths, a few old-style ceiling fans, and a pressed tin ceiling, Lindey's fits comfortably between formal and trendy. It's absolutely lovely in a way that seems more accidental than designed.

The quality of food, however, is no accident. Everything except the ice cream and the bread is made right here from scratch, using strictly fresh ingredients. The menu is a delight—not through cuteness but through the many appealing possibilities. We came for lunch. Foregoing the sandwich and salad options (most $4.50–$6), we started out with a marvelous potato and corn chowder, ruddy and piquant from the red pepper purée base. As an entrée, *al dente* linguine was doused with a creamy white clam sauce and highlighted with capers, a successful variation on the Italian standard ($6.50). Sautéed chicken and apple wedges came in a light, rosemary-scented sauce ($5.95), every bit as good as it sounds.

Dinnertime entrée prices rise to the $10-plus level, except for several pasta dishes in the $7 neighborhood. If our high-grade lunch was any indication, you'll get your money's worth.

HOURS   Mon.–Fri.: Breakfast 7–10:30 am; Lunch 11:30 am–2:30 pm; Dinner 5:30–10 pm (until 11 pm on Fri.). Sat.: Dinner only, 5:30–11 pm. Sun: Dinner only, 5–9 pm. Closed major holidays.

SPECS   169 E. Beck St.; (614) 228-4343; all cards; full bar.

DIRECTIONS   Northbound: Exit 100A puts you on Livingston. Turn right at the fourth light (Mohawk) and go 2 blocks. It's on the right, at the corner of Beck.

Southbound: From Exit 100B follow signs for 23 South. (*Don't* bear right onto 4th St.) Go 2 lights and turn left onto South 3rd, crossing over the interstate. Be sure to get into the center lane or you'll be forced back onto the highway (as we were the first time around). Immediately after the bridge, turn left and then right at the first light onto Mohawk. In 2 blocks **Lindey's** is on the right at the corner of Beck.

COURT OF SMALL CLAMS,
Exits 100A & 100B, Columbus

In Columbus, I-71 and I-70 run concurrently, and it is a simple matter to reach this upscale restaurant that has two entirely different menus. See the description on pp. 89–90.

DIRECTIONS **Northbound:** From Exit 100A, turn left at the second light onto S. High. In 2 blocks the restaurant is on the right, at the corner of Mound.

Southbound: From Exit 100B, go straight, following signs for 23 South (don't bear right onto 4th St.). At the third light, turn right onto S. High. In 1 block, the restaurant is on the right, at the corner of Mound.

SEVA GOURMET RESTAURANT, *Exit 112, Columbus*

University communities can be counted on to provide for the vegetarians and semivegetarians among us (as well as part-time, would-be, and quasi-vegetarians). In the shadow of Ohio State, Columbus' principal purveyor of natural cuisine is the SeVa, a holdover from the '60s, that era of undoctored foods. It's an adorable little restaurant whose strictly homemade fare pleases eaters of all persuasions, not just those who look askance at meat.

Arriving for Sunday brunch, we took a seat on the sycamore-shaded brick patio. Our choices included mushroom crêpes ($3.50) and zucchini pancakes ($2.95), both found to be smoothly textured and full of enticing flavors (the mushrooms sautéed in a wine sauce, the zucchini enlivened with a touch of nutmeg). We bypassed a strawberry-banana omelet, although it is one of the SeVa's favorites, said to be much more appetizing than it sounds. But we figured we didn't need fruit *inside* our omelet when plates came garnished with watermelon, canteloupe, and orange wedges. For an extra dollar we rounded out the meal with our choice of iced or hot tea (herbal or black) and a shot at the salad bar (tabbouli, pineapple, sunflower seeds, multivarieties of lettuce).

Dinner specials at SeVa (pronounced *Say Va*, by the way, Spanish for "It's okay," which indeed it was) are the likes of vegetarian lasagne, eggplant Parmesan, fettuccine Alfredo, and such. For lunch try a "golden delicious" (guacamole and cheese on pita) or a cheesy eggplant sandwich. All meat is Verboten, but each night there is a fresh fish special, usually broiled. Expect to pay $4.50–$6.50 for entrées, $2 extra for complete dinners; at lunchtime the formula is $3.50 plus $1.

Whatever the meal, do end it with SeVa's carrot cake. We realize full well that carrot cake has become a standard of the '80s, and usually it's about as exciting as a doughy birthday cake specked with orange bits. But at SeVa, carrot cake is no begrudging concession to current taste; it's an art form that has been honed to perfection over 14 years, dense and rich inside with carrots, pineapple, and raisins, and teasingly sweet on top with a cream cheese–honey icing. Now that's a piece of cake.

HOURS   Tues.–Thurs. 11 am–9 pm; Fri. & Sat. 11 am–11 pm; Sun. 11 am–9 pm. Closed Mon.

SPECS   2247 N. High St.; (614) 291-5591; V, MC, AE; beer & wine.

DIRECTIONS   See **A La Carte,** below.

A LA CARTE, *Exit 112, Columbus*

A La Carte is the Dimovitch family's gift to Columbus. With a 5-minute detour, passers-through can partake of its many Mediterranean pleasures. We would commend them to do so.

The pleasure comes not from any plastered-on stucco decor, but from an ever-changing menu that delivers unimpeachable quality and variety within an octet of southern European cuisines: French, Italian, Greek, Dalmatian, Macedonian, Middle Eastern, Turkish, and Israeli.

We entered this paradise of exotica with *chopska*, a Macedonian salad of shredded cucumbers and cabbage bound with finely crumbled feta cheese and a fragrant wine vinegar. *Tarator,* a cold Dalmatian cucumber soup, was fuming with garlic and it burned its way to our hearts. From there, things got even better. A piquant Syrian lamb entrée came doused in a creamy wine-and-tomato sauce fit for sheiks. Equally divine was the cannelloni made from razor-thin eggplant slices rolled with a stuffing of ricotta and Romano cheeses, Béchamel sauce, and ground veal.

For these 2 dinner entrées we paid $5.50 and $5.95, respectively, prices that included a fresh vegetable, a fine Vienna loaf, and herbed rice or homemade pasta cut thick and served *al dente.*

The entire menu is available all day, and for those who would prefer something lighter, there are bagel sandwiches and full-meal salads at half the price of entrées.

Our hats off to the Dimovitches. Our steering wheels will be pointed in their direction whenever possible.

HOURS Mon.–Thurs. 11 am–9:30 pm; Fri. & Sat. 11 am–11:30 pm. Closed Sun.

SPECS 2333 N. High St.; (614) 294-6783; V, MC, AE; full bar.

DIRECTIONS From Exit 112 (Hudson St.), turn left if northbound, right if southbound. Go 1 mile to N. High (don't be tempted to bear right onto OH 23/Indianola at the ½-mile point). Turn left on N. High, and in 0.3 mile, **A La Carte** is on the right. **SeVa** is 0.1 mile farther, also on the right.

WALKING HORSE INN, *Exit 165, Bellville*

Who could know that just 3 miles from the truck-stop/gas-station metropolis at Exit 165, the charming village of Bellville awaits visitors without hype or hoopla? Or that one of the best small-town restaurants we found on our midwestern safari would occupy a 125-year-old building in the center of this well-groomed little town?

The Walking Horse Inn belies its aristocratic name by shunning all pretensions to high-priced quaintness. It's a three-meals-a-day family restaurant, attractively rustic but not overdone, and the food is just about faultless. Everything, even the bread, is made right here from scratch. Owners Don and Tina Granter go to great pains to find the best ingredients; their smoked ham, for instance, was the product of a 1-year search. Large rashers of it appear in the bounteous chef's salad. This ham also formed the wrappers for a delicious entree in which ham was filled with broccoli and rice in a velvety cheddar cheese sauce.

For such top-notch offerings, the Walking Horse Inn could command top dollar, but it doesn't. The ham and broccoli roll was $4.20 as a dinner special that included soup, bread, and unlimited access to a much-better-than-average salad bar (its creamy potato salad was particularly outstanding). A complete Sunday dinner is the buy of the week—just $4.65 including soup, salad bar, homemade bread, beverage, and dessert! Lunches are all under $3.

If you happen to be driving by Bellville on a Tuesday afternoon in autumn, there's yet another incentive to stop at the Walking Horse. Then, Tina's mother, as authentic a German cook as ever there was, gives a public demonstration of the making of strudel. She sets up a table in the middle of the dining room, and on it she rolls out immense sheets of the dough, stretching them until they are thin enough to read through. Of course, the product of her labor is served later that evening, so if you miss the afternoon demo, you can still eat its results. We're not sure which we'd rather catch.

HOURS Mon.–Thurs. 7 am–8 pm; Fri. & Sat. 7 am–9 pm; Sun. 7 am–3 pm.

SPECS 93 Main St.; (419) 886-2828; no cards; no liquor.

DIRECTIONS From Exit 165, turn right if northbound, left if southbound, onto OH 97 East. In 3 miles you'll reach the light in Bellville. Turn left and the restaurant is in the first block, on the right.

LYN-WAY RESTAURANT, *Exit 186, Ashland*

"As American as apple pie," we say when we want to describe something close to the heart of America—the America we used to know. The values of an earlier America still thrive in the nation's heartland, and so does apple pie.

In central Ohio, the Lyn-Way is famous for its pie—not just apple, but strawberry, blackberry, banana, peanut, coconut cream, and about a dozen others that change with the harvest. (We were sorry to have missed the ground cherry, a locally grown crop that is unrelated in looks or taste to the ubiquitous George Washington cherry.)

Other than pies, we found a basic meat-and-potatoes menu at the Lyn-Way, with prices so low that there's usually a line to get seated (it moves quickly). A beef liver dinner special, for instance, was priced at an embarrassing $2.85, and that included a healthy smothering of onions and bacon, and a choice of two side dishes; we recommend the macaroni salad, homemade and creamy. There are also sandwiches, eggs, soups (both genuine and canned, so choose carefully), and all the other American standards.

As for the pie, well, we couldn't stop at just one, and even two became impossibly limiting. The sour cream raisin was absolutely scrumptious, and the strawberry was superior. Oddly, our slice of apple pie turned out to be undercooked; based on the quality of the others, we suspect it was an accident.

Next door to the Lyn-Way is a well-equipped public playground in a pleasant city park that helps make this restaurant an ideal stopoff for a carload of restless young travelers. Inside, it's mostly families and senior citizens, well-mannered folks who dress conservatively if informally, and talk about this year's high-school teams, the parade last July 4th, and prospects at the upcoming county fair—all of them subjects as American as the Lyn-Way's apple pie.

HOURS Mon.–Thurs. 6 am–11 pm; Fri. 6 am–midnight; Sat. 7 am–midnight; Sun. 5–11 pm.

SPECS 1320 Cleveland Ave.; (419) 322-8911; no cards; no liquor; children's menu.

DIRECTIONS   From Exit 186, turn left and go about 1½ miles to the sign for Fairground/OH 42, at which turn right to enter an upcurving ramp. Make a right again at the top of the ramp onto OH 42 North. In ½ mile turn left onto CR 1302 (sign for Ashland). Go ¼ mile to stop sign and turn right (Cleveland Ave). You'll see it very shortly, on the left.

Illinois
Indiana

Illinois

ABOUT MOLINE AND THE QUAD CITIES AREA

You can go through the Quad Cities on I-74 or around them on I-80. There's good eating either way. I-80 puts you within striking range of Kernan's, where you'll get some of the best catfish you've ever tasted (see p. 167). I-74 brings you near a wonderful old candy store and lunchroom and a place on the Rock River that serves wild game (see below).

LAGOMARCINO'S, *Exit 2, Moline*

We have to admit we'd recommend Lagomarcino's for its decor alone. This lovely little soda shop, lunchroom, and candy store has been at its Main St. location since 1908, so the tin ceiling is the genuine article and the varnished hardwood of the booths glows with the inimitable patina of age. The floor is of hexagonal tiles in a snowflake pattern, the tables are milk glass, the fountain is marbled, and there's a discreet little Tiffany lamp in every booth.

It's a beautiful place, really, and a visit here may help you understand what Main St. was like in the Midwest before shopping centers nearly killed it off. You will have to make no sacrifice in food quality for the sake of your visit. In fact, Lagomarcino's simple lunchtime fare is excellent. They bake their own rye bread here, cook their own meats, and make the chili, cakes, and ice cream themselves. The humble ham on rye was superb, right down to the mustard. The coffee was the best we had since leaving Chicago, and the fresh strawberry sundae was exactly what it should have been. You just can't do better for this kind of simple food.

The menu's 20 sandwiches get no more unusual than liver sausage ($1.25), corned beef ($2.15), or a Reuben. At Lagomarcino's the flair is reserved for the 14 fancy sundaes. Consider the Bachelor's Kiss for $2.15 (two scoops of ice cream and a banana, topped with hot fudge and marshmallow syrup, sugar wafers, whipped cream, pecans, and, of course, a bright red maraschino cherry).

Not only is the food great, the prices modest, and the restaurant lovely, but the Lagomarcino family seems to be made up of some of the nicest people in the world. If that's not enough to tempt you, how about the fact that it's only 6 blocks from I-74?

HOURS   May–Oct.: Tues.–Fri. 8:30 am–5 pm; Sat. 8:30 am–4:30 pm. Closed Sun. & Mon., major holidays, & for a few unpredictable vacations. Nov.–April: Same as above, but open Mon. 8:30 am–5 pm.

SPECS   1422 Fifth Ave.; (309) 764-1814; no cards; no liquor.

DIRECTIONS   From Exit 2 (Seventh Ave.) turn left if northbound and right if southbound onto Seventh Ave. Go 5 lights and turn right at 15th St. Go 2 blocks and park. It's ½ block to the left.

MOLINE PIZZA WORKS, *Exit 2, Moline*

There's *very* good thick-crust pizza available here in an inexpensive version of that trendy, old-timey decor. The cost was $5.50 for a 9-inch deep-dish pie with fine, spicy sausage. At lunchtime you can get a mini-pizza for just $2.29. There are Italian-style sandwiches ($1.95–$3.25) plus lots of salads, appetizers, omelets, and the standby Italian dinners.

In decor and menu the place was a blend of pizzeria, trattoria, and quicheteria. Nothing classy and nothing offensive. There was no way to try it all out, and we doubt that everything was as good as the pizza. But the pizza really was very, very good, and so are the hours.

HOURS Mon.–Sat. 11 am–2 am; Sun. noon–2 am.

SPECS 417 15th St.; (309) 762-2222; V, MC; full bar.

DIRECTIONS Same as for **Lagomarcino's** above, except go 1½ blocks farther on 15th St. It's on the left.

HAROLD'S ON THE ROCK, *Exit 5B, Moline*

Despite a few touristy gestures, Harold's is still essentially a pleasant hodgepodge of no particular decor. Folks are friendly, things are informal, and the big draw for the families and businessmen who seemed to make up the clientele is the greenhouse dining area that runs along the banks of the Rock River. When water-skiing does not destroy the tranquility, ducks, geese, and peacocks wander about in the 25 feet between restaurant and water's edge, and all sorts of birds go skimming over the water. It's really very pleasant, and we didn't even mind the couple of stuffed raccoons that found their way in among the more usual greenhouse inhabitants.

Another attraction at Harold's is wild game. He claims the largest selection between Chicago and Denver, and we can attest that most fraternal orders are served here (moose, elk, and lions), along with buffalo, raccoon, bear, venison, rattlesnake, and antelope.

We're not sure anyone actually orders these delights at any time of day, but if you order dinner from 3:30–6:30 Mon.–Sat. you can choose from about 10 entrees at the early-bird special price of $3.95 ($4.95 for Harold's famous catfish). The usual steak and seafood dinners are $6.50–$13.95. Luncheons are $2.50–$4.50; $2.95 for a hamburger.

We have to tell you that when we visited Harold's, it seemed to be having a bad day. The service was unbelievably slow and they were out of the catfish we had been told to order (as well as much else on the menu). We figured a bacon-wrapped fillet would be safe, and it was, indeed, okay. No better, however, and what came with it was considerably worse.

This sad experience occurred at the end of a holiday weekend. We think that under normal circumstances Harold's will make a better show of it, but all we'll guarantee is the view.

HOURS Mon.–Thurs. 11 am–10 pm; Fri. & Sat. 11 am–11 pm; Sun. 11 am–10 pm.

SPECS 2600 N. Shore Drive; (309) 764-4813; V, MC, AE; full bar; children's menu.

DIRECTIONS Take Exit 5B (Quad City Airport). At the end of the ramp follow signs for the airport. These will lead you in a long circle back across I-74 and across the Rock River. At the light just across the river turn left and in 1 block turn left again. You're there, ½ mile total.

PAPARAZZI, *Exit 89, Peoria Heights*

Fettuccine alla carbonara in Peoria? Capellini al pesto?? Tortellini alla marinara, veal piccata, saltimbocca??? Will northern Italian play in Peoria?

Lisa Mancuso and Bruce Brown took a gamble that it would, and all indications have been that their show will be in for a long run. For starters, they've recycled a cement-block photo lab into an attractive modern space boldly decorated in green and white (no, not red, green, and white) and appointed with comfortable, if basic, furnishings. And on the tables (set with linen and candle lanterns) they put down some mighty nice plates of food.

For one meal we had excellent pesto (a spinach and basil sauce sparked with pine nuts) on capellini (thin spaghetti); for another, we opted for fettuccine alla carbonara (a bacon, cheese, and cream sauce), a captivating dish made more so here by the quality of the homemade pasta. Prices for these and other entrées average only $4 a la carte (add $2.50 for salad and bread).

Paparazzi, by the way, means "photographers," a name appropriate to this restaurant not only in the building's origins, but also in the superb black-and-white prints on display about the room.

HOURS   Tues.–Thurs. 5:30–10 pm; Fri. & Sat. 5:30–11 pm; closed Sun. & Mon. Reservations usually needed between 6:30 and 8 on Fri. & Sat. Closed major holidays & for a week or two in late July.

SPECS   4315 W. Voss; (309) 682-5205; all cards; beer, wine, & liqueurs.

DIRECTIONS   From Exit 89, take War Memorial Drive east about 2½ freeway miles to Prospect Rd. Turn left onto Prospect and go about ½ mile to Lake. Turn right onto Lake and go 1 short block to Voss. Make a left on Voss and it's on your left. (Takes 5–7 minutes.)

AU BON APPETIT, *Exit 93, Peoria*

Here's a delightfully schizophrenic restaurant. It's a barebones lunchroom with cafeteria service by day, but it becomes a tasteful, if simple, candlelit dining room with silk flowers and linen tablecloths by night. It's got a basic American two-eggs-over-easy menu in the morning; by evening it is serving pork pâté with crackers, beef Bourguignon, and Vietnamese specialties with names like *bun thit nuong* and "Delicacies Island." Run by two branches of the recently immigrated Nguyen family, Au Bon Appetit has begun expanding the culinary horizons of Peorians who have generally looked no further than the Chicago stockyards for gastronomic inspiration.

115

We came for breakfast, before the Vietnamese menu was officially in effect, but had no trouble persuading the Nguyens to prepare a stir-fry of chicken with rice-stick noodles ($3.15 on the lunch menu). Delicious it was, crisp with fresh vegetables and carefully seasoned to gentle piquancy. *Pho,* a strong-flavored full-meal soup, was not quite so much to our liking.

Dinner entrees are mostly in the $4–$5 range, but if you have a friend and a little more cash, you might be tempted to see just how clever the cooks are with a multicourse, multicuisine extravaganza called "Beef Seven Ways" ($16 for two). We didn't have the opportunity to try it, but we got the rundown:

Meatball soup
Nem nuon (ground beef wrapped in bacon)
Beef egg foo yung
Beef cubes grilled at tableside
Vietnamese-style beef kabob
Saigon beef (cubed tenderloin stir-fried with garlic and onion)
Beef rolled with crab fingers

Maybe the Chicago stockyards aren't so far after all.

HOURS　Mon.–Thurs. 7 am–3 pm; Fri. 7 am–3 pm and 5–10 pm; Sat. 10 am–10 pm. Closed Sun.

SPECS　314 Liberty; (309) 673-4720; no cards; no liquor yet.

DIRECTIONS　**Westbound:** From Exit 93B, follow signs to Washington St. On Washington, cross over the expressway, go 4 blocks to Liberty, turn right onto Liberty, and in 1½ blocks it's on the right.

Eastbound: Exit 93 puts you on Washington. In 3 blocks, turn right onto Liberty and go 1½ blocks to the restaurant on the right.

BIG JOHN'S BAR-B-QUE, *Exits 92 & 93A, Peoria*

John Robinson is a hefty fellow, and he's a big man in Peoria. His 35-year-old barbecue is an institution in town by now, having graduated several times into ever larger quarters. In its earliest days, it was a 4-x-8-foot shack from which John made home deliveries in a panel van; now he's got a fleet of delivery trucks parked outside the restaurant, a modern brick structure shrouded with glass and decked out in Formica. It's got about as much soul as a bus station, but Big John doesn't worry about that; he still makes sure that plenty of soul goes into the barbecue.

As with most barbecue, the secret is in the sauce, and quite a secret it is: The recipe is kept in a safe deposit box where it will remain unviewed even by his sons until after his death. Every fall, John and his wife Mary disappear into the woods to make a year's supply of the stuff—about 12,000 gallons! It's an orangey tomato-based sauce that's tingly but not overpowering, sassy but not sweet, and one of the best we've sampled. You'll find it on the table in a little squeeze bottle from which you can dribble it onto your barbecued beef, pork, chicken, fish (!), or—the hands-down favorite—ribs. A "P & P" is *the* way to eat at Big John's: a pitcher of beer and a platter of ribs. But at $15.50, the tariff is a little steep, although two or three can do nicely on it. Of course, there are less expensive routes—small dinners ($6.50), regular dinners ($8), and sandwiches ($2.25).

HOURS   Tues.–Sun. 9 am–11:30 pm. Closed Mon.

SPECS   7th St. and Kumpf Blvd.; (309) 674-4158; major cards; beer & wine.

DIRECTIONS **Eastbound:** Exit 92 puts you on Glendale Ave. which becomes William Kumpf Blvd.; you'll soon see **Big John's** on the right, at the corner of 7th.

Westbound: From Exit 93A, turn left on Jefferson, cross over the interstate, and go 3 blocks to Main. Turn right onto Main, go 4 blocks to Glendale/Kumpf (depending on which side of the street you look to for a sign). Go left and 1 block; it's on the right.

BOB JOHNSON'S RESTAURANT, *Exit 134, Bloomington*

See p. 33 for a description for an up-to-date American Gothic family restaurant.

DIRECTIONS   Take Exit 134 for I-55 Business. Go 3.4 miles to the light at Morrisey. It's on the right.

THE GREAT IMPASTA, *Exit 182A, Champaign*

Once or twice on each of our *Interstate Gourmet* eating safaris, we come across a restaurant so appealing in every way that we leave wishing we could pack it onto a flatbed and ship it home where we would patronize it at least three times a week (possibly three times a day). The Great Impasta is such a restaurant.

It's a breakfast snackerie where you can read the *New York Times* while eating poached eggs and a first-rate croissant. It's a casual lunchroom where for $3.25 you can have a Mediterranean pasta salad or a marvelous lasagne smoothly sauced with Béchamel as well as tomato sauce. Both come with an excellent crust of French bread on the side. It's an uptown dinner spot serving the likes of mostoccioli in Gorgonzola sauce, ravioli Alfredo, or "The Great Impastanoff" (sirloin chunks in a sour cream–based mushroom sauce over homemade pasta or croissant) at prices around $5 or $6 (less for half orders). On top of all that, it's a gourmet deli, pasta shop, and wine bar. And it gracefully wears all of its hats without the slightest bit of pomposity or snobbery.

Before he began feeding the public, Piero Farachi entertained a steady flow of dinner guests who appreciated his culinary finesse. "Have you opened your restaurant yet?" his friends would ask. "Not until I can find a name for it," he replied in what became a standing joke. Anxious to unleash his talents on the public, they came up with the name for him and his fate was sealed.

By any name, the restaurant Piero created is a delight to all the senses. Utilizing the best elements of crisp, modern design, it is cheery and entirely welcoming. And once you've had Papa Piero's magnificent seafood lasagne in a white clam sauce, or a rare roast beef sandwich on his own fine bread, you'll be ready to move in. Or, as we were, to move the restaurant.

The Great Impasta is no imposter. This is the real thing—northern Italian cuisine plus Piero's formidable imagination. The pastabilities are endless.

HOURS Daily 9:30 am–10 pm. Closed major holidays.

SPECS 132 W. Church St.; (217) 359-7377; V, MC, AE; beer & wine.

DIRECTIONS From Exit 182A (Neil St.), head south into town for 1 mile to Church St. (just before a pedestrian mall prevents you from going any farther). Turn right onto Church, 1 block. The restaurant is on the right, across from Robeson's Department Store. Free parking for **Impasta** customers is in Robeson's lot.

Indiana

THE BEEF HOUSE RESTAURANT, *Exit 4, Covington*

Way out here on the Illinois-Indiana border, 100 corn-lined miles from the nearest metropolis, a sprawling restaurant pulls in the crowds like metal filings to a magnet. They come from Indianapolis and Peoria, from Terre Haute and Decatur, and at peak hours on weekends they wait 45 minutes or more, all for one reward: beef—and plenty of it.

Ordinarily, we look right past the red-carpeted steak and sea-food houses that proliferate like clones of each other on every shopping center strip in America. But the Beef House is no ordinary beef house. We'd heard its praises sung before we ever left home, and although some of the rumors proved exaggerated, we were still impressed. No, it's not true that the Wright family raises its own cattle, selecting only the finest steaks for the Beef House, and shipping the rest off to other, presumably inferior, restaurants. But indeed they do shop extensively for the best meat that can be bought, and it's all under glass when you come in the door. Yes, if you so desire, you can pick your own steak before it's cooked and watch it being grilled over hardwood bri-quets on an open-hearth broiler.

When the prodigious portion of perfectly cooked beef arrives at your table, it will be as tender and juicy as you could wish.

And it comes with all the "fixins," literally from soup to nuts, at prices that range reasonably from $9.75 (for an 8-ounce rib eye) to $15.35 (for an extra-large filet). The quality of the meat notwithstanding, we advise you to stay away from the green beans (more gray than green); everything else, even the large popover-shaped dinner rolls, we found to be wonderful.

If the aforementioned price range sounds formidable, you should know that Sunday specials bring the tab down to the $7 level, and weekday luncheons are only $4.75. But even at dinnertime, should you want to eat light, or go light on the wallet, sandwiches are available at all times. And while roast pork and fried chicken can also be had, for most of the folks who drive here from afar, the menu consists of only three things: beef, beef, and beef.

HOURS   Mon. 7 am–9 pm; Tues–Fri. 7 am–10 pm; Sat. 3:30–10 pm; Sun. 11 am–9 pm.

SPECS   (317) 793-3947; major cards; beer & wine; children's portions.

DIRECTIONS   Just north of Exit 4.

THE HOME CAFÉ, *Exit 52, Jamestown*

If a name like "The Home Café" conjures images of an unpretentiously charming place with ruffled tieback curtains, well-worn hardwood floors, and a few wooden tables that greet you with bowls of homemade preserves, then The Home Café will feel like home. And the best part of it is that the hominess extends well beyond the unself-conscious decor.

"At first I thought if we lived up to our name, customers would come in by the flock," reports Carol Lynn, who can be found in the kitchen of her little restaurant 7 days a week, rolling out genuine noodles, hand-shaping fresh dumplings, cutting potatoes for french fries, roasting a turkey or pork butt, and attending to the thousand-and-one details incumbent upon feeding the public the way they would be fed at Easter dinner on the family farm. But it didn't quite work out that way. Weaning folks away from the mass-market eateries took time, but after 4½ years,

Carol has finally developed a loyal clientele. Now, she says, her real problem is finding places like hers when she travels with her family. "My kids won't tolerate anything less," she says with more pride than consternation.

We came for Sunday breakfast (not brunch, mind you), an all-you-can-manage buffet, the hot dishes kept that way on an old wood cookstove (admittedly, a hotplate in the firebox was what kept things warm—insurance regulations, Carol said with regret). Along with fruit juice and 6 kinds of fresh fruit, there was bacon, eggs, lovely light pancakes, and the best biscuits we've had north *or* south of the Mason-Dixon Line. Large and irregular, they were, with slightly browned, rumpled tops, oh, so tender and delicious! And the sausage gravy—creamy, smooth, and thick with small pieces of slightly smoked sausage—was every bit its equal. This thoroughly delightful morning meal cost a mere $2.85, and it is available Saturdays and Sundays until 11 am.

Delighted as we were to have found Carol and The Home Café, we felt a little sadness as we drove back to the interstate, acutely aware of how much smaller are the rewards of serving good, honest food at affordable prices (half portions are at half price) than duping the public into accepting boring plastic food seasoned with large doses of advertising hype.

HOURS Summer (Apr.–Nov.): Mon. 6 am–3 pm; Tues.–Sat. 6 am–9 pm; Sun. 8 am–3 pm. Winter: Sun. & Mon. 6 am–3 pm; Tues.–Sat. 6 am–2 pm and 5–9 pm. Closed Christmas, New Year's, & the first 2 weeks of July.

SPECS 11 W. Main St.; (317) 676-9802; no cards; no liquor.

DIRECTIONS From Exit 52 (Jamestown/Advance/IN 75), turn right if eastbound, left if westbound, onto IN 75 South toward Jamestown.

Go 1¼ miles to the stop sign and turn right. You'll see the restaurant in 1 block, on the left.

Note: When we were there, the exit sign in the westbound lane had no number. This may have been a temporary situation, but keep an eye out for IN 75.

COMPTON'S COW PALACE, *IN 9 Exit, Shelbyville*

If you know the difference between a heifer and a bull, you'll do fine at Compton's Cow Palace, at least in choosing a rest room. You won't do too badly in choosing from the menu if you're willing to settle for simple sandwiches, broiled hamburgers, or butter-grilled hot dogs, along with a dozen or more variations on the ice cream theme. There are soups too—cream of broccoli was quite good, although it should have been served warmer than lukewarm. Prices are uniformly low.

Compton's has been a leading dairy and ice cream producer in Shelbyville since 1938. Although they have six stores in the area, this is their first restaurant, a modern wood-sided building, Friendly-esque inside. While we wish them deserved success, we hope it won't result in a Compton's Cow Palace popping up alongside every pasture.

HOURS   Daily 10 am–11 pm. Closed Christmas & Thanksgiving.

SPECS   318 N. Harrison; (317) 392-4889; no cards; no liquor; children's menu.

DIRECTIONS   From exit marked IN 9/Shelbyville/Greenfield, turn right if eastbound, left if westbound, onto IN 9 toward Shelbyville. Go about 1½ miles and bear left at the light onto Boggstown Rd. In 0.1 mile, it's on the left at the corner of Walker St.

FIRESIDE INN, *Exit 143, Enochsburg*

You've got to time it right, and we didn't. The Fireside Inn is a beer hall 6 nights of the week, but on 3 of them it's also a fried chicken parlor. We hit it on the wrong night.

What we've heard is all superlatives. Best fried chicken in the county, in the state, in the world, etc. But what intrigued us most was the claim that although the chicken is fried, it doesn't taste that way. Somehow, it manages to be crispy but not the least bit greasy. Or so they say.

Owner Joe Kinker was quick to corroborate our reports, but he wasn't about to be talked into proving it on a Thursday night. Nor would he give any details of his cooking procedure, except to say that his secret is more in the kind of chicken he buys than what he does to it. And what kind of chicken might that be? Not on your life, buddy boy.

If you're there on Wednesday, Friday, or Saturday and you want to check out the rumors for yourself, you'll spend $4.80 for ten pieces or $3.75 for three. It doesn't take a calculator to figure out which is the better buy. On Wednesday night there's also catfish, and on the weekends shrimp.

HOURS   Wed., Fri., & Sat. 5–10:30 pm. No food other nights.

SPECS   (812) 934-4174; no cards; beer only.

DIRECTIONS   From Exit 143, turn right if westbound, left if eastbound. Go about ½ mile and turn right on the unmarked road just past Rossburg Cemetery (which is on left). It's 2 miles to the restaurant, on the right.

SHERMAN HOUSE, *Exit 149, Batesville*

What's a sprawling Bavarian-style building with plastered-on half timbers and ersatz beams doing in the middle of a southern Indiana farm town? We don't know and we doubt the residents of Batesville do either, but they've adapted the Sherman House's pretentious Germanic theme in designing their shopping centers, banks, houses—even the town's logo.

But the Sherman House is the most famous eatery between Cincinnati and Indianapolis, and people from both of those cities regularly drive down for a big night off the town, so we felt it fair to close our eyes to the absurd decor and call the Sherman House's food as we tasted it. Here is our scorecard of pluses and minuses.

Plus: The salad bar offered a variety of lettuces (both leaf and head), big chunks of fresh vegetables including broccoli and cauliflower, a tray of nicely toasted sunflower seeds, and good, *real* croutons. Minus: The ham salad was wretched.

Plus: Deep-fried sauerkraut balls were a refreshingly different offering on an otherwise routine German-American menu. Minus: Six of them the size of cherries cost $2.95, and they languished in a floury, wine-flavored glop.

Minus: The thin, pallid, cheddar cheese soup (of the day) was a ghost of what that heady broth can be.

Plus: The sauerbraten had just the right degree of tenderness and tartness, and it was accompanied by a similarly successful sweet-and-sour red cabbage. Minus: Potato pancakes, also on our sauerbraten plate, were raw in the middle. Plus: They were delicious on the outside.

Minus: The dinner rolls were deep-fried; they come out tasting (and looking) like golden-coated Wonder Bread. Plus: You get apple butter to slather all over them, and the combination is undeniably yummy.

Plus: The restaurant employs a baker who makes all the pies in-house. Minus: Her day off was our day in.

And what must you pay for these mixed results? Minus: Most dinner entrees are $8.95 or more, largely because you're paying for all those gratuitous decorations. Plus: Lunches—primarily sandwiches and salads—are in the $2.95–$3.50 range.

On your way out the door, notice the picture of the Sherman House as a masterful example of pioneer architecture, circa 1865, about 85 years before it became, in essence, the Sherman Haus. A sobering lesson in architectural remuddling.

HOURS   Breakfast: Daily 6:30–11 am. Lunch: Mon.–Sat. 11 am–5 pm. Dinner: Mon.–Thurs. 5–8:45 pm; Fri. & Sat. 5–9:45 pm. Sunday dinner: 11:30 am–7:45 pm.

SPECS   35 S. Main St.; (812) 934-2407; phone from Cincinnati, 621-1771; phone from Indianapolis, 632-2630; all cards; full bar; children's portions available.

DIRECTIONS   From Exit 149, turn left if westbound, right if eastbound, and go ½ mile into town. The **Sherman House** makes sure you'll find your way to its door. Just follow the signs.

Ohio
Michigan

Ohio

IZZY'S, *Exits 1F & 1G, Cincinnati*

If you think you've heard "as good as Manhattan" about too many delis that don't know bagels from bialies . . . if you think you might like a potato latke on the side with every sandwich and a couple slices of *real* rye bread to break up and drop into your soup . . . if you thought you'd never again taste a beef-barley soup like the one your Jewish grandmother used to make . . . have we got a place for you!

Izzy's is a Cincinnati institution, what the *Cincinnati Enquirer* called "a bastion of 'studied schlock' since . . . 1901." Since then, it's grown into two locations (no plans for mass expansion). We visited the ingenuously charming no-nonsense Elm Street Izzy's, where the study of schlock has resulted in the placement of Saran Wrap–covered bowls containing Kosher dill pickles, sauerkraut, horseradish, and spicy mustard on every table. It's an orgy of relishes, and we observed more than one customer mounding his sandwich with kraut as high as the meat itself—which was certainly pretty high, in the case of our absolutely first-rate corned beef sandwich on chewy, crusty rye ($2.95). And that beef-barley soup was no paltry portion either; a "cup" of the chunky, vegetable-rich broth came out looking like a bowl to us, but the waitress reassured that bowls are twice the size ($1/$1.25).

When we asked for the check, she told us they didn't bother with such things here. Just go up to the counter and tell them what you had, she advised, and added "If you cheat you'll get caught!"

A sign on the wall says, YOU'RE ONLY A STRANGER ONCE AT IZZY'S. We'll certainly test the claim next time we're in town.

HOURS   Mon.–Fri. 7 am–4 pm (carry-out until 5); Sat. 7 am–3 pm (carry-out until 4). Closed Sun.

SPECS   819 Elm St. & 612 Main St.; (513) 721-4241 & 241-6246, respectively; no cards; no liquor.

DIRECTIONS   **Southbound:** Use Exit 1F, which puts you on 7th St. Go 3 lights to Elm. Turn left onto Elm, go 1½ blocks to **Izzy's,** on the left.

Northbound: From Exit 1G, follow the signs for Linn St. Turn right at the light onto Linn St. northbound. In 1 block turn right onto W. 8th and follow signs for 7th St. At the third light turn left onto Elm. Go 1½ blocks to the restaurant on the left. It's not as bad as it sounds—5 minutes tops.

CAMP WASHINGTON CHILI, *Exit 3, Cincinnati*

Cincinnati is called "the Queen City," but they might as well call it "Chili Town." Frankly, in Cincinnati we found more uplifting meals than the city's unique brand of chili, but regional food buffs wouldn't want to pass through without a shot at this town's nutmeg-scented trademark. Of course, you don't need a book to find a chili parlor in Cincinnati—it's not much harder than finding a June mosquito in Minnesota. At last count, there were 103 such establishments, a number that will undoubtedly be out of date by the time you read this. Directions to a Cincinnati chilery might read something like this: "From any exit in town, turn either way and drive to the first intersection. If it's not on the righthand corner, then it's on the left. Probably there's one on each."

A handful of chains account for over three-quarters of the chileries in town. We sampled four of them, and found more differences in decor than fare. It was all good, to be sure, but it also had a mass-market, fast-food karma about it that seemed to

put it more in league with McDonald's or the Bonanza Steak-house than with the unpretentious corner cafés we thought we'd find.

But we found what we were looking for at Camp Washington —you won't find a clone in each shopping center outside town. The one-and-only Camp Washington is a 1940s-vintage lunch-room that hasn't tried to keep in step with the times.

Architecturally, the product here is the same as everywhere: called "five-way chili," it's a quintet of layers and flavors, starting with a floor of spaghetti, moving upward to a ruddy, aromatic meat sauce, then stories of kidney beans and chopped onions, culminating in a shredded cheddar cheese dome. Spaghetti is the gimmick, onions and beans are like salt and pepper, bright-yellow cheese is icing on the cake, but sauce is the secret and it is in the sauce that Camp Washington excels. For one thing, it's gutsier, chunkier, meatier than that of its competitors. And there is more of it. But there's also something about the spices, some-thing that puts this sauce, and consequently this chili, just a sniff above the rest. There's nutmeg and cinnamon, for sure, and also a heady dash of cumin. Clove and ginger, probably, perhaps mustard and cayenne. Who knows about oregano, tarragon, basil, and bay? Speculation about the ingredients used by the various chili parlors, and their relative proportions, are stock-in-trade for chili junkies, but hard facts are hard to come by. At Camp Washington, the magical powders are stored in a safe; the recipe is stored in the owner's mind.

It will only cost you $1.75 to taste his results. It's a low price to pay for adding this unique gustatorial experience to your life list.

HOURS   Closed Sun. at 3 am (i.e., Sat. night) until Mon. at 5 am; open all other hours, day and night, all week long. Closed for vacation third week of July.

SPECS   3005 Colerain (corner of Hopple St.); (513) 541-0061; no cards; no liquor.

DIRECTIONS   From Exit 3, turn right onto Hopple St. and go 1 block to Colerain. It's on the corner, on the right.

ALPHA RESTAURANT, *Exit 3, Cincinnati*

Jack Gerson is a man who cares about food. In fact, it was frustration from on-the-road eating that led him to quit his $50,000 a year job as a clothing salesman, and drove him toward the restaurant business. Now his concern for food benefits everyone who stops into the Alpha Restaurant.

It's a pert and pretty place, an attractive blend of sandblasted bricks and blond wainscoting, with fresh carnations and alcohol lamps on every table. The Alpha has been written up in every national guide to "health" and "natural" foods restaurants, but Jack is adamant in putting taste before dogma, and he appeals to a wide spectrum of traditional as well as alternative palates. "Health food has the connotation of tasting bad—like if it's good for you it shouldn't taste good," he says, with obvious disdain for those who give it such a bum rap. "But here we'll have one guy eating a juicy steak next to another eating a tofu salad sandwich, and both will consider their own meal delicious." Just for the record, we should add that the steak is from organically raised, hormone-free cattle, and the fresh-baked sandwich bread (like everything else served here) is made at Alpha from scratch.

Jack's has a very large three-meals-a-day menu that ranges from sourdough French toast to omelets galore to melt sandwiches (not just tuna, but artichoke hearts, apple-pecan, and more) to escargots Florentine and eggplant Stroganoff. You can spend $3.25 for a sandwich, $4.95 for an Indian omelet filled with imported chutney, $8.95 for a vegetarian dinner, or $14.95 for tournedos Rossini. 'Taint exactly cheap, but there's a lot of room to move, pricewise, and the entire menu is available all day.

Lately, Jack has been having great fun with his newest kitchen toy, a smoker-oven. It's a wood-fueled device that cooks under pressure, driving the smoke into the food. By playing with various combinations of wood chips (apple, cherry, hickory, mesquite, etc.) he can give new dimension to even the most mundane foods. A year ago, for instance, he invented "smoke-fried" potatoes, the spicy result of a two-step process in which the spuds are first smoked, then sliced and fried. Then came "smoke-baked" potatoes, "smoke-fried" onion rings, smoked chopped chicken liver, and moist-smoked turkey breast (white wine providing the moisture). Who knows what it'll be by the time you get there, but we expect it'll be good.

HOURS   Tues.–Thurs. 8 am–10:30 pm; Fri. 8 am–midnight; Sat. 9 am–midnight; Sun. 9 am–10:30 pm. Closed second week of August.

SPECS   204 W. McMillan; (513) 381-6559; V, MC; full bar; children's portions on request.

DIRECTIONS   From Exit 3, turn left onto Hopple St., cross the bridge, and go more-or-less straight (don't turn north or south onto US 52/27) for 1 mile to the light at Clifton. Turn right onto Clifton for ½ mile to the T. Turn left onto McMillan; the **Alpha** is on the left, at the end of the first block.

MONTGOMERY INN, *Exit 10B, Montgomery*

If you've a taste for ribs—or sports—you'll be happy you made the 5-mile detour to this place. See pp. 99–100.

DIRECTIONS   From I-75, use Exit 10B. Turn right if northbound, left if southbound, onto W. Galbraith Rd. In about a mile, enter Cross County Highway (it goes off at an angle to the left) which in about 4 miles brings you to Montgomery Rd. Take Montgomery Rd. North for 0.2 mile to the restaurant on right; parking is in the rear.

THE GOLDEN LAMB
VILLAGE ICE CREAM PARLOR, *Exit 29, Lebanon*

For good American food in as classically American a setting as you'll find anywhere, try **The Golden Lamb**. The **Village Ice Cream Parlor** will cost you a lot less but its good, simple food may leave you just as satisfied. See pp. 101–102 for descriptions.

DIRECTIONS   From Exit 29 of I-75, turn right if northbound, left if southbound, heading east on OH 63 for 6¾ miles. **The Golden Lamb** is on the left at Broadway. For **Village Ice Cream,** turn left onto Broadway, and it's on your right in the first block.

PEERLESS MILL INN, *Exit 44, Miamisburg*

With a flagstone floor, hand-hewn beams, functional stone fireplaces, and a plethora of 19th-century artifacts, the restaurant inside this 1828 converted sawmill could lean back on its historical laurels and let the food quality slide. Fortunately, it does not, and we were charmed by what was on the plate as much as by what was on the walls.

Chowders change daily; ours was an irresistible spinach soup with a hint of nutmeg. Fish is obtained fresh, and Boston bluefish did credit to its point of origin (we also could have had Florida grouper). Doused in a deliciously tangy house dressing, the Mill's special "seven-layer salad" came on a chilled pewter plate, outdone only by a marvelous, chunky turkey salad entrée, rich with roasted half pecans the size of walnuts. Each bite gave a burst of flavor. Garnishing the plate, a healthy watermelon wedge could have sufficed for dessert.

Ours was a midday meal, and we were pleased to find most entrées in the $4–$5 range, with a few items under $3. At dinnertime, roast duckling is the specialty ($8.55, quarter; $10.95, half); lime-broiled chicken, roast pork loin, and other such Americana run $7–$10. Try the hot fudge pecan ball for dessert. The kitchen seems to have a way with those little nutty nuggets of flavor.

HOURS   Tues.–Thurs. 11 am–2 pm and 5–9 pm; Fri. 11 am–2 pm and 5–10 pm; Sat. 5–10 pm only; Sun. 11 am–7 pm. Closed Mon. & Christmas, New Year's, & July 4th.

SPECS   319 S. 2nd St.; (513) 866-5968; V, MC, AE; full bar; children's portions at dinner.

DIRECTIONS   From Exit 44, turn left if northbound, right if southbound, onto OH 725 West toward Miamisburg. Go about 2¾ miles to 2nd St. and turn left. It's in the middle of the second block, on the right.

THE TROLLEY STOP, *Exit 52B, Dayton*

At The Trolley Stop, there *is* such a thing as a free lunch. Customers build their own sandwiches at the bounteous sandwich bar and pay by weight—34 cents an ounce. Guess the price of your creation and you get it free.

Seven to fifteen people a week walk away without reaching for their wallets, but we weren't so lucky. That's all right, a well-stacked sandwich of rare roast beef, garnished with tomato, avocado, and sprouts, was well worth the $3.22 it cost us. Of course, roast beef wasn't our only option—we could have gone for turkey, salami, pastrami, ham, four different cheeses, tuna and chicken salads, and liverwurst, along with a wide selection of toppings, beautiful leaf lettuce, and a nice selection of breads. Next to the sandwich bar is an equally well-stocked salad bar for which payment is by volume, not weight ($1.50 per bowl).

After 3 pm, salad and sandwich bars move into the kitchen, and although pickin's are the same as ever, the staff does all the sandwich building, at a fixed price of $2.80. Homemade soups, chili, and pies (our peanut butter pie was light and scrumptious) are available all day long.

This is one of several restaurants that dot cobblestoned E. 5th St. in Dayton's renovated Oregon District. The nicest way to appreciate the area's charm is from a shaded table in The Trolley Stop's New Orleans–style courtyard. It's nice inside, too, in a warm and bricky way. There's entertainment nightly, mellow except on Friday and Saturday evenings.

HOURS Mon.–Sat. 11 am–11 pm; Sun. 6–11 pm. Closed during the day on major holidays but open at 6 pm.

SPECS 530 E. 5th St.; (513) 224-1839; V, MC, D; full bar.

DIRECTIONS From the interstate, follow signs for US 35 East/Xenia (Exit 52B). The exit ramp will put you on US 35 East (a freeway). In ¾ mile, take the exit for Main St./Jefferson St. On the ramp, keep right for Jefferson, bearing right onto Jefferson at the bottom of the ramp; then, almost immediately, bear right at the next light onto Patterson. Go 2 blocks and turn right onto 5th St. **The Trolley Stop** is in the middle of the third short block, on the right. There's very little parking on 5th; but you can turn right just past the restaurant onto Wayne and go around the block; you'll find parking on Van Buren or Clay.

THE LEBANESE DELI, *Exit 52B, Dayton*

A stop at the Lebanese Deli is worth the trouble of bucking one-way streets that all seem to go the wrong way. But Dayton's city traffic seems rural compared with New York's or Cleveland's, and we've taken the wrong turns for you; just follow our directions explicitly, and you'll be there in 5 minutes.

It'll take only 5 minutes more to get your food. This is the apotheosis of fast food, and happily, in this case, it is not synonymous with junk food. You can go ethnic or American. Always in the mood for culinary adventure, we sampled the former. Kibbe is a burger of lamb, beef, bulgur, and pine nuts that comes wrapped in a delicious flatbread and topped with cucumbers. Kafta kabob, a sausagelike tube of ground lamb and beef, is also doused in greenery and served in a pita pocket. It's equally satisfying. You'll also find lentil soup, spinach pie, hummus, falafel, baba ganoosh, stuffed grape leaves, and tabbouli . . . and the most you can pay for any of it is $2.05. Baklava and a delicious apricot pastry is for dessert.

Sit at one of a dozen little oilskin-topped tables under a salady wallpaper, or carry your prize out to a fountainside bench in Center City Park.

HOURS Mon.–Fri. 11 am–5:30 pm. Closed Sat. & Sun.

SPECS 20 S. Main St. (at Center City Park); (513) 228-2234; no cards; no liquor.

DIRECTIONS From the interstate, follow signs for US 35 East/ Xenia (Exit 52B). The exit ramp will put you on US 35 East (a freeway). In ¾ mile, take the exit for Main St./Jefferson St. On the ramp, keep right for Jefferson, bearing right onto Jefferson at the bottom of the ramp. Go straight up Jefferson to Market St. (between 4th & 3rd). Turn left onto Market, then park. The deli is in the small city park on your left.

KEWPEE, *Exit 125, Lima*

There are other Kewpees in northwest Ohio, but there aren't any like the original Kewpee. In fact, we've not seen *anything* in the Midwest quite like this sleek, curvaceous, art deco vision of the future as it was predicted in 1927. The building has hardly been touched since then. In downtown Lima, it's as shocking as a cornfield would be in Miami Beach.

Not even the prices seem to have changed much since the '20s. Here we had a 20-cent cup of coffee and a 40-cent chocolate malted that came in a 10-inch-high swirled glass. And not bad, either of them! But the main business of Kewpee is hamburgers. With lettuce, tomato, and mayo, they cost 80 cents. It wasn't bad either, but a little on the salty side.

We think it's worth the drive downtown to sit in the original, museum-quality Kewpee, but if it's the burger, not the decor, that interests you, there's a less-inspired cement-block Kewpee right by the exit. Same burger, same coffee, same prices.

HOURS Mon.–Sat. 7 am–1 am; Sun. 4 pm–12:30 am.

SPECS 111 N. Elizabeth St. & 1350 Bellefontaine Ave.; (419) 228-1778 & 229-1385; no cards; no liquor.

DIRECTIONS **To the original:** From Exit 125, turn left if northbound, right if southbound onto Kibby St., and go about 1½ miles to Elizabeth St. (1 block past Main). Turn right onto Elizabeth, and in ¾ mile, the restaurant is on the left, just past Market.

To the other Kewpee: It's on your right, less than ¼ mile from the exit. Same exit, turn the same way as above; you'll see it.

INGALL'S RESTAURANT, *Exit 142, Bluffton*

If you order carefully and press the waitress about what's homemade and what's fake, you'll be as satisfied as we were at this clean Formica-clad family restaurant. Our pork tenderloin dinner ($3.95) was beautifully browned and succulently sweet, and the home fries showed clear evidence of their spudly origins. Portions are small, as befit the appetites of the mostly senior-citizen crowd. But 60 cents added to the dinner price sets you up for unlimited trips to an unexpectedly lavish salad bar. Here, too, it's best to pick and choose. Selections run from unabashedly wretched (spinach salad in which the star ingredient was out of a can!) to better than decent (marinated zucchinis and onions, cubed date-nut loaf). The spread also included fresh watermelon, tapioca, and rice pudding, obviating any need to order dessert.

Prices are lean, selections are standard (burgers, sandwiches, no-nonsense American dinners), quality varies—there may be better restaurants in rural Ohio, but you'll have to drive a ways to find them.

HOURS Mon.-Thurs. 6 am–9 pm; Fri. & Sat. 6 am–10 pm; Sun. 7 am–2 pm.

SPECS 142 N. Main St.; (419) 358-6056; no cards; no liquor.

DIRECTIONS From Exit 142, turn right if southbound, left if northbound. Go about 1 mile to the stop sign at Main St. Turn left, go through 1 light, and it's on your left.

THE ROCKING U, *Exit 157, Findlay*

A Western-style pizza place in western Ohio? Somehow, it seems doubly anomalous, but the pizza is "right fine, pardner," and that's the bottom line, ain't it?

You can get yours in any of five sizes, from the 6-inch mini ($1.60 and up) through small, medium, and large, to the 16-inch family size ($7.40 and up). All The Rocking U's pizzas come with three cheeses, and although it's possible to build your own combination ingredient by ingredient (peppers and onions free), owners John and Mike Urbanski (the "U" in the restaurant's branding-iron name) have come up with some winning possibilities. There's a tasty Mexican variety that looks something like a taco salad atop a pizza crust, and a vegetable combo piled high with mushrooms, peppers, onions, tomato slices, and black olives. Maybe it's not the "best pizza east of the Mississippi," as the menu modestly boasts, but very likely the best on the banks of the Blanchard River.

Pizza isn't the only crop raised at Rocking U ranch. The brothers Urbanski also put out a variety of respectable salads and sandwiches in the $3–$4 range, most with goofy Western names like the Bat Masterson (corned beef) or Wild Bill Hickok (turkey club). This is a family operation—Mike and John oversee the kitchen, Mom bakes the desserts, Pop does the books, Sis does the artwork. The atmosphere, which falls somewhere between a doctored-up steakhouse and a neighborhood tavern, is casual but comfortable; it's appealing for families and businessmen alike, and equally attractive to couples after the movie and softball teams after the game (especially on Thursday nights when already reasonable draft beer goes two for one).

HOURS Mon.–Sat. 11 am–1 am; Sun. noon–10 pm; holidays, 4–11 pm.

SPECS 320 W. Main Cross St.; (419) 423-4471; no cards; full bar; children's menu.

DIRECTIONS From Exit 157, turn right if northbound, left if southbound, toward Findlay. In 0.6 mile, you'll cross the railroad tracks, and 0.2 mile later it's on the left.

BASSETT'S HEALTH FOODS
BARRY BAGEL'S PLACE, *I-475 Interchange, Toledo*

One peek in **Bassett's Health Foods Cafeteria** and you know that the natural foods movement has reached middle age. No dashikis or shabby knapsacks here—Bassett's is located in a suburban shopping center, and the clientele looks like it would be right at home in Bob Evans' or Bill Knapp's.

But there's no doubt about the culinary philosophy in operation. It's a cafeteria, all right, but there is soy sauce and low-sodium vegetable seasoning and turbinado sugar on the tables. At the head of the service line is a monstrous aluminum juicer and stacks of plump, crisp vegetables just waiting to be smooshed. How about a nice cool glass of Waldorf juice? It's carrot, apple, and celery with a frothy head, and with an open mind (and gullet) you might find it a most pleasant surprise (75 cents). We did.

We also had a spinach lasagne with whole-wheat pasta and a chicken stir-fry on brown rice. Both were well proportioned, reasonable (under $3), and appetizing. There are vege-burgers ($1.75) and even vege-dogs ($1.15) made from soy products, organic roast beef (rare and moist, $2.69 in a sandwich), steamed salmon steaks ($2.85), and honey or maple-syrup sweetened desserts (just 50–85 cents, most of them). And (need we report?) herb teas by the basketful.

If cafeteria-style service appeals but the thought of oatmeal bread and whole-wheat pasta stretches your gastronomic imagination beyond its limits, you'll be happy to know that the flour is all white three doors away at **Barry Bagel's Place.** By Brooklyn standards, the bagels earn a B, fairly high praise considering most of what we saw in Ohio. Get 'em piled with pastrami or roast beef ($2.79) or simply spread with cream cheese and/or jam. Or, forego the bagel altogether and enter the realm of the baked potato. For $2.55, you can get yours topped with nicely steamed stalks of broccoli, still bright green, and doused in a cheesy sauce. Or try a baked potato Stroganoff ($3.15).

It all happens in two pleasant oblong rooms paneled with knotty pine on the diagonal, floored with terra-cotta tiles, and populated by a lively, happy lunch crowd that seems beholden to "Barry Bagel" for proving that the bagels sold in supermarkets are little more than mummified doughnuts.

HOURS **Bassett's:** Mon.–Sat. 9:30 am–7 pm. Closed Sun.
Barry Bagel's: Mon.–Sat. 9 am–9 pm; Sun. 9 am–7 pm.

SPECS Westgate Shopping Center; (419) 531-0334 **(Bassett's);** 537-9377 **(Barry);** no cards (both); no liquor (both).

DIRECTIONS Take the northern entrance to I-475; do not enter the I-475 loop south of the city. Go 2½ fast miles to Exit 17 and turn left. In ¾ mile, turn into the far end of Westgate Shopping Center, after crossing Central Ave.

TONY PACKO'S CAFÉ, *I-280 South Interchange, Toledo*

Tony Packo's. Does the name have a familiar ring? Haven't you heard it before somewhere? Think television. Think "M*A*S*H." Think Klinger. Remember his lusty reminiscences about those super extra-spicy hot dogs he used to get back home in Toledo at . . . Tony Packo's? And perhaps you caught the episode in which the only suturing material available for an emergency surgery on a wounded soldier was . . . the casing from a Tony Packo hot dog!

Well, Tony Packo's *is* a real place and, in fact, Klinger (aka Jamie Farr) really is from Toledo where he grew up on Packo's hot dogs. And he's not the only celebrity to have sampled those hotly sauced sausage dogs. Just about everybody who's anybody goes to Packo when he or she is in Toledo, and before parting they all leave their John Hancocks on . . . yes, a hot dog bun! The autographed buns are on display in plastic bubbles, along with an extensive collection of M*A*S*H-abilia.

Nobody asked us to sign a hot dog bun, but the ladies who staff the self-service counter didn't seem to mind when we asked a lot of dumb questions about what goes inside them. Yes, it's a real Hungarian sausage, not a typical American frank. No, the sauce isn't chili but a ground beef mixture peppered with paprika and a dozen other spices (top secret). Yes, of course the soup is made here and it's loaded with nockerln, those delicious little

Hungarian dumplings. Our questions answered and our trays full, we took our bounty over to a table and started to dig in. Klinger, you were right! If we'd come from Toledo, we'd be fantasizing about Tony Packo's hot dogs on the Korean battleground too. And what soup, a soup that only grandmothers can make, or at least only those with grandmotherly concern for customers. It comes alongside a small bowl of oyster crackers, a wonderful old-fashioned accompaniment we'd almost forgotten about. And our apricot strudel dessert was flaky, fluffy, and fruity.

If hot dogs, no matter how jazzy, just aren't your thing, you'll find stuffed cabbage, several sausage preparations, and what Packo's calls a Hungarian hamburger: a beef patty on rye bread, the whole thing smeared with a tomato-based mushroom-and-paprika sauce.

Prices are uniformly low.

Packo's is probably not at all what you would expect of a self-service hot-doggerie. Actually, it's dressed up more like a trend-conscious tavern, overpopulated by Tiffany-style lamps and old advertising mirrors, and it's disconcertingly dark. However, once your pupils adjust, you'll find not just good food, but an absolutely fascinating assortment of characters and artifacts—and signed hot dog buns.

HOURS   Mon.–Thurs. 10 am–midnight; Fri. & Sat. 10 am–2 am. Closed Sun.

SPECS   1902 Front St.; (419) 691-6054; no cards; full bar.

DIRECTIONS   From I-280 South interchange, go 2 miles south to Exit 9/Front St. Take the ramp for Front St. North, and you'll see the restaurant on the right in under ½ mile, at the corner of Consaul. Turn right on Consaul for Tony Packo's parking.

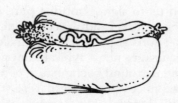

Michigan

ABOUT DETROIT'S GREEKTOWN

Greektown: Detroit's most colorful ethnic strip, a cacophony of music spilling out into the street, a crush of visitors overflowing the sidewalk, a burst of flashing neon. Greektown: a clot of restaurants, bars, nightclubs, bakeries, and coffeehouses. Greektown: good eating, any day of the year, any time of day.

Of course, you have to like spanakopita, moussaka, stuffed grape leaves, and pastitsio. But if you're tired of those Greek standbys and would prefer lamb with okra, octopus in wine sauce, or garlic-fuming codfish, so much the better. Best of all would be an appetite for flaming saganaki cheese, served with panache and an obligatory, guttural, *"Opa!"*

Just where you go for these gustatory delights doesn't really much matter. The mimeographed daily menus, posted in every window, read as if they were run off the same stencil and, in fact, there are rumors that every Greek restaurant on Monroe Ave. is fed from the same underground kitchen. Oh, some will tell you that **New Hellas** is the best (probably it's the busiest), that the **International** is the homiest, the **Pegasus** the wildest, **Golden Fleece** the cheapest, and **Laikon** the most authentic. Who knows? Ask another expert and you'll get another theory. Greektown is a place for wandering and poking; if you see something that looks (or smells) especially delicious, that's the place to go. Chances are you'll be quite satisfied. Prices are uniformly low—$5 is the median for dinner entrees, lunches less.

HOURS   Most Greektown restaurants are open between 11 am and 2 or 3 am, any day you choose to come.

SPECS   Monroe Ave. between Beaubien & St. Antoine; most restaurants have full bars and accept major credit cards.

DIRECTIONS   Exit 51C puts you on I-375, which you should take about ½ mile to the first exit (Lafayette). The first light is Monroe. Greektown is to your right, beginning in 1 block, but it's a one-way street going the wrong way (of course). So, simply go around the block; park anywhere you can.

TRAFFIC JAM AND SNUG, *Exit 53A, Detroit*

An overly rusticated, sprawling tavern decorated with ancient artifacts and a gallery of stained glass implies a certain kind of cuisine. A soda shop merged with a campus saloon implies another. And a restaurant owner who is himself a strict vegetarian suggests something yet again. If you knew that Traffic Jam was all of these things, would you expect Scandinavian fruit and wine soup, Chesapeake shrimp cake sandwiches, scallop seviche, or Szechuan-style wok-fried pork?

That's all right, we were surprised too, and what a pleasant surprise it was, the happy product of Richard Vincent's peculiar kind of culinary panache. Vincent specializes in vegetarian dishes that meat eaters will enjoy and meat dishes that might make veggies reconsider. Even the tofu-pasta paprikash, an unseemly combination if we've ever heard of one, came off smart and snappy. His breads are mind-bending: tomato cheddar, buttermilk–cottage cheese, broccoli-pepperoni. We have a Detroit-area friend who has a freezer full of them. And if variety in solid food is not enough, TJ's wines are dispensed with a nitrogen displacement system that allows Vincent to serve 25 labels by the glass.

What you pay for all of this is hardly representative of its quality. With the exception of fresh poached salmon, all the dinner entrées are under $6. Sandwiches, of course, are several dollars less. We have to wonder how Detroit's high-priced joints can stay in business with this kind of competition.

HOURS   Mon. 11 am–3 pm; Tues.–Thurs. 11 am–10:30 pm (in summer 9 pm); Fri. 11 am–midnight; Sat. 5:30 pm–midnight. Closed Sun.

SPECS   511 W. Canfield (at 2nd); (313) 831-9470; major cards; full bar.

DIRECTIONS   From Exit 53A, a service road takes you to the light at Warren. Head west on Warren (turn left on Warren if northbound, right if southbound) and go about ¾ mile to Cass. Turn left onto Cass and go to the second light (Canfield). Make a right onto Canfield, and go 1 block to 2nd. The restaurant is on the corner, on the left.

CHIC AFRIQUE, *Exit 53A, Detroit*

Feeling adventuresome? How 'bout a nice bowl of *gpawlor?* It's got goat meat, chicken, and all kinds of interesting vegetables like bitterballs and kittily, it's sautéed in red palm-nut oil, and it's spiced with "bonyfish" (a condiment made from dried, ground fish). Doesn't that sound terrific?

It is. The palm oil imparts a slightly nutty taste, the vegetables sing out with mysterious flavors, and the bonyfish ties it all together with a currylike savor.

Okay, what'll you have with your *gpawlor?* We recommend *fufu*, a preparation of ground casava root that looks like two-day-old cream of wheat and leaves a delightfully fruity aftertaste, but if that's not your style you can get rice. Of course, it isn't regular old boring white rice, and neither is it health-conscious brown rice, but a preparation called "check-rice" that is infused with finely chopped spinach and a healthy dose of aromatic herbs.

Now, you really ought to have some rice plantain bread on the side, and for drinks, you *must* have the homemade ginger beer. Wow, taste that ginger! At dessert time, don't pass up the fresh mango cobbler.

Such is the extraordinary fare at Chic Afrique, a delightful West African restaurant that has played host to expatriate Africans, visiting ambassadors and diplomats, dance troupes and entertainers on tour, returned Peace Corps volunteers, and Detroit's most daring diners-out. We feel lucky to have made its acquaintance. Prices are reasonable (most dinner entrées, for example, are in the $5 range), the low-key ambiance is fascinating (there are all kinds of things on the walls to look at and ask about), and the food is not only different—it's delicious.

This converted storefront is across the street from the glass-walled Vernor's factory. Vernor's is Detroit's answer to ginger ale; a good answer it may be, but it simply cannot compare with Chic Afrique's zippy ginger beer.

HOURS   Tues.–Thurs. 11 am–7 pm; Fri. 11 am–9 pm; Sat. & Sun. 1–9 pm. Closed Mon.

SPECS   4644 Woodward; (313) 833-7757; no cards; no liquor.

DIRECTIONS   Exits 53A puts you on a service road which quickly brings you to a light at Warren. Head west on Warren (turn left if you were northbound on I-75, right if southbound) and in about ½ mile, turn left on Woodward. In 2 short blocks, the restaurant is on the left, just past Forest, across from the Vernor's plant.

LA CUECA, *Exit 75, Pontiac*

Don't be fooled by the name. This is not Mexican food—there's not a taco in the house. But if you think you might like empanadas and papas rellenas instead of enchiladas and chili rellenos, give this Chilean restaurant a try. We doubt you'll be disappointed.

It's a '50s-vintage short-order grill room converted into an unself-consciously charming South American restaurant—maps of Chile and its neighboring states are decoupaged onto smooth patches of stucco walls amidst assorted Latin bric-a-brac, and lively Chilean dance music bounces out of two small speakers. (The restaurant is named for the national dance, a word pronounced like *Quaker* without the *r*.)

Empanadas, La Cueca's stock in trade, are pastry turnovers filled with sweet or savory ingredients, then baked or deep-fried. All four variations are available, and from the à la carte menu you can easily put together a complete dinner consisting of nothing but empanadas—a chicken or beef or seafood empanada as a main course, a broccoli or spinach or cauliflower version on the side, and a cherry or blueberry empanada for dessert. Such a dinner would cost you about $4. Or, for the same price, you could choose one of La Cueca's combination dinners that includes a bowl of thick and spicy lentil soup, tossed salad, and *pastel de choclo* (corn pie).

There are enough enticing possibilities to keep you calculating the permutations until your return visit, but no matter what you order, try the fried squash batter cookies—*sopapillas,* in the vernacular spoken here.

HOURS   Mon.–Thurs. 9 am–9 pm; Fri. & Sat. 9 am–10 pm. Closed Sun.

SPECS   975 Orchard Lake Ave.; (313) 335-1224; no cards; no liquor.

DIRECTIONS   Exit 75 of I-75 puts you on Square Lake Rd. Continue straight for about 3 miles (very fast-moving) to Telegraph. Turn right onto Telegraph and in 1½ miles bear right (sign for Orchard Lake Rd.). In another ¼ mile the restaurant is on the right.

THE COOKERY, *Exit 91, Clarkston*

We hit The Cookery on our last day in Michigan, and we couldn't have imagined a more suitable end to 4 weeks of good eating in the Wolverine State. Here, in a former gristmill that also saw service as a small Henry Ford plant, a palette of native Michigan produce is painted onto a seasonally changing culinary canvas. The artist is Ned Barker, whose particular brand of the New American Cuisine is raising quite a few eyebrows—not to mention forks—among discerning diners-out in southeastern Michigan.

In the summertime one can find oven-poached whitefish and roast duckling glazed with Upper Peninsula wildflower honey; the fall menu is graced by Great Lakes fish chowder and mustard-pecan chicken; in winter, guests look for hefty soups in venison stock and appetizers incorporating homemade buffalo sausage; a springtime entrée might be veal medallions sautéed with Michigan morels.

The list could go on and on, one mouth-watering creation after another, but we couldn't have been happier than after our own meal. It began with the best whole-wheat rolls ever (they were replaced after our initial binging with equally divine peanut butter muffins) and moved on to an utterly joyous cold cherry soup (we would have relished the chance to drink it on the rocks, had it been served in a glass). The dinner salad was art in itself, not the obligatorily thrown-together jumble of greens most restaurants serve. As an entree, broiled chicken doused with lime juice was also perfect; it was accompanied by wild rice, fresh mixed vegetables, and cheese pudding.

Ned's decorators have created a strikingly pretty (but not gushingly prissy) bistro, and as with most purveyors of the trend-setting New American Cuisine, the tone is decidedly upscale, although for the quality given, prices could be yet higher up the scale. Dinner entrees, with salad and those magnificent rolls, run $8.50–$13.50. Sandwiches, salads, and light entrees are always available for $5 or less. (Ned has said he keeps the costs in line by sticking with local ingredients instead of flying in Dover sole or Pacific Northwest salmon).

Months later, the Michigan memories linger in our gustatory consciousness. It was a fine farewell.

HOURS Mon.–Thurs. 11:30 am–10 pm; Fri. & Sat. 11:30 am–11 pm; Sun. 11 am–10 pm. Closed Labor Day, July 4th, Christmas, & New Year's.

SPECS Clarkston Mill Mall, 20 W. Washington St.; (313) 625-6800; major cards; full bar; children's menu.

DIRECTIONS From Exit 91, turn left if northbound, right if southbound, onto M-15 South. It's about ¾ mile to the center of town. Go straight through the light at W. Washington, and 1 block later turn right at the sign for Mall parking. The Clarkston Mill Mall is not what you might expect from a mall; **The Cookery,** not a typical mall restaurant, is within.

ANGELO'S CONEY ISLAND, *Exits 111 & 125, Flint*

The Coney Island is king in the northern Midwest, and nobody's conies are more regal than Angelo's. They may be matched, but they aren't exceeded even in Coney Island (where they are known simply as hot dogs). Angelo's is a clangy, bustly, shoulder-rubbing madhouse of a place that has served up short-order food in a jiffy since long before it was classified as "fast food" and associated with chain restaurants. Angelo's fast food is delivered to your table by real waitresses—the kind who wear white uniforms, not cutesy outfits, who know all the regular customers by name, who find time to exchange a few good-humored jibes before rushing off to the next table.

What makes it all work is the food. It's not only fast, and it's not only cheap, but it's good. Real good. The hot dogs (sorry, "conies") give off a telltale *pop* when punctured by a tooth—the true sign of a natural casing. And the just-spicy-enough chili sauce that graces them is so satisfying that we were tempted to take home a half gallon (for sale at the cash register).

Not only conies make Angelo's special. Take a look at the burgers. They aren't made from frozen patties, but fresh-ground beef, and they're served with top-notch trimmings. If you're suffering from acute cholesterol deficiency, try what Angelo's devotees fondly call a "grease bomb": double-meat, double-cheese burgers smothered with grilled onions.

Or, even better, try a roast pork sandwich. Now there's something to rave about. All right, the bread's Wonder, but what goes inside it is what really counts: thick, unbelievably juicy chunks of tender pork loin garnished with red, not pink, tomatoes. Despite its lack of pretensions and its workaday clientele, Angelo's pays attention to detail. Hey, they even serve real half-and-half with coffee. Now there's a place that cares about its food.

HOURS   Daily 5 am–3 am.

SPECS   1816 Davison; (313) 238-3761; no cards; no liquor.

DIRECTIONS   **Northbound:** Exit 111 puts you on I-475 North, which you should take about 8 miles to Exit 8B. Turn right and go 1 block to the stop sign. Turn right and then make an immediate left onto Davison. Go 0.4 mile on Davison to **Angelo's** on the right at the corner of Franklin. After eating, do not backtrack. Return to I-475 North, which will bring you back to I-75, north of Flint.

Southbound: Exit 125 puts you on I-475 South, which you should take about 8 miles to Exit 8B (Broadway). Turn left at the second light, cross under the bridge, turn right at the second light (Lewis), and then immediately turn left onto Davison. Go 0.4 mile on Davison to **Angelo's** on the right at the corner of Franklin. After eating, do not backtrack. Return to I-475 South, which will return you to I-75, south of Flint.

Note: This place is not as far out of your way as it might seem. I-475 is an interstate spur that cuts through Flint; there's little detour involved.

PADDY McGEE'S, *Exit 118, Flint*

The owner's name really is Patrick McGee, the bentwood chairs are green, and the restaurant opened on St. Patrick's day, but despite dishes with names like Wee Irish Salad or Flowers of Tralee, the food served in this barnboard-paneled tavern isn't particularly Gaelic. That's fine with us; they don't eat this well in Ireland.

The fare could be called nouveau American trendy, but it's done so well that you might not realize you've seen it before. The ⅓ pound hamburger, for instance, is ground fresh from chuck steak daily and served on a toothy homemade onion roll with wads of shining leaf lettuce and thick tomato slices ($2.45). It would be hard to find a better burger. Round it out by splurging an extra $1.75 for "Paddy Chips"—curly homemade potato chips that form a 6-inch stack as pretty as a pile of tulip petals. Salads are also excellent—the so-called Irish version really nothing more than a spinach salad sparked with crisps of bacon (*real* bacon) and thick Bermuda onion slices ($2.85). Friday is known in Flint as clam chowder day at Paddy McGee's; thicker than it was authentic, Paddy's chowder was nonetheless delicious ($1.95). Had it been packed with any more of those meaty clam chunks it would have been a clam casserole.

And the custardy bread pudding with whiskey sauce ($1.50) is not to be missed, especially by anyone who starts to doze at the thought of so mundane a dish as bread pudding. This one will redefine the concept.

The Paddy McGee's we found was an incongruous Bavarian wunderland on the outside, an overdecorated mock-Irish pub inside. But it has become so popular that a move to larger quarters (even closer to the interstate) is imminent. We don't know what you'll find in the way of decor, but so long as the food remains unchanged you'll leave in good humor.

HOURS   Mon.–Sat. 11 am–midnight. Closed Sun. & major holidays.

SPECS   2497 Flushing Rd.; (313) 235-3721; V, MC; full bar.

DIRECTIONS   Use Exit 118. First check to see if **Paddy's** has moved to its new location: From the exit turn west (toward Owosso). The restaurant will be on the left, within ¼ mile, directly across from the State Police barracks. If it isn't there, turn around to head east, pass the interstate exit you just used, and in about ¾ mile turn left onto Ballenger Highway. In about 1½ miles, turn right onto Flushing. It's in the first block, on the right. Parking is around back.

TERRY AND JERRY'S O SOLE MIO RISTORANTE,
Exit 162A, Bay City

If you thought that all good Italian restaurants had banished tomato sauce, torn down every decoration save a few stark metal-framed paintings, and pretended that any place south of Naples wasn't really Italy, try this one.

It may be tacky, but they don't have red-checked tablecloths on the tables—the waitresses wear them instead. A curtain of plastic beads separate the two rooms, there are enough plates and bottles on display to outfit a flea market, and exposed beams are purely El Fake-o. So what. It's a place that breathes with genuine character. The guiding spirit, Terry Drake, marches her ebullient personality and gutsy voice onto stage every Saturday night where she is accompanied at the grand piano by the restaurant's maitre d'. (Before Terry's husband Jerry died 5 years ago, vaudeville routines by the couple were nightly fare at the O Sole Mio.)

So much for entertainment and decor. What about the food?

Well, it isn't exactly cheap—entrees run $7.50–$13.75 and there are no sandwiches or full-meal salads as refuge for the budget-minded—but it's as full of successful innovation as the stylish products of the New American Cuisine. Actually, carefully prepared entrées are for the most part traditional (scaloppine alla Marsala, veal sweetbread, scampi marinara, etc.) but the antipasto bar shows off someone's inventive talents. Spaghetti sauerkraut salad, for example, is much, much better than it sounds; red beans with curry is a winner, as are corn relish and an herby bread salad. An Italian dressing with red burgundy and cranberry juice sounded promising but failed to deliver; a tarragon dressing was more successful.

So well established is this dinner-only restaurant that on the occasion of its silver anniversary, the mayor proclaimed O Sole Mio Day in Bay City. Now there's a local institution!

HOURS   Tues.–Thurs. 5–10 pm; Fri. & Sat. 5–10:30 pm; Sun. 4–8:30 pm. Closed Mon. Reservations essential Fri. & Sat. after 7.

SPECS   1005 Saginaw St.; (517) 893-3496; major cards; full bar.

DIRECTIONS   Exit 162A puts you onto Route 25 East. In 2½ miles (just over the bridge), turn left onto Saginaw St. Go 4½ blocks to the restaurant on the left (parking immediately beyond it).

LINWOOD CORNERS RESTAURANT,
Exit 173, Linwood

Once the Linwood Corners Restaurant was an inconspicuous little wing of a crossroads gas station. The owners, Jim and Eleanor Horner, took the time to do everything right—homemade breads and doughnuts, real mashed or fried potatoes, fresh Great Lakes fish, thick homemade noodles, and so on—and eventually folks in the Bay City area began to notice. Soon a growing contingent of I-75 travelers from Detroit began to make Linwood their regular stopoff on the way north. And so the Linwood outgrew its cramped quarters and moved from the gas station to a cement-block building about five times its size.

We can happily report that only the architecture has changed.

Jim and Eleanor have made sure that the food, basic American chow, is as good as it always was. Our $2.55 breakfast, for instance, included three bright orange scrambled eggs, real home fries, two double-thick slices of home-baked white bread, and a huge log of smoked kielbasa served with horseradish. We were too early for the fresh perch special ($4.95) but its reputation for succulence is well established among the Linwood's devotees. However, whitefish, walleye, and salmon, all of them fresh, would have made the choice difficult. On weekday evenings, $3.25 dinner specials like liver and onions, fried chicken, roast beef, etc., will leave you with enough money left over to splurge at a really fancy restaurant on your way back home. But you might decide to come back here instead.

HOURS Sun.–Thurs. 5 am–9 pm; Fri. & Sat. 5 am–10 pm.

SPECS (517) 697-5141; no cards; no liquor.

DIRECTIONS From Exit 173, head east toward Linwood. In 2 miles, turn left onto M-13 North, and it's on your right.

IVA'S CHICKEN DINNERS, *Exit 195, Sterling*

This little red-roofed farmhouse is Sterling's answer to the mammoth eating halls of Frankenmouth, where fried chicken comes out of the kitchen like newspapers off a printing press.

Iva Ousterhout started serving chicken dinners to the oil-rig workers who boarded at her house in the '30s. Now 79, she isn't found in the kitchen very often any more, and the one long table that used to occupy the front room has been supplanted by many smaller ones throughout the house. But Iva's niece, Monica King, who is now at the helm, has not replaced the big black cast-iron pans and old-fashioned techniques that were her aunt's stock in trade.

Choose among several variations on the chicken theme. For starters, you'll have to decide whether you want it stewed or fried, and if fried whether southern style (rolled in flour and pan-fried) or "American fried" (stewed first, heavily battered, and then dropped in the skillet). Four chicken pieces come in a complete dinner, along with relish tray, soup, vegetables, potatoes, biscuits, and beverage. The cost is $8 per person. Add 75 cents and you won't have to stop at four pieces; subtract $3.50 and you'll get your chicken à la carte.

We enjoyed our chicken dinners although we saw room for improvement—the soup, in particular, had an unpleasant after-taste. The biscuits, while fresh and tender, surely weren't the fluffiest we've ever seen. But the chicken itself, in all three of its guises, was quite good, and it should be added that nitpicking at a place like this belies its spirit—nobody ever promised the world's best food, just honest fare competently prepared and served in a charming atmosphere utterly without gimmick or pretension. Despite the presence of twenty tables, Iva's is still furnished more like a house than a restaurant, and it's easy to imagine her scurrying through the rooms with big platters of steaming hot poultry for her hungry and appreciative boarders.

HOURS Mother's Day to Halloween: 11:30 am–8:30 pm, 6 days a week; closed Tues. Mid-February through April and November: Thurs.–Sun. only (same hours); closed Mon.–Wed. Closed altogether in December, January, & first half of February.

SPECS M-76; (517) 654-3552; no cards; no liquor; children's portions.

DIRECTIONS From Exit 195, head east 1½ miles to the stop sign and turn right onto Saginaw St. Go 2 blocks; it's on the left.

PINE PANTRY, *Exit 239, Roscommon*

We couldn't have hoped to find a more aptly named nook in the North Woods for a sprightly meal prepared with the personal attention of a cook who treats her customers as if they were family. No larger than a slightly overgrown closet and paneled with real pine that wears the patina of age, this is an adorable place arranged around a little L-shaped counter with half a dozen booths and one large pine table. Edna Close's father, who weighed 95 pounds, built the restaurant by hand 30 years ago to fit his own dimensions, and even if the booths are a mite tight for most of today's regular customers, they won't let Edna or her husband Jim lift a hammer or saw. "We like it just the way it is," goes the oft-sung refrain.

A thick and tasty bean soup (85 cents) set the stage for the good things that followed. Roast beef is a specialty here, and our stacked beef sandwich on a nicely crusted grinder roll hit the spot with its delicious herb-and-garlic mayonnaise ($2.25). A quiche plate came with slices of tomato and fresh basil, and a raisin muffin; the ham and mushroom quiche itself was delish, but suffered from an unfortunately soggy bottom. Having paid only $1.95, we couldn't kick too hard.

Without even a hint of trend consciousness, the Pine Pantry manages to put across an up-to-date menu that seems like it has always been this way. (That's because it has.) You'll find quiche and Reuben sandwiches and full-meal salads here, but don't come looking for potato skins or fried zucchini or carrot cake. You certainly won't miss the latter when you've had Edna's fresh raspberry pie.

HOURS May 1–Oct. 1 only: Sun.–Tues. & Thurs.–Sat. 7 am–8 pm. Closed Wed.

SPECS   CR 100, Higgins Lake; (517) 821-6532; no cards; no liquor.

DIRECTIONS   From Exit 239, head west (not east toward Roscommon proper) to the first possible right turn (sign for South Higgins Lake State Park). Go 3¼ mile to the blinking light and turn left onto CR 100; it's on the left.

SPIKE'S KEG O' NAILS, *Exits 254 & 256, Grayling*

Okay, it's a bar. Okay, they don't exactly play Mozart on the over-amplified jukebox. But as taverns go, this one is a pine-paneled gem, a North Country classic right down to the jackelope standing sentry over the beer taps. For travelers, there's one good reason to stop at Spike's: those wicked Spikeburgers. So fine these specimens are that the Detroit and Ann Arbor newspapers have sung their praises. We will add our voices to the chorus. This burger was so thoroughly succulent that a mediocre bun went (almost) unnoticed ($2.25).

Not in a burger mood? There isn't much else to order, except for Spike's equally excellent kielbasa dog ($1.75). Order it with ketchup and horseradish, and you won't be disappointed. There's also chili (said to be superlative though we didn't put it to the test), ham and cheese sandwiches, and tacos. You won't find anything else in the way of solid food, not even at 7 am, when Spike's runs what must be the world's earliest Happy Hour, for the third-shift workers at Weyerhauser.

HOURS   Mon.–Sat. 7 am–1:45 am; Sun. noon–1:45 am. Closed only Christmas Eve & Christmas Day.

SPECS   Business I-75; (517) 348-7113; no cards; full bar.

DIRECTIONS   **Northbound:** Exit 254 (a left exit) will take you to a light in about ¾ mile. Bear left there onto M-72, and in 0.4 mile, it's on the left.

Southbound: From Exit 256, turn right. Go ½ mile, just past the fish hatchery to Michigan Ave., on which turn left. In ¾ mile, turn left at the light and **Spike's** is on your right.

BUSIA'S POLISH KITCHEN, *Exit 282, Gaylord*

Poles settled Gaylord to work the great pine forests that spread out in all directions back in the 1880s, but with the growth of Michigan's ski industry in the 1960s, the town took on an Alpine look. You'll come closest to the community's ethnic roots at Busia's, where dishes with names like golabki, pirogi, nalesniki, kluski, and kapusta come rolling off Barbara Mackowiak's bread board.

We have to warn you that—in keeping with the rest of Gaylord, perhaps—Mrs. Mackowiak's Polish menu is somewhat cutesified by such incongruous creations as taco pirogis. But for the most part, it's the real thing, and her husband Al even makes the restaurant's kielbasa himself. The sweet-and-sour cabbage and carrot salad that accompanies all sandwiches is a joy (although the sandwich we had, "beefed-up kapusta," was somewhat dull) and the potato pancakes were perfectly browned and greaseless. There are 4 different pirogi fillings to choose from, and 4 or 5 homemade soups simmering each day. Another dish, called "kwas," is a sweet-and-sour pork broth laced with raisins.

Prices at Busia's are quite reasonable; it's easy to eat lunch or dinner for under $5, and the most expensive item on the menu, pork chops (also known as *kotlety wiepszowe*, whether or not that affects the taste), is $6.50. For dessert, if you can bring yourself to forego Barbara's homemade pies and cobblers, hike 1 block east on Main St. and pop into the delightful **Alpine Chocolat Haus** for ice cream on a cinnamon-peach cone.

HOURS Summer: Mon.–Sat. 7 am–9 pm; Sun. 8 am–6 pm. Winter: Mon.–Sat. 7 am–8 pm; Sun. 7 am–6 pm. Closed July 4th, Christmas; limited hours on some other holidays.

SPECS 324 W. Main St.; (517) 732-2790; no cards; no liquor; children's portions.

DIRECTIONS It's ½ mile east of Exit 282, on the left.

MACKINAW PASTIE SHOP,
Exits 337 & 338, Mackinaw City

Michigan is called "the Wolverine State" even though the only wolverines you'll find there now are the University of Michigan's teams. It ought to be called "the Pastie State." These overstuffed turnovers imported from Cornwall, England, to Michigan's Upper Peninsula are in no danger of going extinct. Lately, in fact, they have been expanding their range, moving from the ore-mining country of the northern U.P. into the tourist country south of there. They've established a particularly strong niche in Mackinaw City.

We combed that town's honky-tonk streets in search of the perfect pastie, and we think we've found it. Dick Hunt and Chuck Brew bought the Mackinaw Pastie Shop from Bill and Wanda Grew, who started it 20 years ago, and with the shop they bought the recipe for pasties that Wanda had learned from her Cornish grandmother. The stuffing—fresh-chopped steak, diced potatoes, rutabagas, and sweet onions—is kneaded together, peppered well, and rolled into a traditionally *thin* crust. The result looks something like the snake that swallowed an elephant in *The Little Prince.* Rutabaga, explained Dick, is the magic ingredient: carrots just won't make a suitable substitute. Most pastie makers settle for carrots only because they are less expensive and easier to obtain year-round; Dick and Chuck, on the other hand, buy an entire summer's stock of rutabagas each May, and stash them in a properly designed root cellar.

Anyway, whatever the secret, we enjoyed the pasties immensely. They may not make a complete meal on their own ($2.50), but with gravy, slaw, and chocolate pudding for an extra dollar, snackers and light diners who want to taste northern Michigan's most famous regional food should be as delighted as we were. Just be sure to ask for the right thing: These turnovers rhyme with "nasty"; if what you request rhymes with "hasty," you'll be talking about something else entirely.

HOURS   Summer: Daily 9:30 am–9 pm. Winter: More limited hours; the owners are not yet sure what they will be.

SPECS   514 S. Huron Ave.; (616) 436-5113; no cards; no liquor.

DIRECTIONS   **Northbound:** From Exit 337, turn right and go 0.4 mile to the blinking light. Turn right and then take the first possible left (unmarked, before RR tracks) which lands you at Huron Ave. Turn left onto Huron and the pastie shop is on the left in ¼ mile.

Southbound: From Exit 338, go straight through the blinking light, then take the first possible left (before the tracks), which lands you at Huron Ave. Turn left onto Huron, and the pastie shop is on the left in ¼ mile.

Ohio

JACK HORNER'S RESTAURANT, *Exit 23B, Akron*

Here's a large, bustling, immensely popular place with about as much character as a gas station. The greenhouse dining area that recently sprouted off one wing of the building certainly looks no more at home here than it would in a subway station. Table-top cards promote fried potato skins, but they seem as futile as pushing tofuburgers at a rodeo. Maybe someone in Jack Horner's management aspired to trend consciousness, but 99 percent of the customers know that it's the place to go for low-priced, high-quality, old-fashioned American cooking.

You won't be able to spend more than $5 on dinner here (even that figure would be hard to achieve)—standards like liver and onions, fried pike fillets, roast beef au jus, and ham steak. Hefty hamburgers on hard rolls are $2.35, and jaw-stretching club sandwiches run $3.80. We decided to opt for a slight innovation —a lamb-burger. Freshly ground, the meat arrived medium-well done, just as ordered, rich with parsley and chopped onion, sided by real home fries and a tossed salad—a most satisfying and complete lunch for $3.95.

Except for the greenhouse, Jack Horner's doesn't look all that different from the service area HoJos on the Ohio Turnpike, but in taste they're miles apart.

HOURS Sun. 6:30 am–midnight; Mon.–Thurs. 6 am–midnight; Fri. & Sat. 6 am–1 am.

SPECS 395 E. Market St.; (216) 434-3976; no cards; no liquor; children's menu.

DIRECTIONS Exit 23B puts you on OH 8 North toward downtown Akron. In about 1 mile, take the second exit (Perkins). Turn left at the first light, cross over the highway, and go left again at the light. Do not reenter OH 8, but go 1 block to the stop sign and turn right onto Forge. **Jack Horner's** parking lot is on the left.

NEW ERA RESTAURANT, *Exit 26, Akron*

The New Era is the perfect ethnic eatery, exactly what we aspire to find in every city. Nobody has gone out of the way to make it pretty or cute or blatantly international. A few framed travel posters are the only external signs that the ethnicity here is Eastern European. Large rooted house plants in window boxes predate the age of plants as obligatory restaurant decoration. Centered above the eleven-stool bar is a photograph of President John F. Kennedy that commands an aura of hallowed dignity as it has since the day it was put up in 1963. The New Era Restaurant breathes—serenades, even—with a genuineness imparted by its location, its clientele and—most of all—its owner.

She is Lucille Juric, who was born in 1898 in the Adriatic coastal town of Kruseuv, in Dalmatia (now part of Yugoslavia). The day in 1938 that Mrs. Juric started a restaurant to serve the rubber-plant workers of Akron marked the beginning of a new era in her life, and the restaurant was so named. But she never forgot her roots, and for almost half a century now she has sent the restaurant's profit back home where it has been used to finance development projects, including a recently completed hospital.

Mrs. Juric's East European heritage is also remembered in her kitchen. Although the menu is more American than anything else, we were drawn immediately to the chicken paprikash, a dish so tender and so utterly imbued with flavor that we will not forget it. Of course, like all good paprikash, it was blessed by nockerln, those soft and tender free-form dumplings whose mild flavor is the perfect compliment to the paprika's tang. Also included in the $4.50 price tag was a spicy cucumber salad that packed a pleasant tingle, and—the real treat—an order of Mrs. Juric's wonderfully flaky, homemade strudel. You'll have to choose between cheese and apple, a tough decision solved best by kicking in an extra 75 cents and getting both.

The paprikash is available every day, but on Saturdays, the

New Era also puts out goulash and sweet raisin bread. On other days, you might find stuffed cabbage or green peppers as dinner specials. Other than that, look for sandwiches (including goose liver) for as little as $1, and American-style entrées—fresh Lake Erie perch, roast pork, turkey and dressing, that sort of thing—most around $4 or $5.

Mrs. Juric's age and a downturn of fortunes for the rubber industry endanger her restaurant's continued existence, but we are hopeful that support from a geographically expanding clientele will prevent this Era from ever closing.

HOURS   Mon.–Sat. 6 am–10 or 10:30 pm. Closed Sun. & first 2 weeks of July.

SPECS   10 Massillon Rd.; (216) 748-0087; no cards; full bar.

DIRECTIONS   Eastbound: From Exit 26, the ramp leads you to a traffic light. You want to turn left here but to do so (legally) you must go straight through the light and then turn around in the McDonald's parking lot. Once faced the way you need to go, drive ¼ mile to the first light (Massillon Rd.), turn left, and you'll see the restaurant immediately on your right.

Westbound: From Exit 26, bear right at the stop sign onto E. Market St. In ¼ mile, turn left at the first light (Massillon Rd.). The restaurant is on the right.

EL CARLOS MEXICAN RESTAURANT,
Exits 48 and 54, Lake Milton

We were charmed by Carlos Alvarado and his little lakeside restaurant. In an age when Mexican food has come to be associated with big-monied shopping center palaces that look more like the Mexican National Museum than a barrio *comedor*, it was nice to find a small-time operator doing a nice job on his own. The local people and Lake Milton vacationers seem to feel that way too, and Carlos serves not only those who arrive by car, but by boat as well (there's an intercom for ordering from the dock). A few customers have dropped in by helicopter.

The food is basically Tex-Mex, but with a few Carlos variations on the tired old standards. He makes a vegetarian chimichanga, for instance, stuffed with sour cream and potatoes; we appreciated its lovely light taste. The stuffed Mexican bell peppers are based on his Yucatanian grandmother's recipe, and Carlos must go to great pains to bring in the right kind of pepper. The chili con queso is his own, a yellow, spicy, tomatoless version of the old bowl of red, used here as a dip with tortilla chips. And for dessert, Carlos has come up with apple and cherry pastelitos, a fruity version of chimichangos, wrapped with a flour tortilla and deep-fried.

Of course, all kinds of dinner combinations are available in this ingenuously tacky but relaxing roadhouse. Prices hover around $5, although à la carte items can be had for much less. Each day a lunch special goes for $3.45.

HOURS   Tues.–Sat. 8 am–11 pm; Sun. 11 am–11 pm. Closed Mon. & major holidays.

SPECS   17679 Mahoning Ave.; (216) 654-3257; V, MC; full bar.

DIRECTIONS   **Eastbound:** From Exit 48, turn right onto OH 225. In ¼ mile, turn left at the stop sign (Mahoning Ave., but unmarked) and go 3¼ miles to the restaurant on the right. After eating, do not backtrack. Continue along Mahoning Ave. for about 2 miles to OH 534 North, which will return you to the interstate.

Westbound: From Exit 54, turn left onto OH 534 South. Go 0.4 mile to the stop sign and turn right (Mahoning Ave.). In about 2 miles, the restaurant is on the left. After eating, do not backtrack. Continue along Mahoning Ave. for about 3¼ miles to OH 225 North, which will return you to the interstate.

IDLE HOUR RESTAURANT, *Exit 16, North Lima*

This little crossroads café is cleaner and cheerier inside than out, and like many lunchrooms of its genre, its finest offerings come at both ends of its meals. Soups are all homemade from scratch; the house specialty is pointedly suggested by a mounted snapping turtle who greets you just inside the threshold. Deep-flavored and chunky with both meat and vegetables, the turtle soup is as worthy a specimen as the fellow at the door. A creamy potato broth was its equal. And, on the other side of dinner are pies made by a local Mennonite lady. Our fresh red raspberry version was bursting with ripe fruit ensconced in a perfect golden crust and sprinkled with light brown sugar.

What comes between soup and dessert isn't at all bad, but it just isn't special. Creamed turkey (pressed turkey loaf) over biscuits (decent) came with mashed potatoes (instant) and coleslaw (the best part) for $2.25. Fried chicken is a house specialty ($3.20 for half a bird, $2.35 per quarter). Most sandwiches are under $1.50, and breakfasts are equally cheap.

It won't be the most memorable meal of your trip, but for a short, sweet stop and a view of small-town Ohio through large picture windows, it'll do just fine.

HOURS   Mon.–Sat. 6:30 am–8 pm; Sun. 11 am–8 pm.

SPECS   11724 South Ave. (OH 164); (216) 549-9105; no cards; no liquor; children's portions.

DIRECTIONS   From the Exit 16 tollbooth, go straight and you'll be put on OH 7 South. In 1 mile, it's on the right at the junction of OH 164.

THE BETSEY MILLS CLUB DINING ROOM,
Exit 1, Marietta

It all started in 1898 as a Monday night sewing class that soon evolved into the "Girl's Monday Club" offering lessons in the "household sciences and arts," and eventually it became a women's club named for its founder. Today the Betsey Mills Club occupies two adjoining buildings that are meticulously maintained with manicured gardens, brick patios, and wrought-iron fences. Among the services the club provides is the rental of inexpensive rooms for young Marietta women, some of whom make their living working as waitresses in the public restaurant downstairs.

In keeping with the setting, the restaurant is decorated with a palatable frilliness that isn't at all precious; in keeping with the menu's low prices, nothing is too terribly elegant and the decor feels a little like a cross between a country inn and a church supper. We liked it. We also liked the food we got—both quantity and quality—for very little money. Nothing gourmet, mind you, just middle-of-the-road American like bean soup, cornbread, and coleslaw ($1.95); pumpkin-nut bread baked in a coffee can and made into four dainty sandwiches (with fresh fruit plate, $2.95); a chicken pot pie dinner special with side orders ($4.45). There are touches of trend consciousness in some of the salad plates, quiche, and Reuben sandwiches, but to call this place trendy would be to overstep its bounds.

HOURS Mon.–Sat. 11 am–2:30 pm and 4:30–8 pm; Sun. 11:30 am–2:30 pm.

SPECS 4th & Putnam Sts.; (614) 373-3804; V, MC; no liquor.

DIRECTIONS   From Exit 1, head west into Marietta. You're on Pike St., which becomes Greene. In about 1 mile, turn right on 4th; it's 3 blocks down, at the corner of Putnam, on the right.

THE CONEY ISLAND, *Exit 46, Cambridge*

Memorable for its pies and respectable for much else, The Coney Island is a simple hop from I-77. Read a description on pp. 92–93.

DIRECTIONS   From Exit 46 of I-77, head west on US 40 toward Cambridge. In about 2½ miles, you'll be in town. The restaurant is on the left, 1½ blocks past the courthouse.

THE INN ON THE RIVER, *Exit 93, Zoar*

The village of Zoar has a colorful history as an early socialistic, communal society that flourished in the mid-19th century. Its history is preserved in a restoration village that documents a social and economic lifestyle not often celebrated in modern-day America. Until a year ago, the town's premier hostlery was the Zoar Hotel, a regular haunt of President William McKinley, who raved about its black pudding, among other things. Alas, the hotel was up on the auction block when we arrived with hefty appetites; its future was considered at best uncertain and for the time being, at least, there wasn't a pint of pudding in the house.

Heir apparent to the Zoar Hotel's legacy is the similarly struc-tured Inn on the River, itself an old hotel that has recently been revived. Despite its venerable history that began in 1829 with the original Zoarites, there is something manufactured about the "country inn" feel it is trying to put across with old weather vanes, farming implements and other paraphernalia, that just aren't as convincing as they're meant to be (especially when ac-companied by Muzak).

Still, it's worth a stop, especially at lunchtime. Bean soup is definitely worth a try. A sausage sandwich of smoked kielbasa topped with grilled peppers and onions came on a hard roll, and made a satisfying lunch for just $2.85; the beef tenderloin, on the other hand, while succulent and medium-rare as requested, seemed overpriced at $4.95, especially considering that it arrived on an outsized platter that might have been filled with salad or fruit garnish rather than merely a pile of potato chips. Other sandwiches include burgers ($2.95), BLTs ($2.85), and turkey clubs ($3.95); spinach salads are sold as side orders for $1.55 or as full meals for $4.95.

Steak and seafood dinner entrees seem on the pricey side, most in the $12–$14 area. Each is named for an early Zoarite, and the tidbits of local history that spice up the menu come at no additional charge.

HOURS   Mon.–Thurs. 11 am–3 pm and 5–10 pm; Fri. & Sat. 11 am–3 pm and 5–11 pm. Closed Sun.

SPECS   Towpath Rd.; (216) 874-4717; major cards; full bar.

DIRECTIONS   From Exit 93, head east 3 miles into Zoar. Take the first right after passing the now-defunct Zoar Hotel; this is the Dover-Zoar Rd. (CR 82). In ½ mile, turn right on Towpath Rd. The first small road leading off to your left, though unmarked, is the inn's driveway.

NEW ERA RESTAURANT, *I-76 Interchange, Akron*

It's only 3 miles out of your way to this superbly authentic ethnic eatery. See pp. 157–158 for a description.

DIRECTIONS Northbound: Stay on I-77 toward downtown Akron; don't take the I-277 loop, even though I-77 through-traffic is routed that way. At the I-76 interchange, take I-76 East for about 3 miles to Exit 26. From there, follow eastbound directions given on p. 158.

Southbound: Approaching downtown Akron, don't take the I-76 West/ I-277 loop south of the city, even though I-77 South through-traffic is routed that way. Instead, stay on I-77 proper as it joins I-76 East toward the downtown area. Where I-77 South breaks off, don't take it; instead, take I-76 East for 3 miles to Exit 26 and then follow eastbound directions given on page 158.

JACK HORNER'S RESTAURANT, *Exit 23B, Akron*

It may not look like much, but Jack Horner's serves top-notch American food at affordable prices. See pp. 156–157.

DIRECTIONS   Note: It is essential to stay on I-77 as it goes through downtown Akron; don't take the I-277 loop. Things get a little confusing, so you may want to consult a roadmap.

Northbound: From I-77 South (not I-277), follow signs for OH 8 North/ Buchtel Ave./Cuyahoga Falls. ■ About 1 mile after entering OH 8, take the Perkins St. exit, turn left at the first light, cross over the highway, and turn left again at the light. Being careful not to reenter OH 8, go 1 block to the stop sign at Forge, turn right, and look for **Jack Horner's** parking lot on your left.

Southbound: From I-77 South, follow signs toward I-76 East, which lead you onto a short stretch where I-76 and I-77 run together. At Exit 23B (a left exit), enter OH 8 toward downtown Akron, then follow directions given above from ■.

DOBIE'S CORNER, *Exit 138, Ghent*

Tucked into the corner of a small, tony shopping center on the outskirts of Akron is one of the most engaging, eclectic European restaurants we have come across, a true purveyor of Continental cuisine in the most genuine sense of the word. George and Evie Dobrin are Rumanians who have traveled extensively throughout Europe and Asia, picking up recipes and cooking techniques everywhere. Akron's discerning diners can now benefit from their expertise. We certainly did.

Given the family's own ethnic background, we chose Eastern European imports from the wide-ranging menu. A tangy cold cucumber soup was thick with sour cream, sprinkled with shards of fresh dill. *Mititei* (pronounced "mee-tee-tay"), fingerlings of charbroiled ground veal, lamb, and beef, was seasoned mysteriously and served sizzling, with three different sauces—horseradish, mustard, and tomato. Its sounds, smells, and tastes were in all manners enticing. Accompanying it, in place of a potato (which we could have had) was *mamaliga,* a cornmeal-based Rumanian peasant dish similar to polenta, layered with sour cream and topped with brick cheese.

And that was only one small part of a menu that also included stuffed cabbage, apricot scrod, eggplant parmigiana, coquilles St. Jacques, sherried lamb stew, and maple-walnut chicken, along with Dobie's delightful appetizers and soups! And for dessert such tempters as orange chiffon charlotte, Macadamia nut pie, frozen mocha cheesecake, and raspberry cake. Need we say they're all homemade?

It's all served in an Old World atmosphere that comes across unforced and without cliché. Prices—$6–$9 for dinner, around $4 for lunch—are most benign, especially considering the quality of the vittles.

HOURS Lunch: Mon.–Sat. 11:30 am–4 pm. Dinner: Mon.–Sat. 5:30–11 pm. Closed Sun.

SPECS Ghent Square, 843 N. Cleveland–Massillon Rd.; (216) 666-1676; V, MC, AE; full bar.

DIRECTIONS From Exit 138, turn left and drive about ½ mile to Ghent Square on the right. It's slightly hidden in there, but you'll find it.

PAN ASIA RESTAURANT, *Exit 155, Independence*

Since opening its nondescript doors several years ago, Pan Asia has startled and delighted East-seeking gastronomes with the distinction and diversity of its cuisine. The name is accurate, for here one can order the foods of India, Korea, Japan, and five separate regions of China (Szechuan, Hunan, Peking, Shanghai, and Canton). We couldn't try all of these entrées, of course, but if our samplings were representative (and word has it they are), then you're likely to be pleased no matter which part of the Orient strikes your palate's fancy.

We loved Yu Shiang pork, a Szechuan meat-and-vegetable dish featuring cloud ears (an aptly named fungus), water chestnuts, and shredded pork; it was hot enough to add character but not so fiery as to overwhelm. The same could be said of the condiments in Bombay chicken curry, to which we added four condiments, or sambals, at the table: shredded coconut, raisins, nuts, and chutney. Both our entrées cost $9.75, which is about average in a dinner menu that runs $6.75–$14.75. (Lunches, of course, are less.)

The Pan Asia's vaguely Oriental decor is not overly atmospheric. Clearly, the emphasis is on the food.

HOURS Mon.–Thurs. 11:30 am–8:45 pm; Fri. 11:30 am–9:45 pm; Sat. 4:30–9:45 pm. Closed Sun.

SPECS 6080 Brecksville Rd.; (216) 524-6830; V, MC, AE; full bar.

DIRECTIONS **Northbound:** From Exit 155, turn right onto Rockside Rd. Go about ½ mile to OH 21 (Brecksville Rd.). Turn left here and in 0.2 mile the restaurant is on the left.

Southbound: From Exit 155, turn left onto Rockside Rd. and go 0.7 mile to OH 21 (Brecksville Rd.). Turn left here and in 0.2 mile the restaurant is on the left.

I-80

Iowa
Illinois
Indiana
Ohio

Iowa

ABOUT MOLINE AND THE QUAD CITIES AREA

You can go through the Quad Cities area on I-74 or around it on I-80. If you go through it on I-74 you will pass near Harold's and Lagomarcino's, these being a wild game restaurant on the Rock River and a wonderful old candy store and lunchroom. I-80 brings you within striking range of Kernan's, where you'll get some of the best catfish you've ever tasted. See pp. 111–124 for I-74 listings.

KERNAN'S RIVERVIEW RESTAURANT,
Exit 306, Princeton

For as long as anyone can remember, the tiny Mississippi River town of Princeton has been known as the catfish mecca of the Quad Cities area. And every time we heard mention of this fact, the name that kept coming up was Kernan's. Seven miles from the exit seemed too long a drive, but then we noticed that the road hugged the Mississippi shoreline.

So off we went for catfish in Princeton. Not only did we get beautiful views of the river and a pleasant stretch of two-lane road, but, which is more to the point, we discovered some of the best catfish we've ever come across. It was both superbly moist and flaky crisp. The light, delicately seasoned breading seemed absolutely greaseless, and the tender flesh quite literally melted in our mouths.

The secret of Kernan's success is not that the fish are plucked right out of the river. These are pond-raised catfish, and only in summertime do a few of their wild cousins find their way onto your plate. The trick is pressure frying. In effect,the catfish at Kernan's are fried in a pressure cooker, with the result that they never lose their moisture as they would under normal conditions.

The salad and home fries were not especially noteworthy. Though Kernan's is known for doing one thing well, the menu includes a variety of fish and beef dishes from $3.95–$11.75 (the catfish is $6.95/$4.96). Lots of sandwiches and appetizers, and even a few salads round out what is really a rather complete menu.

The restaurant's full title is no exaggeration, by the way. The murky Mississippi passes just 10 feet from Kernan's picture windows. The barge and tugboat activity is constant, and the river just keeps rollin'. Riverside restaurants are very popular in the Midwest, but the view from Kernan's was as superior as the flavor of its catfish. It's a great stop if you've got a little extra time for the drive.

HOURS   Mon.–Thurs. 11 am–2 pm & 4 pm–10 pm (9 pm in winter); Fri. & Sat. 11 am–11 pm (10 pm in winter); Sun. 8:30 am–9 pm (8 pm in winter).

SPECS   333 River Rd.; (319) 289-5137; major cards; full bar.

DIRECTIONS   From Exit 306 go north on Route 67 for 7.5 miles. It's on the right.

Illinois

TOWN AND COUNTRY RESTAURANT,
Exit 56, Princeton

Princeton may be a spiffy little town, but it was a young woman who worked in Mother's Kitchen, a trendy little gourmet shop, who told us about the Town and Country. "If you *really* want some good food," she said as if revealing the tawdry truth at the heart of the universe, "go there."

Now some of the best tips we've ever gotten have come from just that kind of person in just that tone of voice. So off we went to this plasticky, bare, "family style" restaurant.

The place was clean and the venetian blinds that ran along two walls let in plenty of light. The long and short of it was this: a dull salad bar with good dressings; good chicken rice soup; Greek baked chicken with a lemony, savory flavor that was much better than just good; roast potatoes, nicely seasoned with oregano; and an acceptable tapioca pudding. Not bad at all, and it cost only $3.15.

The usual fried Americana is on the menu. If you want a burger, you can get it with fries, pickle, and soup or salad for $2.35. Plain sandwiches are $1.10–$1.85. Stick, if you wish, to such basics, but the owners seemed to us to be really trying, and we think you ought to give them a chance to show their stuff.

HOURS   Daily 6 am–10 pm.

SPECS   12 Peru St.; (815) 875-3673; no cards; no liquor.

DIRECTIONS Go 1.7 miles south on Route 26 to the light at Peru St. in Princeton. Turn right, go ½ block, and it's on the left.

THE STRAWBERRY PATCH, *Exit 56, Princeton*

* Untried but likely

Princeton is about as antiquey and boutiquey as a town can get out on the Illinois prairie, and in towns such as this there are almost always good restaurants to be found. Here it's The Strawberry Patch, a place that has an excellent local reputation for French cooking and has been bringing a touch of Chicago to the boonies for over 6 years now. Unfortunately, they serve no dinner on week nights, and even on Fridays and Saturdays you need reservations.

Still we thought you'd want to know about this small, basement restaurant. Where else hereabouts are you likely to get croissant sandwiches or quiche with from-scratch soups ($4.50 for soup and sandwich)? And 50 percent non-iceberg salads? Luncheon specials like steamed mussels in cream sauce and fettucine with ham, peas, and cream sauce are $3–$4.50.

Dinners are the likes of roast duck, beef Stroganoff, and veal Florentine, augmented by specials on the order of pheasant with morels and loin of lamb en croute ($10.50–$15). But, as we said, if such be your pleasure you'd best call well in advance.

HOURS Lunch: Mon.–Sat. 11 am–3 pm; Dinner: Fri. & Sat. 5:30–9:30 pm. Closed Sundays.

SPECS 516 S. Main St.; (815) 872-8011; DC, CB; beer only.

DIRECTIONS Go south toward Princeton on Route 26 for 1.9 miles to the center of town. The restaurant is ½ block after the Apollo Theatre, on the right, beneath the Country Casuals clothing store.

THE RED DOOR, *Exit 75, Peru*

There was something vaguely German at The Red Door, and it wasn't just the schnitzel. It was the hodgepodgey aesthetic of cram-everything-you-can-onto-the-walls-and-cover-the-bare-spots-with-flocked-wallpaper. The result is a sort of "olde-timey" barroom feel that is neither old, nor barroomy, nor German. The truth is that aside from "overdone" we don't know what to call it, which doesn't really matter because the food was very good.

We arrived at dinnertime and asked, as usual, for the house specialty. "Flaming steak Diane," we were told, at $14.75. "Not the chicken marsala or fettucine carbonara at $7.50?" we asked hopefully. "Or maybe the $8.50 trout amandine?" The waitress shook her head politely. So soon a flurry of high-speed knifework provided us with tableside entertainment, while onions, celery, mushrooms, and butter sizzled nicely in a pan. With a flourish the waiter added the fillet and topped it with successive dashes of brandy, Grand Marnier and Bordeaux. A match had the whole thing glowing like a birthday cake, and within a few more seconds the high-speed creation was sitting on the plate.

It was showy and a little vulgar, but there was no denying that the product was a very rich and satisfying meal that turned a mere piece of meat into a real occasion. The spinach salad with vinaigrette was also very good, and a welcome relief from the iceberg-only salad bars we found everywhere else. Even the spaetzles were good. Conclusion: The Red Door's strong local reputation is justified, even if we wish the place would conduct itself with more restraint.

Since 7 small versions of the full dinners run from only $4.75–$7.25, you needn't really spend all that much to enjoy this kind of quality. Lunches are from $3.75 for a burger with potato or vegetable to about $6.26 for a lamb chop luncheon. There's a good selection of interesting salads at around $4.50, and sandwiches of all sorts between $3.50 and $6.

A side benefit of a visit to The Red Door is the opportunity to get a good close look at the Illinois River. The restaurant is but a few feet from the water's edge, and we were fascinated to see how at this point the river rolls and undulates as if it were the swelling sea. Apparently it's the tugboats that cause this. For a full hour after one passes, the river writhes like a snake and puts on nearly as good a show as the flaming steak Diane.

HOURS Mon.–Fri. 11 am–11 pm; Sat. 4 pm–midnight; Sun. 4–10 pm.

SPECS   1701 Water St.; (815) 223-2500; major cards; full bar; children's menu.

DIRECTIONS   From Exit 75 go 2.5 miles south toward Peru on US 51. Then take the exit for US 6W. Go right on US 6 into town. Five blocks brings you to Putnam St. and the **Peru Pizza House** on the left. Turn left onto Putnam and go down the hill 4 blocks to the river. It's on your right.

PERU PIZZA HOUSE, *Exit 75, Peru*

There are very reasonable pizzas and quite good subs to be had here at very reasonable prices. The decor is nil, but the whole place reeks with that just-right vinegary smell.

HOURS   Mon.–Sat. 11 am–midnight. Closed Sun.

SPECS   1620 4th St.; (815) 223-7408; no cards; beer & wine.

DIRECTIONS   See **The Red Door** above.

STARVED ROCK LODGE, *Exit 81, Utica*

We've always been fans of WPA projects, be they the breakwaters of Chicago or the bridges on the parkways of New York. They were true public works that ennobled and beautified the landscape. It wasn't until we stumbled across the Starved Rock Lodge in Starved Rock State Park that we realized the CCC spent a good part of the depression doing much the same sort of thing deep in the forest.

Surely this lodge is a candidate for the most magnificent log structure on earth. In its lobby a massive stone fireplace soars 40 feet before it passes through the ceiling. The floor is natural stone warmed by Indian-style rugs, and here and there is a sprinkling of comfortable old furniture made to look rustic back in the '50s.

The calming, tranquil rooms of the lodge are yours for no more than you'd pay at a modest hotel. And there's a restaurant here, also built with rustic grandeur, and boasting a wall of small paned windows that overlook the Illinois River.

We wish we could tell you that the restaurant was especially good or especially cheap, but we cannot. The concessionaire who runs it is not carrying on the spirit in which the lodge was built. Breakfasts run around $4, which is also the price of a lunchtime hamburger. Luncheons are $5–$6, and dinners are $6.75–$11. The cooking is straight American stuff, and all that we tasted was okay. But at these prices it should be better than that.

No matter. Once you enter the park you are surrounded by a cool, quiet, and unhurried world of oak, maple, and luxuriant ferns. The lodge is superb, and if it's time to stop for the night, there is no way you'll do any better. If you insist on really good food, have dinner in Peru (see pp. 170–172) and sleep here.

HOURS   Mon.–Sat. 8–10 am, noon–2 pm, & 6–8 pm; Sun. & holidays, 8–10 am., noon–3 pm & 6–7:30 pm.

SPECS   (815) 667-4211; no cards; full bar.

DIRECTIONS   From Exit 81 the way is well marked. You can just follow the signs which will take you south on Route 178 for 4.2 easy miles to a left turn onto Route 71. Go 0.8 mile on Route 71 to the park entrance on the left and then follow signs for the lodge.

HEINZ CAFÉ, *Exit 90, Ottawa*

It's not all that hard to find unlikely restaurants that produce their own spaghetti sauce, or even their own spaghetti. But this is the first we've come across that grows and cans its own tomatoes. More "from scratch" than that you simply cannot get unless you gather your own seed!

Mary Seng had been a waitress for 32 years before she took over this old lunch room/coffee shop. It's her big chance, her life's dream, and she's doing everything she can to make it work. That means producing good food in a clean and friendly environment and charging as little as she can. Her 95-cent bowl of chili, let it be said, is superb—spicy but not fiery, and very full bodied. Her hearty vegetable soup (from scratch, of course, with her own tomatoes) is almost as good as the chili, and she goes to the trouble of baking her long, thick potato wedges before frying them.

The truth is that in Heinz's you should reverse the usual rule of eating the simplest possible thing in an unfamiliar restaurant. The hamburgers ($1.45) and Reuben sandwiches ($2.45) don't give Mary a chance to show what she can do. Order instead the spaghetti, the Swiss steak, or the beef tips in noodles ($2.75–$3.95) and see what care and a talented touch can accomplish in even the humblest surroundings.

The place *is* plain—just a curvy lunch counter surrounded by almost-institutional-green walls. The sign outside (which imitates the logo of the national brand) is charmingly '30s-ish, but there's nothing especially antiquey within. Just spotless cleanliness and an old-fashioned warmth that emanates from the people instead of the fixtures.

A lot of that warmth has to be attributed to waitress Beverly Lewen. She is that kind of spontaneous, outgoing counter waitress who puts as much effort into bantering with the customers as she does into keeping their orders straight. Often she stops all that long enough to counsel a high school kid on his or her love life, and every now and then she pulls out a Polaroid to add another mug shot to the restaurant's decor.

The long and short of it is that we had a wonderful time here and recommend it to you highly if this kind of Americana has any appeal at all. And you'll get the added bonus of learning about an Illinois sandwich specialty—the tenderloin. This is a piece of pork tenderloin, pounded to the shape and size of a small pizza, breaded, frozen, deep-fried, and then quite ridiculously served on a normal-sized hamburger bun. Since the meat overhangs the bread by a good 3 inches on all sides, the question, as Beverly put it, is not "Where's the beef?" but "Where's the bun?" Though it's a lot of chewing for $1.95, we liked chili a whole lot better.

HOURS   Mon.–Sat. 5 am–5 pm. Closed Sun., Christmas, Thanksgiving.

SPECS   106 W. Main St.; (815) 434-6995; no cards; no liquor.

DIRECTIONS   Go south from Exit 90 for 1.3 miles to the light at the junction with US 6. Turn right and go 1 block to Lasalle. Turn left onto Lasalle and go 0.7 mile (6 lights) to Main. Turn left onto Main, go ½ block, and it's on the left.

SYL'S, *Exit 130A, Joliet*

Just 1 mile from I-80, off in an industrial section of Joliet, lies a much loved local restaurant that deserves all the affection it gets. Since 1946 the Pekol family has been producing first-rate American food at this location. The neighborhood has changed, but the restaurant hasn't, except to grow bigger and a bit more posh as its reputation spread.

If for nothing else, come to sample the perfectly seasoned apple strudel. Mom's apple pie was never like this! If you want more than that, you might try the barbecued baby back ribs. You'll find them as tender as ribs can be, with a mild but excellent sauce that will win your heart without hitting you over the head.

Excellence at Syl's does not come cheap. Dinners are from $8.25–$13.75, and luncheons are a surprising $4.50–$8.95, with sandwiches at $2.75–$4.95. Part of the reason for the higher-than-usual prices may be the emphasis on beef. As we said, this is a decidedly American restaurant (lobster comes french-fried). If you stick to what's appropriate in a place like this, we're pretty sure you'll go away content.

The decor is sort of ethnic posh. Syl's is large, dark, cool, and quiet, with tablecloths and wooden chairs. There are two walls of brick and a few plants about, but no hint of a trendy brick, plants, and oak routine.

HOURS Mon.–Thurs. 11:30 am–2 pm & 5–10 pm; Fri. 11:30 am–2 pm & 5 pm–midnight; Sat. 5 pm–midnight. Sun. noon–10 pm. Closed Thanksgiving & Christmas.

SPECS 829 Moes; (815) 725-1977; no cards; full bar.

DIRECTIONS From Exit 130A go south on Route 117 for ½ mile to a light. Turn left at the light and go 0.2 mile. It's on the left.

DIE BIER STUBE, *Exit 145A, Frankfort*

Once upon a time Klaus Ditschler ran the biggest, fanciest, most renowned and most overdressed German restaurant south of Chicago and east of Bettendorf, Iowa. Then some financial fancy work left him out in the cold, and though he is struggling to rebuild, the benefit accrues to you. The fact is that this man is a true chef who offered us proudly some of the best German cooking we've tasted anywhere. But at Die Bier Stube it comes relatively cheap, and you don't have to put up with all the tasteless kitsch that seems to characterize midwestern German restaurants. Here it's all simple and tasteful within the limits of a reduced budget—dropped ceiling and plain wall paneling, but clean and light, with white tablecloths and a few amenities.

The venison stew we tasted was simply excellent, and we will long remember the rich flavors of its deep brown sauce. The butter-fried spaetzle were the best we've ever experienced, and even the humble side dish of red cabbage demands a rave notice —it was delightfully tangy, the result of sautéing in duck fat with onions, wine, and a hint of applesauce. Even the house dressing was a truly original creation—a strong and pungent combination of Parmesan, cream, mustard, and other spices, the likes of which we'd not come across before.

Klaus Ditschler really knows what he is doing, and if you're hungry in his vicinity you ought not miss him, especially not when there are specials like an all-you-can-eat farmer's plate for *two* at $11.95 (including, if you can believe it, a pitcher of beer). The Tuesday special is barbecued beef ribs at just $5.50 for an all-you-can-eat dinner!

Klaus's accountant, we are sure, is glad such prices apply only to the specials. On the regular dinner menu you'll find a wide variety of German and American dishes from $7.95–$10.95, with much to choose from at the low end.

Lunch offers 8 German dishes (goulash, sauerbraten, schnitzel, and wurst) at around $4.75, along with a good selection of simple and not-so-simple sandwiches (burgers for $1.95, Reubens for $2.75). Omelets are $2.50. Goulash and liver dumpling soup are just $1.

Absolutely everything we tried at Die Bier Stube had character, originality, and just plain great taste. It's hard to see how you could go wrong here, unless, of course, you can enjoy German food only when it's surrounded by suits of armor and served by someone who looks like she belongs in a fairy tale by Grimm.

HOURS Tues.–Thurs. 11 am–10 pm; Fri. & Sat. 11 am–11 pm; Sun. 11 am–9 pm. Closed Sun. & Thanksgiving.

SPECS 42 Kansas St.; (815) 469-6660; no cards; full bar.

DIRECTIONS From Exit 145A go south on US 45 toward Frankfort. After 3.2 miles and crossing US 30, you should bear left, following signs for the historic district. It's then 4 blocks to Kansas St. Turn right and go 1 block. It's on the left.

Indiana

THE TANGERINE, *Exit 49, La Porte*

One sure way to cope with road weariness is to make mealtime a step into a world so utterly removed from the highway that all thoughts of travel are instantaneously driven from the mind. It costs more, but you rise from the table as from a good night's sleep, refreshed and ready to attack again the rigors of the highway.

We didn't expect to find such an environment in La Porte, Indiana, and it will cost you a 5-mile drive to check out our discovery. Those who make the effort will be rewarded with as handsome and classy an art deco restaurant as we've seen anywhere, and food that, while not quite as spectacular as the decor, was certainly very enjoyable.

We experienced at The Tangerine a lemony veal piccata that was tender, tasty, and subtle; some nice-but-not-very-special appetizers, like shrimp with crabmeat in sherry beneath a cheese topping, and mushrooms in garlic butter. The bread was disappointingly soft and flabby. Dinners are $8.50–$13.95, and someday we'll come back to sample The Tangerine's version of Boston sole—stuffed with creamed crabmeat, mushrooms, and shrimp, sautéed in butter, and finally topped with grapes. That's not the way they do it in Beantown, but it sounds great and sells for only $8.95.

At lunchtime, quiches, crepes, and sandwiches are around $3.50; salads are from $2.25–$3.95. There are only a few entrees, most of them meaty and basic, in the $4–$8 range.

We aren't hiding the fact that it was The Tangerine's looks that made the deepest impression. It is restrained and quiet, yet also daring, posh, comfortable, and relaxing. Soft tones of gray, blue, and pink dominate. The walls are mirrored, and somehow whoever conceived this room managed to get away with moves that would have been excessive anywhere else—things like statuettes discreetly tucked into the mirrored corners and lines of little white Christmas tree lights laid right into the floor.

Step inside and we promise you that within 2 minutes you will completely forget that you're in the middle of a long and boring drive. And you certainly won't feel like you're in La Porte, Indiana.

HOURS   Lunch: Tues.–Fri. 11 am–2 pm. Dinner: Mon.–Thurs. 5–9:00 pm, Fri. & Sat. 5–10:30 pm. Brunch: Sun. 10 am–2 pm. Closed major holidays & first 2 weeks in Jan.

SPECS   601 Michigan Ave.; (219) 326-8000; major cards; full bar.

DIRECTIONS   Turn left at the end of the Exit 49 ramp and head for La Porte. Bear left after 2.5 miles and continue 2 miles farther until you have gone over a long bridge and find yourself at Lincolnway in the center of town. Turn left, go 1 block, and turn left again onto Michigan Ave. Go 1 block, and it's on the right, on the corner.

CORNUCOPIA, *Exit 77, South Bend*

It's not always so terrible when alternative movements make peace with the establishment. Not long ago the Cornucopia's patrons all wore ventilated blue jeans and had their eyes fixed dreamily on The Revolution, or at least upon the spiritual development of the soul. Then the place looked as if it had been hammered together in someone's garage, and it was certainly the most interesting restaurant in South Bend.

Today the hostess looks like a Lord and Taylor ad, and we doubt the dinner-table talk is nearly so intense. Though The Revolution may have faded at the Cornucopia, the food's gotten even better, and the decor has evolved into something that is refined but informally pleasant—here a touch of brass, there a plant or two next to a white latticework room divider. Why, there's even carpeting, but not so much of anything to make the place seem overdressed.

We tried a fillet of sole in crushed walnut breading for $4.50 a la carte. Its delicate, pure, and wholesome flavors revealed the restaurant's health food past, which was just fine, since the moist fish spoke well enough for itself. The whole-wheat bread was really very, very good, and the mocha carob cheesecake was superbly rich without being oversweet or cloying. The coffee was excellent by anyone's standards, and so we just have to give the Cornucopia very good marks indeed.

The health food influence also shows itself in the absence of red meat from the menu. That leaves the likes of quiche; crepes; lasagne; burritos; chicken with mushrooms and almonds in Mornay sauce; and malfatti, which are croquettes of spinach, eggs, Parmesan, and bread crumbs in tomato sauce. All are available a la carte ($1.95–$4.75) or as full dinners ($4.20–$6.95). A wide range of salads ($1.50–$3.50), quesadillas, appetizers, teas, and fruit drinks make for all sorts of interesting lunch possibilities.

The ferment of the '60s may be gone, but one of that decade's lasting benefits has been the improvement of American food. For us, the Cornucopia stands as a symbol of that bit of progress.

HOURS Mon.–Thurs. 11 am–8:30 pm; Fri. & Sat. 11 am–9 pm. Closed Sun.

SPECS 303 S. Michigan St.; (219) 288-1911; V, MC; beer & wine.

DIRECTIONS At the end of the long ramp at Exit 77 turn right onto Michigan St. (US 33). Follow traffic for 2.5 miles through South

Bend to Western Ave. (At 1.9 miles the road will jog right for a block and then left again. Just go with the traffic.) Turn left on Western and then left again as soon as possible. Go 1 block and park in the lot on your left. **Cornucopia** is on the corner near a large sign that says BAER'S.

THE HAPPY HOUSE, *Exit 77, South Bend*

We'd be happier telling you about The Happy House if this nice little Cantonese restaurant was not on the far side of 3 miles of strip development. But if you are willing to brave the clutter you will be rewarded with crisp, fresh vegetables and skillful preparation of the kind of Chinese dishes you knew about before you'd heard of Szechuan—shrimp with toasted almonds is what we mean, plus mushrooms, pea pods, bamboo shoots, and water chestnuts. The food here was marked by clear, lively flavors and attention to detail—not memorable, mind you, but very clean tasting and unobtrusively pleasant, like a really nice person who has only a little to say and says it softly.

The decor at The Happy House is on the plain side of kitschy —but what the place lacks in looks it makes up for with its friendly and efficient personality. And it's not expensive—chop suey dishes run up from $3.85; more authentic cooking is between $5.20 (sweet-and-sour pork) and $6.75 (pressed duck), with about two dozen possibilities in between.

We have knowledgeable friends in South Bend who swear by this place, and you'll be happy with it too so long as you forget everything that's happened to Chinese food in America since 1970.

HOURS Sun. & Tues.–Thurs. 11 am–9 pm; Fri. & Sat. 11 am–10 pm. Closed Mon. & Thanksgiving.

SPECS 3121 US 31; (219) 684-0484; no cards; no liquor.

DIRECTIONS At the end of the long ramp from Exit 77 turn left toward Niles, Michigan, onto US 31. It's 3.7 miles to the restaurant, on the right, just over the Michigan line. You'll pass many alternatives, but patience will be rewarded.

THE RIB SHACK, *Exit 83, Granger*

The Rib Shack is located in an unexpectedly fine old house, but its lace curtains and carpeting do only a little to alleviate the basic decor of cheap paneling and plastic booths. A rib joint is but a rib joint, and who needs more when the ribs are really good?

And they *are* good here—big, tender, meaty, messy ribs, full of real hickory-smoke flavor and drenched with a richly tasty hot sauce that comes in three intensities. For $6.35 you get a half slab with real potato wedges, rolls, and some very good homemade coleslaw; $4.35 will get you a smaller version of the same.

There's barbecued chicken at $3.45 for the four-piece dinner, and $5.90 will buy for the undecided a combination plate of two pieces of chicken and three ribs, accompanied by big, thick potato wedges. If you're not absolutely ravenous, it'll surely feed two of you at lunchtime.

To our minds, rib joints like this make for some of the best possible road food. They're usually at least good. They're always fast, they're fun, and this one is both close to the highway and inexpensive. If the prices quoted above are too much for you, how about a barbecued pork sandwich at $1.15? And if you haven't the time to linger, get your order to go. But we won't guarantee the sauces to be good for the upholstery.

Shrimp, cod, and catfish dinners are also offered ($3.50–$4.50), as are burgers ($1.25), and 10 other sandwiches. They've even got pizza. But it's clear enough what The Rib Shack is about, and it's a pleasure to find a simple eatery that does its thing and does it well.

HOURS   Tues.–Fri. 11 am–9 pm; Fri. 11 am–10 pm; Sat. 4–10 pm; Sun. noon–9 pm. Closed Mon.

SPECS   State Road 23 at Bittersweet; (219) 277-3143; no cards; beer & wine.

DIRECTIONS   From Exit 83 turn right at the end of the ramp and then soon turn right again onto Route 23. Go 2.3 miles to the RR tracks. Continue straight for another ¼ mile, and it's on the left.

GRANGER TAP AND GRILL, *Exit 83, Granger*

So drab and motellike was the interior of Granger's Tap and Grill that we hesitate to tell you about it. Honesty, however, compels us to admit that the Swiss steak we sampled was really quite good, temptingly smothered in a rich sauce of tomatoes, celery, and all sorts of delightful flavors. The mashed potatoes were acceptable, the limas canned, the roll was good, and the beef-barley soup was better than just okay. Not a bad performance at all for a $2 half order of the full $2.75 plate lunch! The soup, of course, was extra, but we shudder to think of what the other 75 cents might have bought—if they had called what they gave us a full bowl, we'd have thought it more than generous.

There are sandwiches, too, the fanciest of which is ham on French for $1.85. Chicken, shrimp, and perch baskets are in the vicinity of $3.25. Dinners run from $3.95–$9.50, with pike, perch, and frog legs putting in an appearance where you wouldn't expect them. Sandwiches at dinnertime are $3.50.

Downstairs is more pubby, and there's one of those mammoth TV screens to keep you from having to make conversation. But upstairs or down, don't come for the charm—just good, straight food at a very decent price.

HOURS   Mon.–Sat. 9 am–11 pm. Closed Sun.

SPECS   12797 State Road 23; (219) 277-6812; no cards; full bar.

DIRECTIONS   From Exit 83 turn right at the end of the ramp and then soon turn right again onto Route 23. Go 2.3 miles. It's on the left, just before the RR tracks.

THE PATCHWORK QUILT INN, *Exit 107, Middlebury*

We weren't able to sample the food at this old farmhouse turned country inn, but we have every reason to believe you may well find dinner here a memorable event. For one thing, there's Arletta Lovejoy's buttermilk pecan chicken that won first prize at the National Chicken Cooking Contest. Even if she had come in tenth we'd figure that anyone with enough imagination to combine those ingredients just had to be at least a good cook, and probably better than good.

Secondly, there's the inn itself, an endearingly eclectic combination of kitsch, crafts, opulence, and down-home coziness that warms the heart and defies classification. But you can be sure of one thing. No one would go to that much trouble and serve crummy food.

The chicken dinner goes for $6.75. Yankee pot roast, ham, trout amandine, roast duck, and Cornish hen are the other possibilities, all in the same price range. If you're feeling both flush and hungry, you might want to spent $11–$12 and convert a mere dinner into a five-course feast. Service is family style, and everything's included, from nonalcoholic drink, soup, salad buffet (with meat salad, pâté, and cheese balls) to two meats, potato, vegetable, rolls, coffee, and dessert.

Should all this somehow fail to please you, we guarantee that you'll at least love the primitive paintings of Mennonite scenes done by a local woman—a sort of middle western Grandma Moses.

HOURS   Dinner: Tues.–Fri. 6–8 pm; Sat. 4:30–8 pm. Lunch: May–Oct. only, Tues. & Wed. 11 am–2 pm. Closed major holidays.

SPECS   11748 County Road 2; (219) 825-2417; no cards; no liquor.

DIRECTIONS   From Exit 107 turn left at the end of the ramp and go 0.3 mile to County Road 2. Turn left and follow the road 1 mile. It's on the left.

VILLAGE INN RESTAURANT, *Exit 107, Middlebury*

We just loved the Village Inn Restaurant. Even had the food not been good or the clientele one quarter Mennonite and Amish, it would still have been worth the 6-mile drive just to be among the people here and feel the warm glow of country friendliness and downright human kindness. Over the counter is a Tab sign that reads: I BELIEVE THAT EVERY HUMAN MIND FEELS PLEASURE IN DOING GOOD TO ANOTHER.

The Village Inn gave us pleasure in its pies, and we can only hope that the woman who starts baking them at 4:30 each morning got as much out of making it for us. In any case, pies are what the restaurant is best known for—cherry, pumpkin, peanut butter, blueberry, toasted coconut, vanilla crumb, apricot, and apple. The list goes on and on and changes with the seasons. But there are always a lot of them, they are always delicious, and they cost only 80–90 cents a slice. The nutmeg seasoning on our custard cream pie was precisely right, and the crust was a bit of tender flaky perfection.

The rest of the menu is not terribly special or terribly Amish, though it is all good country cooking: burgers for $1.30, 20 other inexpensive sandwiches, and a variety of hearty country dinners that are mostly less than $4 (hot beef with potatoes and gravy was $2.60).

Breakfast, however, does offer another chance at a local specialty. Have you ever begun your day with mush and head-cheese? We gave it a try and found that headcheese here is a gray, spicy, loose sausage that arrives in a little dish right next to the mush. The mush in turn is cornbread patties that have been cooked, cooled, and then deep-fried in lard. You eat them like pancakes, and they are, well . . . filling. The headcheese supplies the flavor, so don't eat it all up before you take on the mush.

Regardless of the food, we promise you a good time here if only you will talk to people. Talk to your waitress about local life, or talk to the owner, Junior Schrock. He speaks Dutch and English and considers his restaurant more than just an eating place. People come to him with their problems, and that human contact has for him a flavor more lovely even than that of his pies.

HOURS   Mon.–Sat. 5 am–9 pm. Closed Sun. & major holidays.

SPECS   104 S. Main St.; (219) 825-2043; no cards; no liquor.

DIRECTIONS   At the end of the ramp from Exit 107 turn right for Middlebury onto IN 135. Go 5.6 lovely, easy miles to town. It's on the right.

COUNTRY MEADOWS, *Exit 144, Fremont*

You never know where good food might turn up. At this exit we found it in an unpretentious little golf resort and motel that runs its own restaurant. We knew we were in for a surprise with the first spoonful of the hearty, chunky chicken-rice soup—very tasty and clearly from scratch. The salad bar was iceberg-only, but the blue cheese dressing was perfectly fine. We were finally convinced by the fine taste and handsome presentation of the baked chicken—mildly seasoned but with character and eminently likable ($4.50)—that someone back in that kitchen was really trying.

Whoever it was, they keep at it all day: two eggs, sausage, and toast go for $2.95. Lunch is just sandwiches ($1.35–$2.95) augmented by a chef's salad and a few extras like french-fried zucchini. The small dinner menu runs from $5–$10.50.

Later we got the story and learned that the restaurant had been little more than a watering hole for thirsty golfers until new managers with restaurant experience took over the whole resort. The food improved by leaps and bounds, as did the decor. Out went the linoleum and in came a subtle, tasteful, relaxing scheme in tones of brown. Since the room already had a wall of windows overlooking a meticulously tended golf course, the improvements left nothing more to be desired in the way of a highway stop—gorgeous view, pleasant surroundings, low prices, and good food that's right near the road but as insulated from it as if it were sealed off by glass.

Far, far across the greens, you can just barely see the trucks moving by out on the interstate. The Olympian feeling of removal is quite marvelous.

HOURS   April 1–Thanksgiving: Mon.–Thurs. 6 am–9 pm; Fri. & Sat. 6 am–10 pm; Sun. 6 am–8 pm. Thanksgiving–March 31: Daily 7 am–8 pm. Closed Christmas Day & may be closed from Jan. 1–March 15.

SPECS   (219) 495-4525; V, MC; full bar.

DIRECTIONS   From Exit 144 follow signs for IN 120 for about ½ mile to a light. At the light turn left onto IN 120 and go 0.4 mile to a sign for the resort on the left. It's just up the driveway.

Ohio

4E RANCH HOUSE, *Exit 4, Toledo*

It was the lady in the Maumee Christian bookstore who told us that if we really wanted good, inexpensive home cookin' the 4E was the place to go. Four miles sounded like too much to us, but we went anyway, and if we hadn't we'd have missed as good an adventure in straightforward American eating as the highway offers.

You can tell the 4E is different from the outside—imitation vertical logs shellacked a bright orange-yellow. You don't know quite how to interpret this, but at least it's a sign of individuality. The inside is a warm, knotty pine affair with overhead log beams, a real fireplace, and a collection of ranch house gear that somehow seems quite natural tacked up on the wooden walls.

At midday the customers were happy and noisy. The barbecued short ribs ($4.50) told us why—three superbly tender and meaty ribs smothered in a sauce that was very flavorful even though it was untrendily mild. Less good were the corn (canned but crunchy) and the mashed potatoes (not instant, but no better than okay). Then the 4E scored big once again with its blue cheese salad dressing (not from a bottle) and its homemade black-bottom pie (not too sweet, and miles beyond the usual highway pie). The rolls and desserts, we learned, are all from scratch, and the french fries are not frozen.

The bargains at the 4E are on the specials. There were 9 of them when we visited, running from $3.95–$5.75 for pike or perch, with plain old catfish in beer batter at $5.25. These are available at lunch or dinner, as are the sandwiches that cost between $1 and $2.65. Breakfast anytime—two eggs and sausage for $2.60.

It's a warm, comfortable, happy place with good food and

reasonable prices, well worth the 10 or so minutes it'll take you to find it. And the service was so fast you may end up saving time.

HOURS   Mon.–Sat. 7 am–8 pm; Sun. 9 am–8 pm. Closed major holidays.

SPECS   3428 Airport Highway; (419) 381-9243; no cards; no liquor.

DIRECTIONS   From Exit 4 go north toward Toledo for 2.1 miles on US 20 to Airport Highway (well marked). Turn right and go another 2.1 miles to the light at Byrne. Continue straight 1 block, and it's on the left.

MILLER'S, *Exit 4, Toledo*

If you're hungry at Exit 4 and the 4E is too far, then the best we can do for you is Miller's, an old-fashioned highway restaurant with booths in just *that* shade of dark green. Also featured are little brass chandeliers with diminutive lampshades on each bulb. It's cute, and it won our hearts until we tasted the food. No better, unfortunately, than typical diner food. And by the same token, no worse.

HOURS   Daily 7 am–9 pm.

SPECS   2325 S. Reynolds Rd.; (419) 381-0670; no liquor; no cards.

DIRECTIONS   0.9 mile north of Exit 4 on US 20, on the right.

THE OLD ISLAND HOUSE, *Exit 6, Port Clinton*

The bar in The Old Island House is mellowed by the darkened varnish of its 100-year-old woods, and its high tin ceiling was not ordered from a restaurant design catalogue. There's an inimitable, down-to-earth pubbiness about this restaurant, which makes it a fine place to try out the Great Lakes' best-known contributions to American cuisine—lake perch and walleye pike. The experience will cost you a 12-mile detour, so come only if you're in no particular hurry.

Port Clinton is a pretty little resort town thrust out into Lake Erie by the peninsula that defines Sandusky Bay. The population rises with the summer temperatures and diminishes in winter to a few hardy ice fishermen, but the Island House is the local gathering place any time of year. So it has been since the hotel was first opened in 1886, and so it will still be when you get to this part of the world. (It will still be a hotel, too, with thirty-six rooms to rent, but you'll need 3 weeks' advance reservations in summer.)

Pike and perch have been the house specialties for as long as anyone can remember. If you've never tried walleye, come see why people get so excited over this fish. Our Island House version was gently broiled to a moist and tender perfection—a delicate, subtly delicious collection of flavors, served lobster style, with drawn butter. Bravo! And if you ask for it, the waitress will have all those nasty little bones removed. Expect a tab of about $13.95 for a whole fish (about 18 ounces).

The batter-fried lake perch ($12.95) lacked the subtlety of the pike, but were still very nice. Salad bar greenery was only average, but the avocado and celery-seed dressings made up for it.

Sixteen other predictable dinners are offered ($7.25–$11.95), with California and Ohio wines to choose from. For lunch there's a decent selection of burgers and sandwiches ($1.50–$2.95). Full luncheons run $6–$11.

You may have noticed in the preceding paragraphs that perch and pike do not come cheap. The reason, we were told, is that American game laws forbid (pointlessly, they said) commercial fishing in the Great Lakes. The result is that all the perch and pike in American restaurants have to come from Canadian fisheries, a situation that inflates the price without protecting the fish.

HOURS Summer: Mon.–Thurs. 6:30 am–10 pm; Fri. & Sat. 6:30 am–11 pm; Sun. 7:30 am–9 pm. Winter: Mon.–Thurs. 7 am–9 pm; Fri. & Sat. 7 am–10 pm; Sun. 8 am–8 pm. Closed Christmas, New Year's Day.

SPECS 102 Madison St.; (419) 734-2166; major cards; full bar; children's menu.

DIRECTIONS From Exit 6 go 11.5 miles to Harrison St. in Port Clinton. Turn left on Harrison and go 2 blocks to 2nd St. Turn right onto 2nd and go 3 blocks to Madison. Turn left onto Madison, go 1 block, and it's on the left.

THE HOMESTEAD INN, *Exit 7, Milan*

The Homestead Inn is a grand old Victorian mansion that couldn't quite decide whether it wanted to imitate a southern plantation or a New England sea-captain's house. The result is a 2-story front porch supported by four skinny columns, topped by a mansard roof that in turn bears an elaborate widow's walk —an apparition in the flat Ohio landscape that would look misplaced even if it weren't surrounded by parking lots, motels, and gas stations.

The food was good—nothing really special, mind you, but good, and very modestly priced for a meal in such surroundings (straight American dinners mostly from $6.95–$9.95, luncheons at about $3.95, and quite a few plain and fancy sandwiches for under $2.50). Grand old rooms with all kinds of ornamental woodwork, we have discovered, are very good for forgetting the road, and in this case they are so close to the exit ramp you might almost think they were built by the highway department.

HOURS Mon.–Thurs. 7:15 am–9:30 pm; Fri. & Sat. 7:15 am–10 pm; Sun. 7:15 am–8:30 pm. Closed major holidays.

SPECS 12018 Route 250; (419) 499-4271; V, MC, AE; full bar.

DIRECTIONS From Exit 7 bear left toward Milan. It'll be on the left, hard by the exit.

MITCHELL'S BARBECUE, *Exit 8, Elyria*

We really liked the ribs in this concrete-block soul food restaurant that is decorated with only a Coke machine, the ancient TV that sits atop it, and the friendly warmth of the people who work here. James Mitchell, who is in his 60s, will buy only the tiniest baby back ribs. That, he says, is half the secret. The bigger ones are meatier, to be sure, but tougher, too. Smoke 'em up in the backyard, as Mr. Mitchell does, and add a sauce that is spicy without being hot. The result is about as good a full dinner as $4.50 will buy, and if that's too much, try a rib sandwich at $2.60.

We have to confess, though, that it wasn't the ribs that knocked us off our seat at the four-stool counter. It was the sweet potato pie, which, we swear to you, was only a shade less spectacular than the pie at Mrs. Bonner's Private Club in Crawfordville, Georgia. You'll have to buy our southeastern volume to realize what lavish praise that is, but in any event, *do* try this pie. Try also the mix of turnip and mustard greens. James Mitchell's Murphysboro, Tennessee, recipe is the equal of anything we found in the South, and so were his distinctive home-baked pinto beans.

You can buy a Delmonico here for $6.50, but if you haven't come for the ribs then we think you should try a ham-hock dinner for $1.25. Since there are always some specials for less than $2, you can be assured of holding on to your cash even if you don't like ham hocks.

It's a great place, and, as we said, the people were as warm, friendly, helpful, and welcoming as any we have met in any restaurant anywhere.

HOURS   Mon.–Sat. 11 am–8 pm. Closed Sun. & all major holidays.

SPECS   1519 West Ave.; (216) 322-8474; no cards; no liquor.

DIRECTIONS   Go south from Exit 8 on Lorain Blvd. for 1.1 miles to Lake Ave. Turn left onto Lake and go ½ mile. Then bear right with the traffic under the bridge and onto West. Go straight on West for 1.3 miles. It's on the right.

DELI ON THE COMMONS, *Exit 8, Elyria*

The menu describes this establishment as "a delicatessen of a sort," a qualification that we imagine arises because the place is run by a charitable institution for boys in trouble with the law. There was no need to qualify the corned beef sandwich, however. It may not be the match of a New York deli, but it was good enough. The rye was real, and the corned beef is cooked up fresh daily. It was, we grant, a somewhat assimilated corned beef sandwich, the bread being square and the meat being sliced just a bit too thick. But it was a good one all the same, as were the pickle and the horseradish *(sic!)*. All of which was enough to make us think you won't do too badly with any of the 20 sandwiches at $1.80–$2.90.

What is really strange about this place is the unclassifiable decor—twenty little tables covered in oilcloth and decked out in a random assortment of parasols, plants, mobiles, bells, and assorted Goodwill knickknacks that hang from overhead beams. There are fresh flowers on the tables and seventeen edifying mottoes on the walls. We can tell you only that it all creates a gay, but slightly tawdry carnival atmosphere that seems to please the lawyers and businessmen who are the deli's principal patrons.

HOURS   Mon.–Fri. 8 am–3 pm; Sat. 11 am–2:30 pm; Sun. 11:30 am–2:30 pm.

SPECS   144 Middle Ave.; (216) 322-2711; no cards; beer & wine.

DIRECTIONS   Go south from Exit 8 on Lorain Blvd. for 1.1 mile to Lake Ave. Turn left onto Lake and go ½ mile. Then bear right with the traffic for 0.2 mile to Broad St. Turn left onto Broad and go 0.2 mile to Middle Ave. Turn right onto Middle, go 1 block, and it's on the left.

SZARKA'S TASTE OF HUNGARY,
Exit 9, North Olmsted

It would have been a pleasure to find Szarka's Taste of Hungary anywhere, but on the food-barren Ohio Turnpike, it was a real joy. Alex and Helen Szarka are Hungarian immigrants

191

whose parents had restaurants in the old country. The family tradition is being continued with their son Laszlo, who, after studying culinary arts in Budapest and Vienna, now holds the reins in the restaurant's kitchen.

We have to admit a bias toward flavors of well-prepared Hungarian cuisine, but we think that even Zsa Zsa Gabor would say "Mahvelous, dahling" after a meal at Szarka's. Not that it's a classy, high-priced joint. No, Szarka's is meant to appeal to families, and although the Hungarian bric-a-brac on the walls is less than restrained, it's all done in the right spirit.

Even among those whose tastes do not run to the unfamiliar, Szarka's is popular for the quality of its veal, all of which is butchered on the premises. Wiener schnitzel and veal paprikash are tops here, the former a gigantic breaded veal steak seasoned with just the right tension between spicy and savory ($7.25). The paprikash ($7.50) comes in a wonderful, velvety sour cream sauce red from an abundance of paprika; be sure to request the angelically tender spaetzle-like dumplings available (in place of a potato) to sop up the delicious juice. Chicken paprikash is a dollar less, as is the stuffed cabbage—huge, delightfully piquant rolls of greenery filled with ham and veal. For those with a pot-luck-supper outlook, it's possible to get a little bit of many things in either of Szarka's two combination plates ($6.25 and $7.50).

The lunch menu echoes dinner, with a slight fall-off in portion size; prices are also lower, of course, most around $4 or $4.50.

HOURS Tues.–Thurs. 11:30 am–4:30 pm; Fri. & Sat. 11:30 am–midnight; Sun. noon–8 pm. Closed Mon.

SPECS 29691 Lorain Rd.; (216) 779-8166; MC only; full bar; children's menu.

DIRECTIONS From Exit 9, go straight (sign for North Olmsted). You'll be on Lorain Rd./OH 10 East. In 2½ miles the restaurant is on the right (5 minutes).

HUDSON HOUSE DINING ROOM,
Exits 12 & 13, Hudson

The town of Hudson was once the capital of the Western Reserve of Connecticut, an area encompassing what is now all of northeast Ohio. At one time it was the home of Western Reserve College, established by Connecticut residents who intended it to be the Yale of the West. (Later it moved to an upstart town called Cleveland, where it became Case Western Reserve University.) In keeping with its history, Hudson is a beautifully preserved, not-too-terribly quaint, New England-style town, worth a detour just as a break from the decidedly unquaint turnpike. As it turns out (no surprise), you can also eat very well there.

Subdued and tasteful, with floral wallpaper, crystal stemware, and a delicious lavender/dusty-rose color scheme, the Hudson House has the charm of a country inn (which it's not). Quality is equally evident in what comes out of the kitchen: rich soups, gorgeous salads, well-sauced and innovative entrees, and *au courant* sandwiches.

Though everything we had was superb, salads are truly the specialty of Tracy Sveda, who (with her architect father) is responsible for creating this restaurant out of a former Plymouth-DeSoto car dealership. Her spinach salad, for instance, was no ordinary bowl of rabbit food; it came with hard-boiled eggs, chunks of bacon, orange wedges, and a strongly fragrant orange dressing on a bed of crisp, bright-green spinach leaves ($2.50/ 4.25). Prior to that, we dipped lustily into a potent potato, mushroom, and wine soup ($1.35), and a costly but worth-it appetizer of baked Brie encrusted in slivered almonds ($4.95). Other lunchtime tempters include quiche, crêpes, omelets, and croissant sandwiches, most $4–$5; at dinner, look to spend $9–$12 for entrées like chicken Veronique; shrimp tempura; and Tracy's original "tower of crêpes," in which three flat shells are layered over alternating fillings of scallops, broccoli, and mushrooms, the whole stack doused with Swiss cheese sauce, and surrounded by a thick marinara. We'll be back.

HOURS   Mon. 11 am–3 pm; Tues. & Wed. 7 am–3 pm; Thurs.–Sat. 7 am–11 pm; Sun. brunch 10 am–3 pm. Hours may change. Closed first 2 weeks of Jan.

SPECS   60 W. Streetsboro St.; (216) 650-1686; V, MC; full bar.

DIRECTIONS   **Eastbound:** From Exit 12 tollbooth, go straight, following signs for Akron/South. You will be put on OH 8 South, which you should follow for about 1 mile to OH 303. Go left on 303 East, and 2.6 miles to the restaurant, on the right. (If you reach the junction of OH 91, you've passed it.) After eating, don't backtrack; instead, reverse westbound directions, below, to reach to the next exit on the turnpike.

Westbound: From Exit 13, go straight (south) and you'll be on OH 14 East. In about 1½ miles, turn right onto OH 303 West toward Hudson. Go about 4½ miles to the junction of OH 91. Cross it, and the restaurant is the second building on the left. After eating, do not backtrack; reverse eastbound directions, above, and you will reach the next exit on the turnpike.

TOWN HALL TAVERN, *OH 193 Exit, Youngstown*

Art Carnahan was the Liberty Township fire chief when the whole town got gerrymandered into Youngstown, leaving idle the old brick Town Hall that had housed the firehouse. He hated to see it go, so he put it to "adaptive reuse." In other words, he started a restaurant.

We arrived at Town Hall Tavern in its first month of reincarnation and we were impressed by what we found. Art and company have not gone all out to create the kind of plush firehouse theme restaurant we've seen in at least a dozen cities. Instead, he offers something less common, four choices of atmosphere: a bare-bones counter service area, an enclosed patio under a carnival-type awning, a pleasant but unaffected carpeted dining area (Scotch plaid carpeting, unfortunately) with waitress service, and the somewhat cushier Ballot Box Lounge (Liberty's former polling place).

No matter where you sit, the fare is light and sandwichy: hamburgers, meatball subs, BLTs, breaded veal hoagies, etc.

($1.50–$2.50). Plump, truly juicy hot dogs are big, offered with a variety of toppings (only 69 cents). And there are a few salads, fried veggies, dinner specials, and—get this—homemade ice cream. That creamy treat costs a most reasonable 95 cents per two-scoop portion.

There's no denying that the Town Hall Tavern is trying to be trendy, but they're doing it so innocently that the result is refreshing. We don't know if the other folks there felt the same way as we did, or if they were simply starved for anything that bespoke the 1980s, but they sure seemed to be enjoying themselves.

HOURS   Sun.–Wed. 11 am–midnight; Thurs.–Sat. 11 am–2:30 am.

SPECS   4316 Belmont Ave., Liberty; (216) 759-8509; V, MC, AE; full bar.

DIRECTIONS   **Eastbound:** From Belmont Ave./OH 193 Exit, turn right at the stop sign, go 1 short block to the light, and turn left onto 193. In 0.4 mile the restaurant is on the left.

Westbound: From Belmont Ave./OH 193, turn right at the light and in 0.1 mile the restaurant is on the left. Couldn't ask for it much closer.

Wisconsin
Illinois
Indiana
Ohio

Wisconsin

MR. HARVEY'S GOURMET, *Exits 106 and 108, Portage*

It is always wonderful to come across a restaurant so truly unique that it defies all our attempts at glib classification. Start with a typical old small-town restaurant on Main Street that's heavy on the plastic. Then add behind the Formica counter a sufficient quantity of liquor bottles to leave the novice unsure whether he's entered a bar or a restaurant. Then tack up a lot of wood, stained "dark oak," to hide some of the plastic, and mix in a flea market's worth of pots, mugs, pitchers, hats, and statues. Don't forget the World War I German helmet so that people can guess that all this is a cheap version of gemütlichkeit.

Now, just when they think they've got you figured out, keep the place open for 24 hours a day and draw in a late-night clientele from the Portage proletariat. Give the nervous whisp of a waiter a black vest and tie, and choose for your cook a man who looks like the counterman in a Dagwood comic strip.

That, friends, is Mr. Harvey's Gourmet, and what it all means we wouldn't dare say on the basis of one quick visit. Let us therefore stick to the bare facts. The menu offers about 35 entrees from braised chicken livers at $2.75 to prime rib for $7. Most are less than $4, as was the all-you-can-eat meat loaf special for $2.85 and German-style barbecued spareribs with sauerkraut for $3.50.

For reasons that we could not make out, the waiter did not want us to order the meat loaf. We did it anyway and found it savory and full of vegetables—more interesting than good, really, but, like the restaurant, unique unto itself. The corn was canned, and the gravy was just okay, as was the fresh strawberry pie. But the cream of broccoli was terrific—a rich, buttery, and absolutely delightful cup of soup that would have required no apologies anywhere. About 25 sandwiches are available, the most expensive of which is the rib eye at just $1.85. You can get a salami sandwich and soup for just $1.65.

If you've an adventurous soul, you really ought to give Mr. Harvey's a try. We promise you nothing, however, but an experience.

HOURS　Daily 24 hours.

SPECS　100 E. Cook St.; (608) 742-5116; no cards; full bar.

DIRECTIONS　**Eastbound:** Take Exit 106 for Route 33 East toward Portage. Go 4.3 miles on Route 33 to the second light in Portage. It's on the right, on the corner.

Westbound: Take Exit 108 for US 51 North toward Portage. Go about 2 miles and turn right onto Route 33 East for Portage. Go about 2 more miles to the second light in town. It's on the corner, on the right.

ELLA'S DELI AND ICE CREAM PARLOR,
Exits 135A & 138B, Madison

We've visited delis in Manhattan and delis in Atlanta; we've checked out the lox in Littleton, New Hampshire, and the pastrami in Peoria, but we had to come to Madison, Wisconsin, to find the world's only carnival-cum-corned-beefateria. The original Ella's was a fairly straightforward sort of place that made its name serving chicken soup to homesick students at the University of Wisconsin. But for the new Ella's, which is far more convenient to the highway, they pulled out all the stops.

This veritable museum of glorious gadgets is designed like a merry-go-round, with tables and worn bentwood chairs radiating outward from a beautiful old marble ice cream fountain. There are toys just about everywhere, from steamboats, cars, and flying saucers to an assortment of Rube Goldberg machines, all of them illuminated, animated, and nicely crafted in their details. The place is infectious, like Small World at Disneyland. You can't help but get caught up in the silly, happy, bright, and childlike spirit.

And they do have food—a cup of earthy, respectable matzoh ball soup, for example, at $1.10, or a good but not perfect pastrami sandwich for $2.95 (the rye was a little too soft, but the pickle was perfection). Skip the chopped liver, but by no means fail to taste Ella's own custard ice creams ($1.35). The French vanilla was superb. Ours came beneath real hot fudge and real whipped cream with some huge, delicious waffle cookies—as good as Rumpelmayer's, but only $1.95.

The menu is huge. Nothing is very expensive, and you can sneak out with a kosher frank for just $1.95. Be prepared, however, to spend a lot of time gawking at the gadgets.

HOURS   Sun.–Thurs. 10 am–11 pm; Fri. & Sat. 10 am–midnight. Closed Christmas, New Year's, Yom Kippur.

SPECS   2902 E. Washington Ave.; (608) 241-1595; no cards; no liquor.

DIRECTIONS   **From I-90/94 eastbound:** Take Exit 135A onto US 151 South toward Madison. Go 3.6 miles to **Ella's,** on the right. There will be traffic.

From I-90 westbound: Take Exit 138B onto Route 30 and go 3 expressway miles to US 151 (E. Washington St.). Go left on Washington 0.1 mile. It's on the right.

THE MANOR, *Exit 185, Beloit*

This is one of those restaurantized, southern-style mansions where the plush chairs roll around on wheels over the red and black carpet, where the curtains are lacy, and where there's an illuminated fountain that makes one room, at least, feel like it's always the Fourth of July. Music from 7:30, but we got out in time.

Quite decent dinners are mostly from $4.70–$9.95, and we're pleased that many of them are down in the $5.50 range—Swiss steak and barbecued beef ribs, for example. Chicken Kiev is but $6.50, and even steak Diana is only $6.95.

HOURS   Tues.–Sat. 4:30–10:30 pm; Sun. noon–8:30 pm. Closed Mon., Christmas.

SPECS   (608) 365-1608; V, MC, AE; full bar.

DIRECTIONS   From Exit 185 go about ½ mile west. Turn right and go 0.2 mile. It's on the left. It is really right at the exit and hard to miss except that it's set back a bit.

THE BUTTERFLY SUPPER CLUB, *Exit 185A, Beloit*

We experienced in the Butterfly's handsome, plush, and very modern lounge a strongly flavored version of linguine in white clam sauce, in which the strength came from the clams, not the garlic, the spices, nor even its ample doses of oniony crunch. It was not subtle, mind you, and the sauce had been over-thickened, but straightforwardly good, and certainly good enough for a roadside dinner.

They make the pasta themselves and charge around $6.50 for the eight different ways they serve it. Other dinners run up to $12.50 and are mostly straight steak and seafood stuff. Chicken, however, comes fried or alla cacciatora ($7.95).

Insist on the lounge. The dining room is tacky even though it's got a view.

HOURS Tues.–Thurs. 5–10:30 pm; Fri. 4:30–10:30 pm; Sat. 5–10:30 pm; Sun. 11 am–8:30 pm. Closed Christmas & New Year's.

SPECS (608) 362-8577; V, MC, AE; full bar.

DIRECTIONS From Exit 185A go east on Route 15 for 1.2 miles to Exit 6 (Hart Rd.). Turn right at the end of the ramp and go 0.1 mile to a T. Turn left at the T and go 0.4 mile. It's on the right.

Illinois

THE SAUSAGE SHOP DELIKATESSEN
DER RATHSKELLER, *US 20 Exit, Rockford*

Would you go 9 miles out of your way to experience the world's best Lyonnaise potatoes? What if the potatoes came with perfectly cooked, delightfully mild, absolutely delicious Thueringer bratwurst? What if you got a full, fat, 16 inches of the sausage with a heaping mound of those most wonderful potatoes for just $4.50 with some excellent pumpernickel thrown in? Not even if the atmosphere was ancient, pubby, authentic, unpretentious, and friendly, and that absolutely nothing had changed in the place since Fred Goetz opened it in 1931?

We were tipped off to **Der Rathskeller**'s existence by a rave review in the 1942 edition of Duncan Hines' guide to American restaurants. Forty-two years ago Hines described this place as his absolute favorite for sausage. We hardly believed the restaurant would still be there; even less did we suspect they'd still be using the same cast-iron skillet to fry the potatoes! That's right, for over 50 years these astonishing potatoes have been made in skillets that have never, never, never been used for any other purpose whatsoever. Maybe that's where the flavor comes from, but whatever the secret we can do nothing but pay homage to this straightforward dish here raised to heavenly heights.

But let us not forget the wonderful German-style ribs (ever so tenderly simmered in sauerkraut juice and sugar, and served without the sauce that is so familiar to southern-style rib lovers —$6.50). The red cabbage, too, was excellent, and so was the light, homemade cheesecake, enlivened by a whisp of lemon. Thirty kinds of sandwiches are available, from Milwaukee beer cheese ($1.95) to peppered corned beef with Roquefort ($2.95) with a whole world of sausage sandwiches in between.

All this is served downstairs at twelve cozy little tables where there's so much authentic charm and "atmosphere" you'd be delighted with the experience even if the food were lousy. Upstairs is **The Sausage Shop** that gave rise to Fred's entire business. They still make their own, but activity upstairs is much reduced from the days when Fred offered over 50 different kinds of sausage for sale.

HOURS   Tues.–Fri. 11 am–2 pm & 5–9 pm; Sat. & Sun. 8 am–midnight. Closed Mon. Except during summer there is often a wait on Wed., Fri., & Sat. nights—reservations then advised.

SPECS   1132 Auburn St.; (815) 963-2922; no cards; full bar.

DIRECTIONS   Go west on US Business 20 (State St.) for 4 miles to Alpine. Turn right onto Alpine and go 2.3 miles to Spring Creek. Turn left onto Spring Creek and go 2.7 miles. It's on the left. (Spring Creek changes its name to Auburn after it passes over the bridge.)

STASH O'NEIL'S, *US 20 Exit, Rockford*

Stash puts out good fun food in a restaurant and bar gaily decked out with a pleasant jumble of plants, tools, antiques, and even a racing shell that hangs from the ceiling. Yes, this is one of those "eating and drinking establishments," only here the subtitle is "a neighborhood gathering place." As at all such places, the menu is cute and unintimidating. There are lots of nachos ($3.45), potato skins (about $4), fried mushrooms ($1.95), and ½-pound hamburgers ($3.76–$4.45), which were actually very good, though we feel a need to apologize for the menu prose that introduces them. Salads, too, from chicken with nuts to spinach, taco, and chef's (around $4.25). Lots of fancy sandwiches (around $3.75), croissants, and a truly beautiful salad bar boasting grapes, pineapple, and big, fresh, luscious red strawberries ($3.45 by itself, $1.95 with a sandwich).

O'Neil's is deservedly a very popular place in Rockford for enjoyable light meals. There are, nevertheless, a few basic steak and seafood dinners available from $5.75–$10.95. But we think this is the place to order a Dublin Dip, described as follows on the menu: "Stash has got the Polish dip. Thinly sliced roast beef piled high on Irish French bread, complimented with a slice of raw onion and 'aw Juice.' "

HOURS Mon.–Thurs. 6 am–10 pm; Fri. & Sat. 6 am–11 pm; Sun. 7 am–9:30 pm.

SPECS 4846 E. State St.; (815) 396-4182; major cards; full bar.

DIRECTIONS The restaurant is 3.8 miles west of the exit on Business 20 (State St.).

THE CLOCK TOWER INN, *US 20 Exit, Rockford*

Funky little owner-operated restaurants are more our style, so seldom do we include "inns" that are actually mammoth resort complexes with at least three different restaurants in them. But our other Rockford eateries are far from the road, while The Clock Tower sits abreast the exit ramp as eagerly as any Wendy's. You'll pay $3.95 for a hamburger in the very ordinary-looking coffee shop; the prices and decor go up from there.

It's really not bad for this sort of thing.

HOURS   Coffee shop only: Mon.–Thurs. 6 am–11 pm; Fri. & Sat. 7 am–midnight; Sun. 6 am–11 pm.

SPECS   7801 E. State St.; (815) 398-6000; major cards; full bar.

DIRECTIONS   Immediately east of the exit for US 20. Its huge tower can't be missed.

BEEF VILLA
CANDY CANE RESTAURANT, *Exit for Route 25, Elgin*

We came across a very good Italian beef sandwich at this mercilessly bare, fast-food setup that could boast only a few unhappy little tables. The sandwich wasn't as good as **Al's** (see pp. 211–212), but the roll was. The seasonings were more than just respectable, and the hot peppers were truly hot.

We also tried the two-piece broasted chicken dinner at the **Beef Villa** and were astonished to find that it too was very good —tender and juicy on the inside, crunchy on the outside.

The sandwich was $2.05 (Italian and Polish sausage versions, too) and the chicken was $1.99. Here the chicken comes in two degrees of hotness (as if it were Szechuan cooking or Buffalo chicken wings). We ordered it hot, but, frankly, after the peppers on the sandwich we couldn't tell how hot that was.

If you want something with just a bit more class than this, try the **Candy Cane Restaurant** right across the street. It's clean, neat, and pleasant, decorated with an oil-painted photo of someone's grandmother and crossed candy canes that look like shepherds' hooks. Any place that sweet can't be bad.

HOURS   Villa: Mon.–Thurs. 10:30 am–10:30 pm; Fri. & Sat. 10:30 am–11:30 pm; Sun. 11 am–10:30 pm.
Candy Cane: Mon.–Thurs. 6 am–8 pm; Fri. 6 am–9 pm; Sat. 6 am–2 pm; Sun. 7 am–1 pm.

SPECS   No address; no phone; no cards; no liquor.

DIRECTIONS   Go south on Route 25 for 0.6 mile. It's just past the light at the Congdon Ave. intersection, on an island between the two legs of a fork.

THE MILK PAIL, *Route 25 Exit, Elgin*

Here's a "nice" place—safe, clean, respectable, and very, very American. The Milk Pail began life 50 years ago as a roadside stand that sold cottage cheese made in the farmhouse behind it. Success breeds growth, and you won't find much true farm life here now. You will find pheasant, trout, duck, and turkey, however, along with steaks, grouse, chicken, and shrimp, well enough prepared and wrapped up in a farmy atmosphere that is more hokey than a rib shack and less so than Disneyland. Full dinner prices are $10–$15, luncheons for around $6, and sandwiches mostly from $3–$4. Big weekend breakfasts are $4–$5.

Bring the kids.

HOURS Tues.–Thurs. 11 am–9 pm; Fri. 11 am–9:30 pm; Sat. 9 am–9:30 pm; Sun. 9 am–8 pm.

SPECS (312) 742-5040; V, MC, AE; full bar.

DIRECTIONS Take Route 25 Exit and go north on Route 25 for 0.8 mile. It's on the left in a wooded area.

PRINCE

ROLLIE'S, *Exit for I-294, Des Plaines*

A 1-mile drive north on I-294 will bring you to a very good Chinese restaurant in a slightly frumpy motel, and also to some good sandwiches, fast and cheap. See pp. 277–278 for details.

JERRY'S RESTAURANT, *Exit 81A, Harwood Heights*

We got an above-average breakfast at Jerry's Restaurant—fresh eggs, substantial bread, good coffee, and home fries that were frozen but not greasy. The place is a new, plastic, semiglitzy neighborhood restaurant and lunch counter. The accents are Polish; the menu and prices are the usual, unless you go for four eggs and a huge chunk of steak at $3.69.

HOURS Daily 6 am–9 pm.

SPECS   5209 Harlem Ave.; (312) 775-5467; no cards; no liquor.

DIRECTIONS   From Exit 81A (Harlem Ave.) turn left if westbound and right if eastbound onto Harlem Ave. Go 0.4 mile, and it's on the left.

CARSON'S, *Exit 81A, Harwood Heights*

Carson's is one of Chicago's best rib joints, now grown so popular that four of them dot the city, two of which are very close to interstate highways. In truth, Carson's eateries are far too classy to be called "rib joints," and this one is all done up in muted tones of gray and red, with white tablecloths and two walls of mirrors—modern good taste, a bit clichéd, but certainly pleasant enough.

The Harwood Heights Carson's is also distinguished by lunch hours, during which the price of a half order of ribs falls to a mere $5.95, and during which rib tips in that same wonderful sauce can be had for just $3.95. Sandwiches, omelets, and barbecued chicken are in the $4–$5 range.

See p. 236 for a description of the sauce that made Carson's famous.

HOURS   Mon.–Thurs. 11 am–11 pm; Fri. & Sat. 11 am–midnight; Sun. noon–10 pm.

SPECS   5050 N. Harlem Ave.; (312) 867-4200; major cards; full bar.

DIRECTIONS   From Exit 81A (Harlem Ave.) turn left if westbound and right if eastbound onto Harlem Ave. Go 0.6 mile, and it's on the right.

PIZZERIAS UNO AND DUE, *Exit 50B, Chicago*

If we cannot authoritatively claim that this is the world's best pizza, it is only because we haven't checked out every last pizzeria in Tucson and have to admit there might still be a more delicious pizza in some as yet undiscovered Italian village. All we really know for sure is that Ike Sewell invented Chicago-style deep-dish pizza on this very spot, and for 20 years it has been the best pizza ever to have passed our lips—no ifs, no ands, no buts.

If by some chance you have not experienced the true deep-dish Chicago pizza, let us tell you that it does not feel right to refer to this meal by the same word that denotes a thin layer of dough topped by tomato sauce and cheese. Deep-dish pizza is a real oeuvre, and should be thought of as akin to moussaka or lasagne, and other full-status meals. The crust at Uno's or Due's is thick but never soggy and rises up crunchy for 2 inches or so around the edges. Into this bed is poured the zestiest and most flavorful of tomato sauces, bulging with huge hunks of ripe tomato. The cheeses are excellent, the sausage tangy, and just two pieces are more than enough for even a good-sized appetite.

Tiny, crowded Uno, with its graffiti-decorated walls and dim lights, was the first of Ike's creations. So successful was it that he opened up Due just a block away—a carbon copy of Uno except that there was a bit more in the way of decor. Trio, Quartro, and Cinco followed, though not in Chicago, and we have to admit we were a bit distressed to learn that by now there are franchises in seventeen cities. We checked out the originals on our recent visit to see what's changed, and we can happily report that nothing had. Chicago pizzaphiles have gone in for more trendy variations (double-crust pizza, for example), but Uno and Due keep turning out the same excellent product that put the words "Chicago-style" in front of the word "pizza."

Since it is not hard to reach these restaurants from the road, and since enough pizza for two costs only $5.10 (add-ons are 50 cents to $1), Uno and Due would be perfect highway stops were it not for the parking in this near-north area (you'll have to use one of the many lots) and the lines (which seem always to be there in the evenings). What can we say? Excellence always requires some kind of sacrifice, and remember that this is an experience, not just a meal—something you will tell your children about for years to come.

HOURS   **Uno:** Tues.–Fri. 11:30 am–1:20 am; Sat. 11:30 am–2:20 am; Sun. 1–8:20 pm. Closed Mon.
Due: Mon.–Fri. 11:30 am–3:20 am; Sat. 5 pm–4:20 am; Sun. 4 pm–12:20 am.

SPECS   **Uno:** 29 E. Ohio St.; (312) 321-1000; major cards; full bar.
Due: 619 N. Wabash St.; (312) 943-2400; major cards; full bar.

DIRECTIONS   Exit 50B puts you on an expressway spur that leads right into Ohio St. Continue straight ahead to Wabash (1.2 very quick miles from I-94/90). **Uno** is on the right at the corner of Wabash and Ohio. **Due** is 1 block to the left on Wabash.

SU CASA, *Exit 50B, Chicago*

Ike Sewell not only invented Chicago-style pizza, he also opened the city's first Mexican restaurant. Now that may seem like overreaching oneself, and perhaps it is, but we remember years ago tasting some of the very best of Mexican seafood here. We checked it out again recently and have to report mixed results —good rice and a very good taco that featured a subtle jalapeño in cheese sauce, but uninspired carne asada, plus enchiladas and chiles rellenos that were merely okay.

Nor did we remember the excessive collection of Mexican kitsch (including the strolling mariachi guitar). The menu is large and there are still a lot of classy Mexican dishes to choose from (trout with coriander, for example, or shrimp Veracruz). Prices at lunchtime run from $2.25–$6.50; dinners are $4.25 to $11.50. Same parking problems as for **Uno,** but no lines.

HOURS   Mon.–Fri. 11:30 am–12:30 am; Sat. 5 pm–12:30 am.

SPECS   49 E. Ontario St.; (312) 943-4041; major cards; full bar.

DIRECTIONS   See directions for **Pizzeria Uno** and **Due** above. **Su Casa** is ½ block east of **Due,** on Ontario St.

THE GREEK ISLANDS
DIANA'S, *Exits 51E & F, Chicago*

I-90/94 passes within a block of Chicago's Greektown, a 4-block stretch of restaurants, taverns, and travel agencies that's well-known all over town. Despite the fact that this neighborhood is at the virtual back door of downtown Chicago, it's as easy to get to as a service area in Iowa. Parking is free, the food is cheap, and it is a stop that has to rank near the top in the way of good tastes and local color.

Unfortunately, we found the food in one place and the color in another. **Diana's** had the most funky-wonderful good looks we've ever come across. Imagine a nightclub setup with dozens of little red-checked tables surrounding a tiny dance floor. Above the dance floor put a recessed, mirrored dome, and for the band picture a diminutive stage adorned with gilted Corinthian columns and an earthy mural of Diana, her hounds and her maidens on a boar hunt in a jungle far greener than anything you'll find in Greece.

Looks like that you have to love, but we could have passed on the combination plate of roast lamb, moussaka, pastitsio, rice, and vegetables ($5.95). It may have been good when it was born, but it had just been hanging around the kitchen too long to have much zip.

The Greek Islands, which is right next door, has just undergone a modernizing face-lift. We gather that once it had a lot of character, but now, though far from unpleasant, its spaciousness, its latticework ceiling, its tile floor, its bricks, plants, and blue-checked tablecloths all just seem too new, too clean, and their edges too sharp, to warm the cockles of the heart.

But the food is a different story. We ordered roast lamb in a feta-laced sauce and sat back prepared for the worst. Though the meat was indeed fattier than we'd have liked, the sauce was not greasy or the least bit heavy. In fact, it was light and very tasty, the best we've had of this simple kind of Greek cooking. We ate it all and enjoyed the good, crusty bread that accompanied it, but then found ourselves wishing we had room enough left for the seafood dishes ($4.75–$5.05) we'd heard so much about.

We suspect you'll do well at The Greek Islands whatever you

try, and in no case will you go broke. Full meals are $4.95–$7.35 at dinnertime, a few cents cheaper at lunchtime.

HOURS   **Greek Islands:** Sun.–Thurs. 11 am–midnight; Fri. & Sat. 11 am–2 am.
Diana's: Daily 10:30 am–2 am.

SPECS   **Greek Islands:** 200 S. Halsted St.; (312) 782-9855; major cards; full bar; children's menu.
Diana's: 212 S. Halsted St.; (312) 332-1225; AE, CB, DC; full bar; children's portions.

DIRECTIONS   **Westbound (actually northbound at this point):** Take Exit 51E for Monroe St. Go left at the stop sign at the end of the ramp and then over the bridge, 1 block to Halsted. Go left 1 block. It's on the right.

Eastbound (actually southbound at this point): Take Exit 51F for Adams St. Turn right at the stop sign and you're just about in the parking lot.

THE BERGHOFF, *Exit 51i, Chicago*

Let it be said right off that The Berghoff is not the ideal place for a quick highway stop. For one thing you have to park your car in a downtown lot ($2.50 for the first hour, 75 cents an hour thereafter), and for another there are usually lines at mealtimes (albeit fast-moving ones). On the other hand, maybe a brief tour of the Loop would be a welcome diversion, and maybe you'd like to taste some excellent and relatively inexpensive German food in what often gets called "the atmosphere of Old Chicago."

The Berghoff *is* a Chicago institution—since 1898 the kind of old downtown restaurant where the waiters wear black, the woodwork is ancient oak, and the tone is noisy, quick, efficient, and informal all at once. You'd almost expect to see peanut shells on the floor, but The Berghoff comes off with more dignity than that. Perhaps it's the height of the ceilings or the art deco chandeliers pinched from the *Queen Elizabeth I.*

No matter—the place is lots of fun and the food is mostly very good. At dinnertime just $6.85 bought us three ample slices of tender, flavorful sirloin in delightfully tangy sweet-and-sour brown sauce. The creamed spinach that came with them was really excellent, and if the buttered noodles and apple strudel ($1.25 extra) were not of the same caliber, well, they were better than just okay.

Other dinners, both German and American, run from $6.25–$11.95. Most are less than $7.50. Sandwiches are available at $4–$5, and there are some interesting salads in the $5–$6 range (consider, for example, the sirloin salad with egg and tomato wedges and slices of fresh melon). The lunch menu parrots the dinner offerings, except that entrees are about $2 cheaper, there are more sandwiches, and they cost about $1.50 less.

Finally we must mention the beer situation at The Berghoff. These days restaurants pride themselves on the number of imported beers they can offer, but for years The Berghoff has been doing them one better. This is the only restaurant we know of that actually brews its own—and very good brew it is. Chicagoans must like this sort of thing, because The Berghoff also has its distillery in Kentucky, where the restaurant's own bourbon is made. Or perhaps it's just a leftover from prohibition days, Old Chicago style.

HOURS   Mon.–Thurs. 11 am–9:30 pm; Fri. & Sat. 11 am–10 pm. Closed Sun. & major holidays.

SPECS   17 W. Adams St.; (312) 427-3170; no cards; full bar.

DIRECTIONS   Take Exit 57i (Congress Parkway). This will automatically put you in the right direction on an expressway spur that goes into the Loop. Go straight ahead for 1.1 miles until you cross Michigan Ave. and go ½ block to the park. Turn left at the light, following a sign for South Garage. Then turn right into the underground garage and drive to the far end. Park, emerge into daylight, and walk ½ block north to Adams. Turn left onto Adams, go 2 blocks, and it's on the left, near State and Adams. You'll be in the heart of downtown Chicago, which is unbelievably easy to negotiate.

AL'S
(and MARIO'S ITALIAN LEMONADE),
Exit 52A, Chicago

The Italian beef sandwich is one of Chicago's many contributions to America's ethnic specialties, and **Al's** has been voted again and again the best place in town to find out what it's all about. We did so, and learned that an Italian beef is a mound of thinly shaved roast beef that has been simmered with the meat's own juices and seasoned with a host of lively, garlicky spices. This is then unceremoniously dolloped onto a good, crusty, submarine roll. The juices thereupon mix with the bread to make for the most mysteriously mushy, spicy interior, and if you eat this creation without allowing the counterman to go one step further, you'll be very happy.

But no true Chicagoan would do that. "Hot or sweet?" you'll be asked at this point. The man wants to know what kind of peppers you want, and if you choose hot be prepared to gulp down at least a quart of Coke.

Al ought to know just about all there is to be known about Italian beef. His family's been turning it out for 40 years, and for 17 years Al's own sandwich stand has stood at this spot on Taylor St. Be warned that Al's is no more than just that—a sandwich stand. Its walls are overhead garage doors that are open all summer, cooling the countermen a bit perhaps, but still not enabling the tiny edifice to house the crowd that pours in at lunchtime. It's a bit of a mob scene, and you must take a number and wait about 15 minutes for one of the lightning-fast countermen to get to you. You shouldn't hold him up by thinking once your number is called. The menu is sufficiently simple that you ought to have made up your mind by then: Italian beef—$1.90; Italian sausage—$1.80; sweet pepper sandwich—$1.70; and a hot dog for $1.10. Except for Cokes and fries, that's about it. When you do one thing just about perfectly, there's no need for more.

Whether or not you go for the hot peppers, we earnestly recommend that you wash your sandwich down with the best lemonade we've ever tasted. **Mario's** tiny stand is right across the street from Al's. For $1 he'll sell you a glass of iced, deliciously flavored, not-too-sweet *tutta frutta* laden with lovely chunks of real fresh fruit.

Both these places are sure winners, the best in their classes. But if for some reason you're not satisfied, the neighborhood here is just loaded with restaurants, most of them Mexican or Italian.

HOURS   **Al's:** Mon.–Sat. 9 am–1 am. Closed Sun. & major holidays.

SPECS   1078 W. Taylor St.; (312) 733-8896; no cards; no liquor.

DIRECTIONS   Take Exit 52A for Taylor St. Turn left if eastbound and right if westbound onto Taylor. Go 3.5 blocks, and it's on the left.

TOSCANO, *I-55 Exit, Chicago*

See p. 37 for a restaurant in an old Italian neighborhood that will not give in to blight or gentrification.

Indiana

PHIL SMIDT AND SONS, *Exits 0 & 5, Hammond*

At the edge of Lake Michigan, in grimy, industrial Hammond, Indiana, hard by the Lever Bros. plant, there stands a little stucco restaurant that since 1910 has been serving what may well be the best lake perch in the world. Phil Smidt's is famous, so famous there's no need for it to move to a more fashionable address. And believe us, it would take real excellence to bring the world to Hammond.

Do not conjure up images of a frowsy waterside fish house. Phil's is remarkably calm, quiet, and dignified, what with starched tablecloths, upholstered bentwood chairs, and waitresses in black-and-pink uniforms. It gets a little glitzy here and there, as in the Rose Room, where three huge rose murals stand out against a black background, Tijuana-style, but once past the door you immediately forget that you are surrounded by one of the world's heaviest concentrations of industrial development.

Nor is it cheap. The perch at lunchtime go for $8.25 in butter, $8.95 boned, and $9.25 boned and buttered. But you get enough to call it dinner. All the entrees include potato salad, cottage cheese, coleslaw, beets, and kidney beans, plus potato, rolls, and butter. These condiments may not seem very exciting, but at Smidt's they're different. Each was excellent, with a unique flavor, and a delightful little bite. The kidney beans with celery were the best ever.

Finally there arrives the pièce de résistance—a delicious mound of lightly battered perch almost afloat in drawn butter. The fish are perfectly cooked. Their wonderfully light, mild flavor is accented by the butter to make them not just a lovely and unusual meal, but a whole new experience.

Other lunchtime specialties are frog legs ($8.50, and the restaurant is as famous for them as it is for its perch), walleye pike ($8.50), and half a chicken ($6, also served in butter). In addition, there are a few steaks plus shrimp, scallop, and catfish dishes. The dinnertime menu is nearly identical except that prices go up $5.50 on the house specialties and they become all-you-can-eat affairs. The chicken goes up only $1.25, making it a true all-you-can-eat bargain at $7.25.

Honestly though, it would be a shame to eat here and not try the perch. We sampled them all around the Great Lakes area, and nowhere did we find them better than at Phil Smidt's.

HOURS Mon.–Thurs. 11:15 am–9:30 pm; Fri. & Sat. 11:15 am–10:30 pm. Closed Sun. & major holidays.

SPECS 1205 N. Calumet Ave.; (219) 659-0025; major cards; full bar; children's menu.

DIRECTIONS **Eastbound:** Take Exit 0 at the end of the Chicago Skyway and go east on Indianapolis Blvd. for 1 mile to the light at Calumet (US 41). Turn left onto Calumet for 1 long block. It's on the right.

Westbound: You may save time by taking Exit 0, but it will put you on Indianapolis Blvd. in the wrong direction. Make a U turn and proceed as above. Or take Exit 5 onto Calumet Ave. (US 41) and go 3.7 trafficky miles to the end of the road at Lake Michigan. It's on the right.

TRAVELER'S ADVISORY

Between Hammond, Indiana, and Elyria, Ohio, I-80 and I-90 run together, forming the major part of the Ohio and Indiana Turnpikes. Entries for this stretch of highway are found on pp. 177–191 under I-80.

Ohio

MITCHELL'S BARBEQUE
DELI ON THE COMMONS, *Exit for Route 57, Elyria*

See pp. 190–191 for descriptions of a good soul food restaurant and an okay deli.

DIRECTIONS   Go south on Route 57 for 1 mile to the junction with I-80/90 (the Ohio Turnpike). Then follow directions given.

HECK'S CAFÉ
and others, *Exits 161 & 162, Rock River*

Heck's Café began life as Cleveland's most distinguished purveyor of gourmet hamburgers and has gone on to become one of the city's best continental restaurants. The result is that the dinner menu offers 15 variations on the ½-pound Heckburger ($4.45–$5.95) and also the likes of an absolutely delicious veal Alouette (medallions of veal stuffed with Alouette cheese, covered with mushrooms and Bordelaise sauce, and served over braised spinach, $14.95). Not cheap, to be sure, but worth every penny to judge from what we sampled.

If Heck's is too pricey, but good eating is your mood, do not despair. Heck's is in a tony gentrification area, which means there are other possibilities nearby. The far less expensive **Le Café Croissant** is right across the street, and **Otto's Brauhaus** lies but 3 blocks to the east. What's more, the **Pearl of the Orient,** featuring Szechuan and northern Chinese cooking, was about to open up a branch in the same renovated movie-theater-become-very-tasteful-little-shopping-center that houses Heck's. **The Pearl** is also one of Cleveland's best, with dinner prices at $6–$10 and lunches for $4–$5.

Heck's has the kind of excellence that comes when business sense gets combined with a real love of what one does. Cooking, it seems, was the owner's hobby, and so serious was he about it that he went to Europe to better sharpen his skills. This led to the restaurant, and now you can end the tedium of the road by stepping so far out of the world of cars and highways that you'll forget you're traveling.

The world you'll step into is one of art deco splendor. It's slightly trendy but good taste prevails—pink tablecloths, plants, mirrored walls, and bamboo chairs—plush but not pompous, classy but not intimidating. At dinnertime most folks are dressed, but there are no rules.

Fourteen items constitute the dinner menu. We're afraid to discourage you by listing prices ($10.50–$16.50), so consider instead a few of the appetizers: snow crab claws Dijonnais ($4.95); warmed Brie with apples, almonds, and French bread ($3.95); escargots with angel hair pasta, sweet garlic, cream, parsley, and Parmesan cheese ($4.95); or bay oysters wrapped in bacon, fried in beer batter, and served with béarnaise sauce ($4.75). Just right for a light meal, and it sure beats HoJo's. Lots of interesting ways to eat lunch, mostly from $3.95 to $6.95.

HOURS   (Heck's only) Lunch: Mon.–Sat. 11:30 am–3:30 pm; Dinner: Mon.–Thurs. 5:30–11 pm; Fri. & Sat. 5:30 pm–midnight. Closed Sun.

SPECS   19300 Detroit Ave.; (216) 356-2559; major cards; full bar.

DIRECTIONS   Eastbound: Take Exit 161 (marked Detroit Ave./ Rock River) and turn left at the end of the ramp onto Detroit Ave. Go 1.4 miles to the restaurant on the left in what was once the Beachcliff Movie Theatre (the sign is still there).

Westbound: Take Exit 162 (marked Hilliard/Rock River) and turn right at the light at the end of the ramp onto Westway. Go 1 block to Lakeview and turn right. Then go ½ mile on Lakeview to Detroit. Turn right on

Detroit and go 0.4 mile to a building marked Beachcliff Movie Theatre, on the left. It's in there.

MILLER'S DINING ROOM, *Exit 164, Lakewood*

Just 1 easy mile from I-90 is Miller's Dining Room, a unique Cleveland institution that is an oddball combination of daintiness, decency, and a few irresistible delights.

The daintiness is in the decor, which reminds us of those old restaurants in downtown department stores that set out to create grandeur but give up halfway and settle for a kind of overblown homeyness. Tall ceilings is what we mean, with Napoleonic wallpaper and suggestions of fluted columns that produce an old-ladyish effect.

The food is generally decent. Sometimes it's better than that, and you get enormous quantities of it for very little money. For example, $6.95 bought us the full-course scallop dinner, and at Miller's "full-course" means appetizer, salad, two vegetables, potato, rolls (of which more later), beverage, and dessert. It's more than you will want, in all probability, but just in case you're ravenous, fear not. Our motherly and superbly efficient waitress (who had no idea what we were doing there) was distressed that we didn't seem to be eating enough and kept bringing still more without fattening the bill.

The scallops were not wonderful, but they were good, with a kind of substantial, straightforward flavor. That about describes the cream of mushroom soup and the tapioca with (frozen) strawberries. The mashed potatoes we have to tell you were drab, the broccoli fresh but overcooked.

Miller's greatest delight, however, is its rolls, served by a gnomelike young woman who showed up at tableside every 2½ minutes. "Wanna roll?" she queries as she shoves at you a banged-up octagonal tray full of sticky buns, blueberry muffins, cornbread, etc.

We admit to our prejudices. At first we scorned the thought of munching on sticky buns midmeal, and the first taste of them did not impress us. But we noticed that we kept on eating them, despite all the food before us, and concluded they were really quite good after all.

This sort of service is a large part of Miller's charm. Another girl brings the salad on a similar tray, and you make your choice from little dishes of coleslaw, Jell-O, shaved carrots, and tiny mounds of cottage cheese dotted with a maraschino cherry.

Finally there arrives the finger bowl, the most appropriate of endings, somehow, for dinner at Miller's.

HOURS   Lunch: Mon.–Sat. 11 am–3 pm; Dinner: Mon.–Sat. 3–8 pm; Sun. 11:30 am–7:30 pm.

SPECS   16707 Detroit Ave.; (216) 221-5811; no cards; full bar; children's menu.

DIRECTIONS   From Exit 164 (McKinley) go to the light and turn left if eastbound and right if westbound onto McKinley. Go 0.9 mile to Detroit Ave. Turn right and it's 0.2 mile to **Miller's,** on the right.

MIHELICH'S HOMETOWN RESTAURANT,
Exit 184, Euclid

Slovenians are one of Cleveland's largest ethnic groups, and Mihelich's Slovenian cooking is said by some to be Cleveland's contribution to America's culinary melting pot. From the outside it's one of those little brick houses that has been Bavarianized by the addition of some stucco and beams. On the inside everything is dark, red, and relaxing. The quiet little bar, which seems also to serve as a neighborhood tavern, is discreetly separated from the dining area by a latticework partition that matches the kitschy paintings to a T. Just about exactly what an inexpensive ethnic restaurant should be.

217

The Slovenian part of the menu is less than extensive. It consists, in fact, of just 4 dishes, one of which is Wiener schnitzel,
and another of which is Hungarian goulash. That leaves only a
spicy tripe stew and stuffed cabbage leaves for those in pursuit
of the real thing. We settled for the goulash, which to us seemed
unsubtly tasty—good seasonings and fine tender chunks of beef,
but with too much flour in the sauce and with dumplings that
were coarse. Not great, but not bad either. The apple strudel was
better, the rice pudding about the same, and the salad was acceptable, but nothing more.

These "gourmet" dishes were all around $5.50. Most of the
menu was straight American, running from $5.25 for fried perch
to $10 for what is called here a "Boston" strip steak. Sandwiches
are always available and cost something over $1.

We can't say that Mihelich's was a dining experience we will
never forget, but the truth is that we won't forget our trip to
Mihelich's. The people were wonderful, and somehow the place
seemed to summarize what it stands for quite perfectly. We left
feeling warm and good about the ethnic groups that make up so
many of the Midwest's great cities.

And it's very close to the road.

HOURS   Lunch: Mon.–Fri. 11 am–2 pm; Dinner: Mon.–Sat. 5–9
pm. Closed Sun.

SPECS   830 Babbit Rd.; (216) 731-9689; V, MC; full bar; children's
menu.

DIRECTIONS   **Westbound:** Take Exit 184 for Babbit Rd. Go 0.3 mile
to the first light and turn right onto Babbit. It's just 0.1 mile, on the left.

Eastbound: Take Exit 184A for Babbit Rd. and go straight on the service
road for 0.5 mile to Babbit. Turn left and it's 0.2 mile, on the left.

ARMAO'S PIZZA, *Exit 186, Euclid*

An easy 1-mile drive from Exit 186 will bring you to what may
well be the best pizza in Cleveland. And the nice thing is that
though *Cleveland* magazine has twice bestowed that honor upon

it, Armao's remains the cozy, friendly neighborhood place it has always been.

The pizza really was good—a medium-thick crust that was superb; a sauce that was mild but flavorful; the whole thing greaselessly delicious. The cost was just $2.75 for a four-cut version, $4.10 for an eight-slicer. The usual add-ons were about $1 apiece.

To sample these offerings you will not have to bear the usual pizzeria decor of fluorescent and Formica. Armao's dozen booths are bathed in the unaffected warm glow of wood, with the result that the place feels more like a pub than a pizzeria. The flirty, friendly waitress was more than efficient.

Armao's offers more than bare pizza. Aside from pressure-fried chicken dinners ($4.95) and a variety of pasta and seafood dinners ($3–$6), there's a good selection of simple sandwiches (including whitefish) in the vicinity of $2.75. For a few cents more you can get a good sub, but remember—the place is really a pizzeria.

It's also a good choice and easy to reach.

HOURS   Mon.–Thurs. 11 am–1 am; Fri. & Sat. 11 am–2:30 am; Sun. 3 pm–midnight.

SPECS   25571 Euclid Ave.; (216) 731-7446; no cards; full bar.

DIRECTIONS   From Exit 186 turn right onto Euclid Ave. and go 1.2 miles to a tiny shopping plaza on the right. It's in there.

DIME STORE RESTAURANT AND BAKERY,
Exit 212, Madison

We got some pretty good homemade chili at this eighteen-stool, marble-countered sandwich and soda shop. It even had those old green milkshake machines and mirrors etched with ads for Bowman's Cleveland Ice Cream. That alone would justify a lunch stop, but when you add to this a bakery and very, very modest prices, how far wrong can you go?

The bakery is downstairs, and from it comes the usual assortment of pies, horns, brownies, and so forth. We wish we could tell you that everything was superb, but it wasn't. Come for the fun of it, for the chili, or maybe for the kielbasa with sauerkraut ($1.25), or for a 75-cent ham salad sandwich. Pass on the canned soup, and be happy that you've found a plain and simple local eatery that's close to the road.

HOURS   Mon.–Sat. 5:30 am–5:30 pm. Closed Sun.

SPECS   70 Main St.; (216) 428-3305; no cards; no liquor.

DIRECTIONS   From Exit 212 go north 0.8 mile on Route 528 to the stop sign at Route 84. Turn right and it's on the left in ½ block.

THE OLD TAVERN, *Exit 212, Unionville*

Though said to have been born as a log cabin in 1798, today The Old Tavern looks like a cross between an antebellum manor house and something that would be at home on a New England farmstead. Within it is a pleasant, unpretentious hodgepodge of tiny, low-ceilinged rooms and small-paned windows. The floor tilts a bit, as well it should in so venerable an establishment. Here and there are some real antiques, but the working furniture is mostly Ethan Allen. The Tavern isn't gussied up, or really historical or authentic or glitzy or brash. It's just kind of homey, and almost sweet, run by the same Harry Carver for the past 23 years.

The house specialty at lunchtime is ½ pound of chopped sirloin on a soft roll that is smothered in cheese and (canned) mushrooms. It turned out to be surprisingly good, especially when followed by the other Tavern specialty—lemon sour cream pie.

Our noontime experience would lead us to have no hesitation trying the Swiss steak in pan gravy ($7.25) that we were told is the dinnertime favorite. The roast duck with wild rice dressing, however, would seem a risky choice. About 15 other dinners, including pike fillets ($7.55), are available, and only a few are over $8.50.

The remainder of the lunch menu is the usual, except for the lake perch, offered in a sandwich for $2.75 or with fries, coleslaw, and a roll for $4.95. Corn fritters make an unexpected appearance at 75 cents a serving.

HOURS   Mon.–Sat. 11 am–2:30 pm & 5–9 pm; Sun. noon–7 pm. Closed 3 weeks in January.

SPECS   7935 S. Ridge Rd.; (216) 428-2019; V, MC, AE; full bar.

DIRECTIONS   From Exit 212 go north on Route 528 0.8 mile to a stop sign at Route 84. Turn right onto Route 84 and go 2.5 miles. It's on the left.

HULBERT'S, *Exit 228, Ashtabula*

Hulbert's is a bricks, plants, and oak café with a spanking new tin ceiling from which hangs an entire flock of shiny ceiling fans. It is in the Ashtabula harbor restoration area, and we should tell you right off the bat that the restaurant alone will not justify the 6½-mile drive. You'd have to want to see the industrial waterfront of Lake Erie. That desire will be well satisfied by the drive, and Hulbert's perfectly fine and juicy hamburgers ($1.95) will provide the perfect excuse.

The same could not be said for the chicken noodle soup ($1.10 a bowl), which was mediocre despite its fresh mushrooms, or the chicken wings (20 cents a piece), which we found more fiery than flavorful.

We concluded that Hulbert's was a pleasant and cheerful but otherwise undistinguished restaurant. Dinners run up to $7.95 for a rack of ribs and begin at $3.95 for spaghetti and meatballs. Spinach salad is $3.35 and a good selection of interesting sandwiches are from $1.95–$3.95.

HOURS   Mon.–Thurs. 8:30 am–8 pm; Fri. & Sat. 8:30 am–10 pm; Sun. noon–8 pm.

SPECS   1033 Bridge St.; (216) 964-2594; V, MC; beer & wine.

DIRECTIONS   From Exit 228 go south on Route 11 for 5.6 miles to the end of the road. Turn left and follow the road for 1.1 miles through an industrial landscape. You'll see **Hulbert's** on the right, not far past the second bridge.

DETRICK'S RESTAURANT,
Exit 235, Kingsland

The pendulum of the electric cuckoo clock jerks spasmodically to the left and stands silently still when it should swing to the right. Detrick's is not the place for class, or for fine food, either. But for absolute convenience and some decent downhome cooking, this former drive-in will do just fine. Local folks only, here —state troopers, farmhands in Caterpillar hats, little old ladies— all of them reasonably friendly.

The "barbecued" chicken was just a batter-fried bird with a topping of tangy sauce. The made-here strawberry pie wasn't super either, but it *was* full of honest strawberry flavor, and it wasn't oversweet. Do not miss the mashed potatoes and gravy— outa sight, the pride of any diner. Their own bread, too. Modest prices.

HOURS Sun.–Thurs. 7 am–9 pm; Fri. & Sat. 7 am–10 pm.

SPECS (216) 224-1166; no cards; no liquor; children's menu.

DIRECTIONS **Westbound:** Go left at end of the Exit 235 ramp, over the bridge, and then turn immediately left onto Route 84. Go 0.1 mile, and it's on the left.

Eastbound: Go straight at the stop sign at the end of the Exit 235 ramp. It's 0.1 mile on the left.

Minnesota
Wisconsin
Illinois
Michigan

Minnesota

CEDAR AVENUE RESTAURANTS,
Cedar & Twenty-fifth Avenue, Minneapolis

By the time you reach the Cedar Ave. Exit on I-94 a good many of the restaurants that line it will have met their maker. That's the way it goes in a trendy university neighborhood, but you can be fairly sure that new ones will have risen to take their places. When we passed through our eye was caught by **The Joy of Eating** (325 Cedar Ave.—burgers, quiche, and tortellini); a Cincinnati-style chili parlor (411 Cedar); a gourmet pizzeria (523 Cedar); and **Sgt. Preston's** and **Trumps,** both of them "saloon and eatery"-type places with appropriate gimmicks (6 blocks from the exit ramp, opposite one another just before the road forks). Of course there were Japanese and Chinese places, too, and Lord knows what else.

What's happened to the Midwest, anyway?

DIRECTIONS **Westbound:** Take Cedar Ave. Exit and turn right at the light onto Cedar. The next 6 blocks are full of restaurants.

Eastbound: You must go to the Twenty-fifth Ave. Exit, cross over I-94, and come back on I-94 for ¼ mile to the Cedar Ave. Exit. Then go as above. Easy enough.

CHEROKEE SIRLOIN ROOM,
Lafayette Bridge & 9th Street Exits, West St. Paul

There are moments when we tire of sushi and sauces; when fettuccine seems merely fattening, and just the thought of something in French fills us with indignation. In such moments we want meat—plain and simple, deeply charred on the outside and juicy, tender-pink within. And we want it without a lot of baloney—no potted plants, thank you, or stained-glass windows; no menus on blackboards, and no wine list that gets beyond Almaden or maybe Inglenook.

We wish we might always be in St. Paul when these attacks of gastronomic patriotism occur, because the Cherokee Sirloin Room is absolutely the perfect place to satisfy them. Friendly and informal, but with white linen for just a bit of class, this lovely restaurant has grown from a neighborhood eatery to one with a citywide reputation. There are dozens of newspaper reviews around to prove that its steaks are as good as any in town—but with prices that are only two thirds of its ritzier competition's. The dinner menu actually begins at $5.95, but we blew the bankroll on the near-top-of-the-line 16-ounce sirloin at $9.95. It arrived precisely as we visualized it, except that it was a full 2 inches thick, came beneath a pretty garnish of one demure onion ring and one fresh strawberry, and tasted even better than we had hoped—the second-best steak to pass our lips in 75,000 miles of eating. The rolls and au gratin potatoes that came with it were good enough, and we discovered Grain Belt Premier beer, a St. Paul brand that ought to go national.

While steak is obviously the Cherokee's thing, they are also very proud of the half dozen fish dinners ($6.95–$8.95). There are only a few sandwiches ($4–$5, with fries) and a chef's salad ($5.25) that is not particularly imaginative. Luncheons are $4–$5.

An unusual touch at the Cherokee is that the menu closes with a prayer that thanks God for all we take for granted. We inquired and found out that Dorothy Casper, the mother of the family who owns the restaurant, decided to inject religion into business when management meetings began getting acrimonious. She insisted that the meetings begin with a prayer, and ever since they have been quietly productive. Perhaps it's also worth noting that on Thanksgiving the Casper family foregoes its own feast and opens the restaurant to the poor for dinner.

HOURS Lunch: Mon.–Fri. 11 am–2:30 pm; Dinner: Mon.–Thurs. 5–11:30 pm, Fri. & Sat. 5 pm–midnight, Sun. 3–10 pm. Closed major holidays.

SPECS 886 S. Smith St.; (612) 457-2729; no cards—checks accepted, will even send a bill; full bar.

DIRECTIONS **Eastbound:** Take 9th St. Exit and go 2 blocks to Smith. Turn right onto Smith. In 3 blocks Smith bears right. Stay on Smith and go about 2 miles, through some turns, and over the bridge. It's on the left, at the corner of Annapolis and Smith.

Westbound: (Not quick, unfortunately.) Take Lafayette Bridge Exit (which is an exit to the left). In the exit ramp bear right as you go around a long loop that will lead you over the bridge and onto another freeway. Go 2.7 miles to the Butler Ave. Exit. Turn right onto Butler and go 1.8 miles to Smith. Turn right onto Smith, go 0.4 mile to the restaurant, on right at the light.

THE LOWELL INN
THE FREIGHT HOUSE
(and Stillwater generally),
Route 95 Exit, Stillwater

Seven miles north of I-94 and hard by the banks of the St. Croix River lies the beautiful, red brick and boutiquey town of Stillwater, Minnesota. As usual in such towns, the restaurant current runs as deep as the river's. Choose a lovely old inn that looks as if it were transplanted from Williamsburg, or a bricks, plants, and oak café that has the inevitable river view. There's also a fine sausage shop, and a very good Italian restaurant.

The Lowell Inn is lovely indeed, but forget it if you're in search of a bargain. Its basic American lunch menu runs $7.95–$13.25. The chicken a la king was good, but not that good, we thought, though you just may be in the mood for starched linen, attentive service, and fresh flowers at any price.

The Freight House has a true-to-form QRS menu (quiche,

Reuben, and spinach salad), and charges at least $4 for anything at all, which makes it, too, something less than a superbargain. The taco salad was very enjoyable, however. Sandwiches and salads are available at nighttime in the $5–$6 range. Dinners with salad and potato or rice are $8–$10—no big surprises.

Stillwater's best, we thought, were **Das Wurst Haus** and **Vittorio's,** for which, read on.

HOURS   **Inn:** Breakfast—Daily 8–10:30 am; Lunch—Sun.–Fri. noon–2 pm; Dinner—Mon.–Thurs. 6–8:30 pm; Fri. & Sat. 5:30–10 pm, Sun. 5–8 pm.
Freight House: Summer—Sun.–Thurs. 11 am–10 pm; Fri. & Sat. 11 am–11 pm. Closed 1 hour earlier in winter. Closed Christmas, New Year's, Thanksgiving.

SPECS   **Inn:** 102 N. 2nd St.; (612) 439-1100; all cards, full bar.
Freight House: 305 S. Water St.; (612) 439-5718; V, MC, AE; full bar; children's portions.

DIRECTIONS   Go about 7.2 miles north on Route 95 to Stillwater. For **The Freight House** take the first right in town. It's 1 block, on the left. For **The Lowell Inn** continue straight into town and go 1 block past the second red light (Myrtle St.). Turn left, and go 1 block. It's on the right, on the corner.

DAS WURST HAUS, *Route 95 Exit, Stillwater*

Two years ago Don Kielsa decided to move from St. Paul to the quieter life in Stillwater. With him came his butcher and sausage shop, and now it's Stillwater instead of St. Paul that, according to some, has the best bratwurst outside of Germany. Our bratwurst experience isn't wide enough to verify the claim, but we can tell you that Don's product is very, very good indeed, and so are the light whole-wheat rolls and the sauerkraut that come with it for $1.85.

About 5 other kinds of wurst get made in the small shop, along with Don's own smoked turkey legs, beer sticks, beef jerky, and pepi-pol, an original synthesis of pepperoni and Polish sausage.

The shop itself is as pleasant a place as there could be to

munch away at a quick lunch. Where would a real butcher-block table be more appropriate than among those dangling sausages? The fact that you don't know who you'll end up sharing it with makes the whole adventure just a bit more fun.

HOURS Mon.–Thurs. 9 am–5:30 pm; Fri. 9 am–8 pm; Sat. 8 am–5:30 pm; Sun. 11 am–5:30 pm. No Sunday service in winter. Closed major holidays.

SPECS 312 S. Main St.; (612) 439-4022; no cards; no liquor.

DIRECTIONS Go 7.4 miles north on Route 95. It's on the left in the second block once you hit town.

VITTORIO'S, *Route 95 Exit, Stillwater*

We weren't all that encouraged by Vittorio's looks, which seemed to be made of the bones and other earthly remains of two or three other restaurants that had inhabited this site. The red-checked vinyl cloths were okay, but for seating there were only glorified kitchen chairs, and off to one side was one of those indoor shingled mansard roofs. Here a touch of wrought iron, there an arch, and high up above a bare wood ceiling that really seemed to want to be in a bricks, plants, and oak café.

Things got spiffier in the lounge, where plush chairs and stone walls prevailed, but it seemed more fake than inviting.

When the mediocre bread arrived, we were sure we'd wasted another check, but next there arrived a cannelloni in white sauce that knocked our socks off and had us believing everything we were told about how the Gozzi family brought over the recipes from Novellara, a small town in northern Italy.

Wherever it came from, the dish was terrific—nice fat cannelloni cooked *al dente* and stuffed with ground beef, ham, spinach, and ricotta, then topped with a light, delicate cheese sauce abundant with subtle flavors.

It's $5.25 for the cannelloni at lunchtime. Other pasta dishes go as low as $3.75, and you can get pizzas for $6.25 and $7.25. Add chicken cacciatore and steaks at $8.50–$11.50 and that just about gives you the dinner menu.

We promise you'd be happy with the cannelloni bianchi at twice the price.

HOURS   Daily 11 am–11 pm.

SPECS   402 S. Main St.; (612) 439-3588; V, MC, AE; full bar; children's menu.

DIRECTIONS   Go 7.2 miles north on Route 95. It's on the left almost as soon as you hit Stillwater.

Wisconsin

KERNEL RESTAURANT, *Exit 41, Menomonie*

It's open 24 hours and it has unspecial, honest food (ribs, steaks, mashed potatoes) in a decor that avoids the red-velvet-and-dark-wood-brothel look only because it is too plainly and inexpensively done plausibly to suggest luxury. So far as we could tell, it was the best around—inoffensive, clean, and locally popular. Country music, too. Keep your expectations reasonable, and you won't be disappointed. Modest prices.

HOURS   Daily 24 hours.

SPECS   (715) 235-5154; V, MC; no liquor.

DIRECTIONS   On the left just a bit south of Exit 41.

NORSKE NOOK, *Exit 88, Osseo*

Helen Myhre is a modest, pleasant woman, who doesn't understand why everyone makes such a fuss about her tiny village restaurant. There's no denying, however, that her pies are famous. There's a whole wall of restaurant reviews to prove it, and lots of people must be reading them because the place was packed at 3:30 pm on Monday. Only half the clientele were local,

even though Osseo is a mile from the highway and Helen doesn't advertise.

Helen learned to cook by feeding the farmhands who helped with the harvest on her parents' farm. Now the farmers come to town for her fare and (much to her chagrin) roll dice to see who will put up the 95 cents it costs to sample a piece of rhubarb pie —or banana, or strawberry, blueberry, apple, pecan, custard, chocolate, etc. The list goes on and on, changing with the seasons to take advantage of what's fresh. Our slice of raisin–sour cream pie was enormous, piled high with the lightest, airiest, heavenliest meringue we've tasted yet—a wholesome, hearty chunk of pure Americana.

Despite the name and despite the fact that Helen is half Norwegian, there's almost no Norwegian cooking here. For three special events a year she makes lutefisk, a Norwegian salted fish specialty that requires 4 days of soaking just to remove the brine. But that's not really for the public. Expect instead just hamburgers at $1.40 and specials of barbecued ribs and smoked pork chops ($3.50–$7.25 for dinner). There's just not time for much else when you have to turn out 50 pies a day and people from Milwaukee keep wanting to walk off with half your stock.

HOURS   Mon.–Sat. 5:30 am–9:30 pm. Closed Sun. & major holidays.

SPECS   7th & Harmony Sts.; (715) 587-3069; no cards; no liquor.

DIRECTIONS   From Exit 88 go 1 mile west on US 10 to Route 53. Turn left and go 2 blocks to 7th St. Turn left again, go ½ block, and it's on the right.

THE RIVER HOUSE, *Exit 115, Black River Falls*

Black River Falls is a funky-but-charming little farm town with a Main Street that looks just a bit like a set from a Wild West movie. The barber shop repairs electric razors and Rick's Place is not a nightclub but a bowling alley.

The brand new exterior of The River House stands out from the town's tired storefronts like a city slicker among a gang of field hands. All is new inside, too—a sort of small-town imitation of the trendy stained-glass-and-wood look, but it's hometowny enough so that it ends up feeling comfortably unpretentious.

The creamy tomato soup was really very good, and so was the imaginatively seasoned pan-fried chicken. It took some while for the chicken to reach us, even though the restaurant was not busy, but when it came, it came in more than ample quantities—two big breast pieces and a crunchy wing. Refreshing little balls of fresh honeydew and cantaloupe added to what would have been an admirable salad bar even without them. The dressings were a mixed bag, and the little square of carrot cake that finished out the $4.25 meal was too sweet for sure.

Our general impression is that someone is really trying to do things well here, and we doubt you're likely to get a better $4.25 dinner for many miles in any directon. Deli sandwiches (on Kaiser roll, wheat, pumpernickel, or white) are just $2.75, and for another dollar you get access to that excellent salad bar.

HOURS   Mon.–Sat. 6 am–11 pm; Sun. 9 am–2 pm. Closed major holidays.

SPECS   38 Main St.; (715) 284-7141; no cards; beer & wine.

DIRECTIONS   From Exit 115 go 0.9 mile south on Route 27 to Black River Falls. Turn right at the stop sign. It's ½ block, on the left.

TRAVELER'S ADVISORY

From Madison to Tomah, I-90 and I-94 run together. See I-90, pp. 205–210, for entries along this stretch of road.

ELLA'S DELI AND ICE CREAM PARLOR,
Exit 240, Madison

For a good-tasting stop that's lots of fun to boot, see p. 198.

DIRECTIONS From I-94 westbound take Exit 240 onto Route 30, which is another limited access highway. Go 3 miles to the end of Route 30 at E. Washington St. Turn left 0.1 mile. It's on the right.

MADER'S, *7th Street and I-43 Exits, Milwaukee*

See pp. 13–14 for a description of this excellent and pricey Milwaukee institution that specializes in German food.

DIRECTIONS **Westbound:** Take the exit for I-43 North near central Milwaukee and then follow directions on p. 14. It will take you less than a minute to reach the exit off I-43.

Eastbound: Take exit for 7th Ave./Civic Center which will lead you to 7th St. going north. Go 7 blocks to Highland, turn right, and go 4 blocks to 3rd St. It's on the corner, on the right.

THREE BROTHERS, *Exit 312, Milwaukee*

We were in town on Monday afternoon, and Three Brothers is open only in the evening from Tuesday to Sunday. So we weren't able to check out this locally renowned, funky focal point of Serbian cooking. But from what we've heard, if you're in the mood for raznjici, kajmak, or slivowitz, you won't go away unhappy.

If looks are any indication, there's certainly nothing to worry about. The restaurant is in an ancient tavern left over from the days when Milwaukee's breweries owned their own retail outlets. Behind the marble bar there's a faded mountain scene mural. The bentwood chairs and ceiling fans really belong here, and though all is clean and pleasant, the old kitchen-type tables make it clear enough that this is not a place where the money has gone into the decor.

It's true, of course, that you can't judge a book by its cover. Well, then, how about the fact that it's the *Milwaukee* magazine restaurant reviewer's favorite? Or the fact that they give you goat's milk butter instead of cow's?

We're sorry we missed it. Write us a nasty letter if you don't like it, but know that your wallet won't be severely dented in any case. Prices are moderate, but *do* spend the few cents to call ahead and make reservations.

HOURS Tues.–Thurs. 5–10 pm; Fri. & Sat. 4–11 pm; Sun. 4–10 pm.

SPECS 2414 S. St. Clair; (414) 481-7530; no cards; full bar.

DIRECTIONS **Westbound (actually northbound):** Take Exit 312A and bear right in the exit ramp for Becher St. ■ Turn right onto Becher and go 0.2 mile to a three-way intersection and bear gently right onto Bay. Follow Bay for 1 mile to Russell. Turn left onto Russell and go 1 block to St. Clair. Turn left onto St. Clair, go 3 blocks, and it's on the right.

Eastbound (actually southbound): Take Exit 312B and follow the signs for Becher St. east. Then as above from ■.

NANCY'S RESTAURANT, *Exit 335, Sturtevant*

Nancy's is a cute new little place all neatly decked out in ferns and oak and booths in British racing green. The details have been attended to, both in the decor and in the good, solid, honest American cooking at moderate prices. Real homemade soups and dressings; above average rolls. The barbecue sauce is especially recommended, and the mashed potatoes did not come out of a box.

HOURS Daily 6 am–10 pm.

SPECS 2811 Wisconsin St.; (414) 886-2408; V, MC, AE; full bar.

DIRECTIONS From Exit 335 turn right and go 2.5 miles to County Road H (Wisconsin St.), just after the RR tracks. Turn left and go 3 blocks. It's on the right.

Illinois

THE VILLAGE SMITHY, *Exit 30B, Glencoe*

If you're looking for a dignified and tasteful little place, where the waiters wear vests, the food is very good, and where there's enough class to make you thankful for your blessings, then the tony village of Glencoe has just what you're looking for.

There's no iceberg at all in The Village Smithy's salad, and the vinaigrette was good, both on the greens and when dabbed onto the excellent, crusty bread. They even make their own very fine saltless potato chips here, served as an aside at lunchtime! The principal affair was our shrimp Dijonnais (just $4.95) which at first seemed a bit stodgy but then burst into lively flavor when prodded by a generous squirt of lemon.

All soups, sauces, dressings, muffins, biscuits, and desserts are made absolutely from scratch, and though owner Bill Lepman would rather be known for his triple chocolate mousse dessert than for the ever-popular apple crisp, the popularity of the latter is well deserved. The people of Glencoe, it seems, want their French food only in France, not in their own backyard. Which is okay with us. American food done with style and excellence is good enough. Dinners cost mostly $8–$10, lunches in the vicinity of $5.50.

HOURS Lunch: Mon.–Sat. 11:30 am–2:30 pm; Dinner: Sun.–Thurs. 5–10:30 pm, Fri. & Sat. 5–11:30 pm.

SPECS 368 Park Ave.; (312) 835-0220; major cards; full bar.

DIRECTIONS Westbound (actually northbound): Take Exit 30B for Dundee Rd. Go right on Dundee for 1.2 miles to the stop sign at Vernon. Turn right onto Vernon and go 0.4 mile to the stop sign at Park in the center of the village. Turn right onto Park, go 1 block, and it's on left.

Eastbound (actually southbound): You'll have to go to Exit 31 (Tower Rd.) and double back on I-94 to Exit 30B. Then as above.

ASHKENAZ RESTAURANT & DELI
LOU MALNATI'S PASTA AND PIZZA
CHICK-N-RIB JOYNT
IRVING'S FOR RED HOT LOVERS,
Exits 34A & 34C, Wilmette

Immediately east of these exits lies one of the finest concentrations of inexpensive specialty joints we have ever found so close to the road. Twenty seconds of driving time will bring you to a pleasant little suburban shopping area where you can choose between inexpensive versions of Jewish, soul, and Italian specialties or explore the wonders of the world's best-named hot dog shop. We aren't going to try and review all this. It was too much at once even for us, and nothing was open after 9 pm. But we sincerely doubt you'll do badly, and deciding which to try is sure to be fun.

DIRECTIONS Westbound (actually northbound): Take Exit 34C for Lake St. East. Just east of exit ramp. (**Irv's** is just behind the first shopping plaza.)

Eastbound (actually southbound): Take Exit 34A for Skokie Rd. Go straight at the end of the ramp for 0.3 mile to the second light. You're there, right across the street. (**Irv's** is in the plaza slightly to the left.)

WALKER BROS., *Exits 34A & 34C, Wilmette*

We very much appreciate Chicago's way of taking American favorites and turning them into something grand (see **Pizzeria**

Uno and **Carson's,** for example). All that seems very right for Carl Sandberg's city of heavy shoulders, and to us it looks as if the owners of **Walker's** set out to be the Ike Sewell of the pancake world (see p. 205). His famous apple pancake ($4.95) even looks like a pizza, except that the bubbling, beautiful brown crust is made of apples, cinnamon, sugar instead of mozzarella cheese, and the crust is far, far lighter than anything in a pizzeria—an airy, delicate sort of thing that starts to lose its heavenly quality within 5 minutes of leaving the oven.

The thing looks great, and it *is* a Chicago favorite. All the same we have to tell you we found it much too sweet—a lot more flair than flavor, and there was no way to tell that there was something like a pancake under all the teeth-gluing brown stuff.

The restaurant itself is like the apple pancake. Its looks are fantastically beautiful—the most opulent and lavish bricks, plants, and oak decor we've ever seen, with the finest collection of stained and leaded glass and the most luxurious use of oak moldings. It's undeniably handsome, but it's also overdone, and there is something kinda nutty about spending so much to decorate a suburban pancake house.

Crêpes, omelets, French toast, and pancakes of every kind (with Cointreau and sour cream filling, for example, all between $2.25 and $4.95). We suspect that if you stick to what is simple you'll actually do quite well. Walker's really does use the very best of ingredients, including whipping cream with the coffee, and the service was very fast, even if less than friendly.

HOURS Sun.–Thurs. 7 am–10 pm; Fri. & Sat. 7 am–midnight. Closed Christmas, New Year's, & early on other holidays.

SPECS 153 Green Bay Rd.; (312) 251-6000; no cards; no liquor.

DIRECTIONS **Westbound (actually northbound):** Take Exit 34C for Lake St. East and go 2.6 miles to Green Bay Rd. Turn right and go 0.6 mile to **Walker's** on the right.

Eastbound (actually southbound): Take Exit 34A for Skokie Rd. and go straight at the end of the ramp 0.3 mile to the second light. Turn left onto Lake and go 2.6 miles to Green Bay Rd. Turn right and go 0.6 mile to **Walker's,** on the right.

CARSON'S, *Exit 37B, Skokie*

For many Chicagoans, Carson's means ribs the way Kleenex means tissue paper and Coke means soft drinks. The honor is well deserved. Carson's ribs are big, meaty, and very, very tender, clothed in a sticky, deeply flavored sweet sauce that makes them go down like honey. A delicious, spicy tang provides a counterpoint that builds as you eat, without trying to sear its way into your heart. The hot stuff is unobtrusive and perfectly balances the sweet, and you are left gnawing the discarded bones like a hungry puppy.

More than that we do not ask from a plate of ribs, except perhaps that they be a bargain. At Carson's, the full order costs $11.95 and is almost certain to be more than you can eat. The half order (six big ones) is $8.95, and both versions are preceded by tasty rolls and a good anchovy–sour cream dressing on an iceberg salad. Fried skins, bakers, or potatoes au gratin come with the meal.

No mere rib shack, Carson's is a dressed-up, spiffy-looking place that boasts real paneling on its walls, trendy mirrors, and dignified white tablecloths. Not really stylish, mind you, and the tone, though very informal, is still refined enough to make you forget the rigors of the road.

We find it hard to imagine eating anything but ribs at Carson's, but the barbecued chicken ($8.95) and pork chops ($6.95) just can't be bad. The steaks ($12–$17) and even the pike ($12) have good reputations, as does the goldbrick sundae.

At lunchtime the price of a half slab of ribs falls to $5.95, and if that's too much you can get the idea from an order of rib tips in the same sauce for $3.95. Sandwiches, barbecued chicken, and omelets are in the $4–$5 range.

We admit with a bit of chagrin that Carson's is a chain. It's a local chain, however, with only four locations, all of which are in Chicago. There may someday be a Carson's in every American city, but Chicago's local restaurants have a way of surviving such success. Consider, for example, Pizzeria Uno. Even if one day there are thousands of little Carson's all across America, we'll not hesitate to recommend them so long as the quality remains this high.

HOURS   Mon.–Thurs. 4–11 pm; Fri. & Sat. 4 pm–midnight; Sun. noon–11 pm.

SPECS   8617 Niles Center Rd.; (312) 675-6800; major cards, full bar; children's menu.

DIRECTIONS   From Exit 37B go straight for 0.8 mile to Niles Center Rd. Turn right and go 0.2 mile. It's on the left.

THE BAGEL, *Exit 41B, Lincolnwood*

We were just about to order our standard Jewish deli tester—corned beef on rye with matzoh-ball soup—when we spotted the lox and onion omelet that was rapidly disappearing into our countermate's belly. So powerful was the dish's appeal to both eye and nose, that we pointed unceremoniously at the poor man's dinner and asked for "one of those." Sara Leff, our lovely, motherly waitress, gave us an understanding smile. Our neighbor halted his staccato gulping. Both agreed it was one of the restaurant's best dishes, made in real butter, mind you, and not at all greasy.

Such exchanges breed intimacy and the revealing of secrets. "There aren't many real Jewish delis left in Chicago," he said. "Used to be a lot, but now they've all been sold to Greeks." Whether that's true or not, we can attest that The Bagel is indeed the real thing. True, the decor is a bit more subdued than you'd expect, maybe even just a little chic, but the place is properly noisy, the tables are still bare Formica, and the menu covers the entire gamut from kosher franks, corned beef, and chopped liver, to schmaltz herring, tzimmes, blintzes, whitefish, kishka, kasha, and kugel. What's more, The Bagel is a relocated version of a 35-year-old storefront deli from the Jewish neighborhood of Albany Park. Things got a little fancier after the move, and prices probably took a very noticeable jump (the corned beef sandwich is $4.95, and the omelet cost $5.50; but dinners are $8–$9). So far as we can tell, however, the cooking remained the same, or maybe it got better. Who knows? But we do know that everything we tried was excellent, and we spotted many a rave review tacked proudly to the deli's walls.

HOURS   Daily 5 am–10 pm. Closed Jewish holidays.

SPECS   3000 W. Devon Ave.; (312) 764-3377; no cards; no liquor.

DIRECTIONS   Exit 41B puts you in the right direction on Paterson Ave. Go 2.7 miles east to Sacramento (a small side street just after Weinstein and Sons Funeral Home). Turn left onto Sacramento and go 4 blocks to Devon. It's on the left, on the corner.

TRAVELER'S ADVISORY

Through downtown Chicago I-90 and I-94 run together. See I-90, pp. 205–212, for entries along this stretch of road.

Michigan

HYERDALL'S RESTAURANT, *Exit 16, Bridgeman*

Maybe you don't want fancy cooking. Maybe you'd prefer to save a few dollars and have plain-but-terrific home cooking in a nice, comfortable, clean and entirely pleasant little roadside restaurant. If so, you simply cannot do better than Hyerdall's, where the service is so fast you will not believe it could produce such excellent eats.

You can tell from the outside that it's going to be good. The restaurant is housed in a quaintly inviting, little black-and-white building that sits right by the old highway. Inside it's a heart-warmingly old-fashioned roadside restaurant so pristinely manicured it seems to have been built yesterday. Any remaining doubts are dispelled when you realize that the mashed potatoes are the real thing, and that everything—soups, dressings, biscuits, etc.—is made from scratch under the supervision of Evelyn Pschigoda, who has been at this job for 43 years.

The menu offers considerable variety, from ribs ($5.25), shish kabob ($5.25), and scallops ($5.75) to the all-time Hyerdall favorite, stewed-till-it's-falling-off-the-bone chicken with powder biscuits, mashed potatoes, and gravy ($5.25). We sampled the oven-fried chicken just to see what the contradictory-sounding dish was, and found it to be a less greasy, more tender, but just as tasty version of plain old fried. We were entirely delighted with it, as we were with fresh rhubarb-strawberry pie, even though it was a bit sweet for our tastes. The house dressing was superb.

When you get this kind of quality at these kinds of prices, the word tends to get around. You'd do well to call ahead on weekends, alas, but such is a small price to pay before you get there, given that you'll pay so little once you're inside. A hamburger is but $1.50. Sandwiches go up to $2.50 and are available at all times.

HOURS   Tues.–Sun. 11:30 am–3 pm & 5–9 pm (until 8 pm in winter). Closed Mon. & from Thanksgiving to Christmas.

SPECS   9673 Red Arrow Highway; (616) 465-5546; no cards; no liquor; children's menu.

DIRECTIONS   From Exit 16 turn left if westbound and right if eastbound. Go 1 mile. It's the second building on the right after the light.

GRANDE MERE INN, *Exit 22, Stevensville*

There's no lack of fine restaurants in the Stevensville area. **Tosi's** near Exit 23 was once called by *Time* magazine one of the twenty-two best country restaurants in America. It's quite expensive, however, and reservations are suggested (4337 Ridge Rd.— [616] 429-3689).

That leaves **Schuler's** and the **Grand Mere Inn,** of which the Grand Mere seemed to us to win hands down. Virtually everything we tried was excellent, from heartily flavored barbecued spareribs ($10.95) and scallops Shamay ($9.25) to the cakey, light, chocolate cheesecake that abounded in rich, natural flavors. A light, refreshing taste distinguished the artichoke heart appetizers that were stuffed with crabmeat and topped with a dill sauce. The salad was a crisp, fresh mixture of more than just iceberg lettuces. Only the house dressing was a disappointment, but one that was more than made up for by the mushrooms with garlic and tarragon stuffing.

The Grand Mere has a pleasant, spiffy sort of informality about it. Its fine view of Lake Michigan is the principal decoration, augmented by cotton print tablecloths, fresh flowers in Perrier bottles, and enough wood all around to make things feel natural but not trendy.

You can lunch here on sandwiches, entrees, and salads such as crabmeat Louis or spinach and bacon, all for around $4–$5.50. The seafood, be it lake perch or the scallops that had *Bon Appetit* requesting the recipe, is always fresh, and the service is friendly.

In general, it seemed to us that the Grande Mere was delivering $20 quality for $10. If you're in the mood for a really good meal, don't hesitate to take advantage of it.

HOURS   Tues.–Thurs. 11 am–3 pm & 5–10 pm; Fri. 5–10 pm; Sat. 5–11 pm. Closed Sun., Mon., & major holidays.

SPECS   5800 Red Arrow Highway; (616) 429-3591; V, MC, AE; full bar; children's menu.

DIRECTIONS   From Exit 22 turn left if westbound and right if eastbound. Go ¼ mile to the light. Turn right and go 1 block. It's on the right.

THE WARNER WINE GARDEN, *Exit 60, Paw Paw*

We didn't know it either, but Michigan is the third largest wine-producing state in the country. The wineries are concentrated in the southwestern part of the state; Paw Paw alone boasts three. All have tasting rooms, but one comes to the aid of the motorist's appetite as well as thirst.

A more idyllic setting would be hard to imagine: You walk a swaying footbridge across a gushing stream, follow a brick path, and end up on a wooden deck that juts out over the Paw Paw River. A small waterfall wooshes underneath, and a spreading tree shades you from above. Sit at a table made from old oak wine casks, and peruse an adorable little menu cut out to resemble grapes. Your mood will be so refreshed that Saltine crackers and Velveeta cheese would probably taste divine. Indeed, the fare is simple, but not that simple.

Instead, try the Vintner's lunch: nice, crusty French bread, their own herbaceous cheese spread, wedges of fresh fruit, and smoked bratwurst ($3.75). Perhaps you'd prefer a shrimp salad sandwich on a croissant? It's $3.95, including a glass of wine. Or maybe a Reuben, a spinach salad, or a roast beef sandwich. We can't think of a more pleasant way to wash it all down than with a champagne slush (95 cents), but if you prefer your wines in the liquid state, those are available too—6 whites, 4 reds, and 2 rosés, by the bottle or the glass (95 cents).

Regardless of what you drink, the Warner Wine Garden is such a dream that you'll float all the way to Ann Arbor.

HOURS   Summer and Fall: Mon.–Sat. 11 am–4 pm; Sun. noon–4 pm. This year for the first time, **The Wine Garden** will be open year-round, moving to indoor quarters for the winter. It is considered experimental, however, and hours are yet to be determined.

SPECS   706 S. Kalamazoo St.; (616) 657-3165; V, MC, AE; wine only.

DIRECTIONS   **Warner Winery** and **Wine Garden** are about ½ mile north of Exit 60. Just head into town: it's on the left.

MI RANCHITO, *Exit 76B, Kalamazoo*

How nice to find a little Mexican restaurant that isn't trying to look like the high-priced spread. One that's located in a converted gas station paneled with barnboard, light on the sombreros but heavy on authentic cuisine. One that doesn't even have a liquor license at a time when margaritas are the biggest money-maker in most north-of-the-border Mexican establishments. In the Tex-Mex–crazed Midwest, it was a pleasure to find a Mexican restaurant that cared a whole lot more about its food than its image.

Mi Ranchito is run by three Mexican families. Now that they're in the United States, finding the right ingredients is a major challenge, but the owners have risen to it; one of them drives a van to Chicago every week to pick up fresh peppers, spices, herbs, and Mexican avocados (smaller, pricklier, and not as sweet as the California-grown variant, but essential for a properly tangy guacamole).

It's the peppers, says Lucia Franco, whom we interviewed after our meal, that makes Mi Ranchito's food so special. Using a canned chile for chiles rellenos would be like serving canned green beans in a three-star restaurant, she believes. In many dishes, different peppers must be combined for the right flavor; the richly pungent enchilada sauce, for instance, uses jalapeños, poblanos, japones, and cascabel serranos. And for cheese, the *queso* of choice is Chihuahua—creamier, slightly oilier, and more mature than Monterey Jack.

The difference this kind of care imparts was obvious in everything we tasted: the corn tamale (made in the husk by Lucia's 73-year-old mother, $1.35 a la carte); the quesadilla ($1.50); the mildly spiced chicken chalupa ($2.50); and the fiery beef enchilada ($2.25). As combination dinners, you'll spend $5–$7, but keep an eye out for daily specials that run all day long for under $4.

HOURS   Mon.–Thurs. 11 am–9 pm; Fri. & Sat. 11 am–10 pm. Closed Sun. There is another **Mi Ranchito** in nearby Oshtemo open 1 hour later Mon.–Sat., and open Sun. from 2–10 pm. Both are closed major holidays.

SPECS   **Kalamazoo:** 3818 S. Westnedge; (616) 343-7262; no cards; no liquor.
Oshtemo: 3112 S. 9th St.; (616) 375-5861; major cards; full bar.

DIRECTIONS   Kalamazoo: Exit 76B puts you on Westnedge North. The restaurant is about 1 mile north of the interstate, on the left.

Oshtemo: Use Exit 72 and head north for 1½ miles; it's on the left, just past the first light.

T. E. MURCH'S CAFÉ BAKERY AND
COUNTRY MARKET, *Exit 76A, Kalamazoo*

You don't expect a shopping mall lunchroom, squeezed somewhere between Baskin Robbins and the Wrangler Wranch, to take the pains to do most everything right, but T. E. Murch's seems to be such a place.

For one thing, the breads are baked right here, fresh daily, and they're excellent. Choose between white, rye, pumpernickel, cracked wheat, and oatmeal; the latter was crusty, soft-textured, and light. And then, look what goes on the bread. First a spread, like the grainy, imported Pommery mustard (sorry, *moutarde*), then rare roast beef or sausage or hickory-smoked turkey breast. Top that with any of 6 cheeses, or combine them however you like if you're ordering a cheese sandwich. If you want your cheese melted, they'll broil it in an oven, not a microwave. (Sandwiches run $2.66–$3.33.)

There are also some lush-looking salads, good coffee, and a choice of many teas—both black and herbal. For snacking or desserting you've got blueberry-bran muffins, pumpkin roll slices, and mint-cream chocolate cake.

We can't give an entirely glowing report on Murch's, however. The soup had a disappointing, manufactured taste about it, and the lemonade was chemical tasting and oversweet when we hoped it might be homemade. But all in all, we were glad to have stopped, and glad to know that occasionally there are rewards for the hungry traveler who stalks the suburban shopping mall.

HOURS   Mon.–Sat. 9:30 am–9 pm. Closed Sun.

SPECS   Southland Mall; (616) 323-3781; no cards; no liquor.

DIRECTIONS   Exit 76A puts you on Westnedge South. In ½ mile, pull into Southland Mall on the right. Use main mall entrance and turn right.

Note: Should you be headed downtown, there is another **Murch's** in the Kalamazoo Center, underneath the Hilton Hotel, on Michigan Ave. It's open Mon.–Sat., 10:30 am–5:30 pm.

CASCARELLI'S, *Exit 121, Albion*

An Albion institution since 1905, Cascarelli's began as a fruit stand, added a candy shop, soda fountain, bar, and now—what else?—an Italian restaurant. Despite its metamorphosis over the years, it's still a warm and friendly old place that wears an air of gentle dignity and appeals to all ages and social strata in this college town.

We were told it had the best pizza in town, and after tasting it we're prepared to believe the boast but wouldn't increase its geographical bounds tremendously far. We preferred the "Cascariffic," a worthy sandwich thick with good, spicy ham and far spicier pepper-jack cheese on a decent Italian bun ($2.50). A sandwich called "Ripon" (named for the Wisconsin college?) is grilled salami and cheese with onions and mustard on rye. Not bad, although the bread won't win any awards in "Canarsy" ($2.25). The rest of the Italian-American menu holds few surprises, but prices hold the line at $6 for dinner, with the exception of fresh Lake Michigan perch—all you can eat for $7.95.

HOURS   Mon.–Sat. 9 am–midnight. Closed Sun.

SPECS   116 S. Superior St.; (517) 629-3675; no cards; full bar.

DIRECTIONS   From Exit 121, follow signs for Albion/Business 94, which will take you through two jogs into the town center. Continue straight as Business 94 puts you on Superior St. (it turns to the left but you shouldn't). The restaurant is on Superior, 1 block past the light at Cass, on the right.

GRASS LAKE CAFÉ, *Exit 150, Grass Lake*

It's the kind of place where the waitress asks an assembled party of regulars if anyone needs a menu and the answer is sure to be no. We took one, though, and quickly learned about "The Warrior," a ½-pound burger that came out nicely seared, its slightly irregular surface a giveaway to its freshness. Smothered with bacon, melted Swiss and American cheeses, it came juicy and full flavored on a chewy onion bun ($3.25). At the same price was stuffed cabbage—not your usual blue plate special, and very nicely done indeed, with potatoes and spiced apple slices on the side.

Much as we enjoyed our lunch, we were about 4 hours early to partake in the Grass Lake Café's weekly highlight—the Friday night perch fry. True, you can get prebreaded frozen fillets of fish any time of the week, but on Fridays after 4 pm, Bill and Barb Naylor do fish right, starting with whole, fresh perch and finishing with golden brown, flaky fillets. (Or so we are told by a reliable source.) For $4.75 you can stuff yourself to the gills with repeat visits to the salad bar for nonpiscine variety.

Grass Lake Café's pies are all homemade, and our peach boasted an exquisite latticework shell unfortunately stuffed by a filling of canned peaches. A disappointing end to an otherwise delightful lunch. Perhaps the raspberries were fresh.

HOURS   Summer: Mon.–Sat. 6 am–9:30 pm; Sun. 7 am–8:30 pm (in winter, the café closes at 8:30 every night). Closed only Christmas, Thanksgiving, & New Year's.

SPECS   114 W. Michigan Ave.; (517) 522-8800; no cards; no liquor.

DIRECTIONS   From Exit 150, head south for 2½ miles to E. Michigan Ave. Turn right and go ½ mile; it's on the right, just past the light.

ZINGERMAN'S DELICATESSEN, *Exit 172, Ann Arbor*

If we tried to sprinkle the page with even a hint of what you'll find in this overflowing emporium of gustatory sights and smells, it would be impossible not to bombard you with an orgy of meats and smoked fish, soups and salads, cheeses and charcuterie, sandwiches and sides, breads and crackers, cookies and cakes and pastries. If we said that Zingerman's is the definitive deli, *la crème de la* cream cheese and lox, the Zabar's of the Midwest . . . you'd probably say you've heard it before. But unless you've been here, you've not seen it before. Or tasted any better.

Choosing among 100 sandwiches, we somehow settled on one—good old pastrami on rye ($3.25). The meat was perfect— soft, juicy, just fatty enough, properly peppery; the bread was moist, chewy, crusty, just right. Its thickness was impressive but we managed to find enough room for another test: chopped liver ($2.75). Would it be dark and strong-flavored, we wondered, or light and savory from the combination of chicken (not beef) liver with hard-boiled egg? It passed the test brilliantly. At that point there was no stopping us. We backed up a little to a rich and heady barley-mushroom soup just crammed with brisket ($1.25), then zoomed ahead to the best ruggelach (almond cookies) we've tasted in a very long time, pausing long enough to check in with some curried turkey salad and pickled herring, finally staggering out the door stuffed but ecstatic.

And we highly recommend that you do the same.

Before we leave Zingerman's, we should say that it's packed during peak hours but serene in between, when classical music wafts between the deli cases. Perhaps the nicest place to sit, when the weather cooperates, is out on the shaded slate patio. With a copy of the *New York Times* (provided gratis), a bagel spread thickly with cream cheese and whitefish, and a mug of good steamy coffee . . . you'll feel right at home. We did, anyway.

HOURS   Daily 7 am–8:30 pm.

SPECS   422 Detroit (corner of Kingsley); (313) 663-3354; no cards; no liquor.

DIRECTIONS   Westbound: From Exit 172, take Business 94 East (West Huron) about 1¾ miles to Main St. Turn left onto Main and go 3 blocks to Kingsley. Turn right onto Kingsley, go 3 short blocks to the deli at the corner of Detroit.

Eastbound: Directions identical to above, but you'll be on Business 94 for 2½ miles before reaching Main.

SIAM KITCHEN, *Exit 172, Ann Arbor*

Once we became inured to fast-food alleys and shopping-center strips, we pretty much stopped combing them for food worth writing about, but Ann Arbor breaks all the rules. The University of Michigan seems to have brought Ann Arbor more than just Rose Bowl titles over the years; there's a United Nations of dining in this college community, and more of it than the downtown area can contain. Within yards of the expressway on both sides of the city are refuges of sanity and calm, and some of the most enticing ethnic eating that the Midwest has to offer.

Step into Siam Kitchen, for example. While not in the least bit rarefied, there's an air of hushed dignity about the place and a distinct sense of Oriental tranquility. Weavings and framed stone rubbings on rice paper grace the walls, culinary tapestries decorate the plate. Thai cuisine is an amalgam of many others, its influences reaching as far west as Arabia, as far east as Polynesia, but most strongly to India and China. Order the delicious spicy and sour soup called *tom yum goong* and you'll detect the Szechuan factor; in an appetizer called *s'tay gai,* chicken strips are marinated in coconut milk (shades of Hawaii?) and served with a sweetish peanut sauce (an Indonesian touch?). For an entrée, try *gaeng gai,* chicken stewed in a coconut milk curry, and you'll get whiffs of the Indian subcontinent. But ponder the mysteriously smoky flavors imparted to stir-fried shrimp and broccoli by a variegated multispice sauce in the dish called *goong phad prig phaow,* and you won't know where in the world you're eating. That's Thai cuisine for you.

We didn't bother contemplating the origins of the fresh coconut ice cream that was our dessert, but we sure didn't mind contemplating its flavorful richness.

For this kind of artistry, you'll probably spend between $6 and $10 on a dinner entrée; add another $3 or $4 if you fall prey, quite understandably, to one of the appetizers. Lunch specials run $5–$6. Certainly it won't be the cheapest meal you've ever found in a shopping center, but it quite possibly will be the most surprising.

HOURS   Lunch: Tues.–Sat. 11:30 am–2 pm. Dinner: Tues.–Thurs. & Sun. 5–9:30 pm; Fri. & Sat. 5–10:30 pm. Closed Mon., and in summer closed Sun. as well.

SPECS   Westgate Shopping Center, 2509 Jackson Rd.; (313) 665-2571; major cards; no liquor license at time of writing (pending).

DIRECTIONS   **Eastbound:** Exit 172 puts you on Jackson Ave. In ¾ mile, you will pass under the interstate; immediately afterwards, turn right into Westgate Shopping Center. It's in the corner of the L.

Westbound: From Exit 172, turn right and, almost immediately, turn right again, into Westgate Shopping Center. It's in the corner of the L.

AFGHAN HOME RESTAURANT, *Exit 180B, Ann Arbor*

Ten miles across town from the **Siam Kitchen**—in a motel rather than a shopping center—is another ethnic restaurant no less exotic and every bit as serene as its Thai counterpart. Here the flavors are Afghan, also a compendium of many influences, and here we had the most exquisite dessert of our midwestern adventure.

But that's getting a little ahead of ourselves, and we wouldn't want to deemphasize any of the courses that came before it. To describe the soup called *aush* as "hearty" would be to understate our case; the beefy, minty broth spoke with fully defined flavors and intriguing textural contrasts smoothed off by a yogurt roux. We were also taken with *bulanee gandana,* a piquant vegetable turnover drizzled with an aromatic Afghan sauce. As lunch entrées, we chose *sabzi chalau,* subtly flavored chunks of lamb on garlic-infused spinach; and the spicy scallion dumplings called *aushak.* Those with at-home tastes can stick with an "Afghan burger" on flat bread, but if we come again we'll go for *kofta kebab,* skewered spicy beef, or *mahee biryon,* fresh rainbow trout marinated and pan-fried. (Lunch entrées are $3–$5; the same basic fare in dinner-sized portions runs about $2.50 more.)

Now, about that dessert. They called it *firni.* It's a silken custard, divinely creamy, sprinkled with pistachios and flavored throughout with cardamom. There's the magic: cardamom. This intoxicating condiment has oft been called "the seed of paradise," and in paradise we were with the first spoonful.

No matter where you sit, you'll float away on a cloud of newfound flavors, but the best table in the house is no table at all. It takes a little planning and a party of at least four, but if you can reserve the velvet-pillowed Afghan Room, your meal will be served on a tablecloth spread on an Oriental rug—as close an approximation as we've found to the fabled magic carpet of yore.

HOURS Mon.–Sat. 11 am–3 pm & 5–10 pm; Sun. 11 am–10 pm.

SPECS Varsity House Motel, 3250 Washtenaw Ave.; (313) 971-7166; major cards; full bar.

DIRECTIONS Exit 180B puts you on Business 94. Take it for 1½ miles to Exit 37B, which puts you westbound on Washtenaw Ave. Go

0.6 mile to Varsity House Motel, on the left at the corner of Huron Parkway. The restaurant is inside and down a flight of stairs.

JUDY'S CAFÉ, *Exits 204 & 210, Detroit*

If you've seen the sign HOME COOKING so many times you don't believe it anymore, try **Judy's** home cooking. One stop and you'll be a believer again. It's well worth the 3–5-mile detour. See pp. 260–261 for a description.

DIRECTIONS   Eastbound: Exit 204B puts you on Southfield Freeway North (M-39). It's 4 fast freeway miles to Exit 8. Turn right on Warren Ave., and in about ¾ mile, **Judy's** is on the left, between Forrer and Montrose.

Westbound: From Exit 210B, turn right at the stop sign onto Addison, then quick left onto McGraw, which becomes Ford Rd. Two miles will take you to Greenfield Rd. (watch signs). Turn right onto Greenfield for 1 mile to Warren. Turn left onto Warren, and in 2½ blocks, **Judy's** is on your right, between Montrose and Forrer. It's not difficult, but if you'd rather take the Southfield Freeway, you can use Exit 204 and follow the directions above.

GREEKTOWN, *Exit 216A, Detroit*

This 2-block melange of restaurants is easily accessible to I-94 travelers wishing to make a short detour. See pp. 139–140.

DIRECTIONS   From Exit 216A, follow signs for I-75 South, which you should take for about 2 miles, then entering I-375 for about ½ mile to the first exit (Lafayette). The first light you'll reach is Monroe. At this intersection you would want to turn right for **Greektown, which begins 1 block away, but you can't because it's a one-way street, so just go around the block. Park anywhere in the neighborhood.

CHIC AFRIQUE, *Exit 216A, Detroit*

It's a 2-minute detour to the exit for this unusual West African restaurant. See pp. 141–142.

DIRECTIONS   From Exit 216A of I-94, follow signs for I-75 South, which you'll take to Exit 53A (Warren), the very first exit. Turn right at the light onto Warren and go about ½ mile to Woodward. Turn left onto Woodward and go 2 short blocks to the restaurant, on the left, just past the light at Forest.

TRAFFIC JAM AND SNUG, *Exit 216A, Detroit*

This surprising restaurant is a simple skip over from I-94. See description, pp. 140–141.

DIRECTIONS   From Exit 216A of I-94, follow signs for I-75 South, which you'll take to Exit 53A (Warren), the very first exit. Turn right at the light onto Warren, and go about ¾ mile to Cass. Turn left onto Cass to the second light (Canfield). Turn right onto Canfield, and go 1 block to 2nd. The restaurant is on the corner, on the left.

THE COPPER KITCHEN, *Exits 271 & 274, Port Huron*

Michigan's "Thumb," the eastern appendage of the mitten-shaped state, has a claim to culinary fame: bean soup. Considering that the region is a primary grower of navy beans, the distinction is not surprising, although such logic does not always prevail in the agri-rich Midwest.

Not only is The Copper Kitchen's wondrously zesty bean soup at the top of its genre, but the restaurant itself—truly a "hole in the wall" of the kind we always seek—is a gem. Actually, it's several holes in the wall, a delightful little labyrinth of minuscule rooms in the basement of a venerable brick building recently converted to shops and studios—what they call "adaptive reuse" in the renovation biz.

For $1.65 you can sample The Copper Kitchen's specialty, accompany it with cornbread, and refill your soup bowl. There are other soups too—clam chowder on Fridays, chili every day, and all of it cooked up from scratch. Prefer your lunch between two slices of bread? Roast beef, corned beef, and ham sandwiches come on a variety of good breads, and you can dress them up with Michigan cheddar cheese ($2–$3, depending on the fixin's).

Also, a number of full-meal salads and salad spreads ($3–$4), fresh-baked cream pie, and that's about it—there aren't many more menu items than there are rooms.

Nothing elaborate, but real good, wholesome food and a taste of the Thumb.

HOURS   Mon.–Sat. 11 am–3 pm. Closed Sun. Breakfast may soon be added.

SPECS   609 Huron Ave.; (313) 984-4726; no cards; no liquor.

DIRECTIONS   Northbound: From Exit 271, follow signs for M-21 into Port Huron. This puts you on Oak St., which moves right along and in 3 miles brings you to a downtown intersection at Military. Turn left, and in about ¾ mile, the restaurant is on the left, in the Citadel Building, just after crossing Bard.

Southbound: Exit 274 puts you on Route 146, a short spur that delivers you onto Lapeer in about 1 mile. Turn left onto Lapeer and go 1¾ miles to Military. Turn left onto Military and go 0.4 mile to the restaurant, on the left in the Citadel Building, just after crossing Bard.

Michigan

COOK'S RESTAURANT, *Exit 30, Grand Rapids*

Once, everybody who was anybody (and under 20) in Grand Rapids spent summer evenings cruising the "Monroe Strip" in a '57 Chevy. No serious cruising could be complete without a stop at Cook's Drive-In, predecessor to the A & W's of today. But there's a big difference between Cook's and A & W: one of them was changed by success. At Cook's, the root beer is still custom made, from raw ingredients, on the premises. It's the creamiest, spiciest, most invigorating root beer we've ever had, bubbly, handsome, and jet black in a frosted mug.

And at Cook's the only socially acceptable thing to wash down with root beer is a hot dog—a 100 percent beef dog doused with "the works," meaning mustard, onion, dill spears, tomato wedges, cucumber slices, and a jalapeño pepper. Not a sauce of those ingredients, but a veritable salad proudly crowning the all-beef barker ($1.25).

Cook's never did go national, but it added another location in Grand Rapids, all to the benefit of the expressway traveler, for the new place is much more interstate accessible. Unfortunately, it's not a vintage drive-in foaming over with character; it's a no-frills sit-down restaurant with self-service counter, heavy on the plastique. The posted menu is somewhat more comprehensive than at the original Cook's: nothing elaborate, mind you, but standard short-order fare like two-eggs-over-light, omelets, and ham and cheese sandwiches at bottom-of-the-line prices. Best of all, they've got that incredibly good root beer. For nostalgia's sake if nothing else, it should be used to wash down Cook's tube steak spectacular.

HOURS Mon.–Wed. 6 am–10 pm; Thurs. & Fri. 6 am–11 pm; Sat. 6 am–10 pm. Closed Sun.

SPECS 3576 Alpine Ave., NW; (616) 784-2737; no cards; no liquor.

DIRECTIONS **Westbound:** Exit 30B puts you on Alpine Ave. North. In ½ mile you'll see **Cook's** on the right.

Eastbound: From Exit 30, turn left on Three Mile Rd. and go 1 block to Alpine Ave. Turn left onto Alpine and in ½ mile **Cook's** is on the right.

SCHNITZELBANK
LITTLE MEXICO CAFÉ, *Exit 37, Grand Rapids*

If you're continuing on I-96, it's only 5 fast miles out of your way to reach this well-loved German restaurant (pp. 267–268) and this interesting Mexican café (pp. 265–267).

DIRECTIONS Exit 37 of I-96 puts you on I-196 (Gerald R. Ford Freeway). In 3½ miles, take Exit 76 and follow directions given on p. 267 for **Little Mexico.** For **Schnitzelbank** use Exit 77B and follow directions on p. 268.

HUAPEI, *Exits 95 & 106, Lansing*

A dingy brick building in a not-exactly-charming section of town is *the* undiscovered spot for Chinese and Korean food, boasted our resident restaurant expert. But skip the Chinese, he instructed; just ask for the Korean menu.

He must have chuckled inwardly as he said it, mischievously neglecting to inform us that the Korean menu, handwritten on looseleaf paper, has nary an English word on it. But mercy had tempered his ploy, and he did tell us to order Number 24, spicy garlic chicken ($7). So, 24 it was.

Looking around, we knew we were on to something good. Over half the customers read the Korean menu with ease. The remainder, Caucasians-in-the-know, did as we did: they ordered by number, based on recommendation or previous experience. A few went one step farther, pulling crumpled receipts out of pockets and pointing at Korean words that had been penned by the waiter of a previous visit.

On a tip from one of these Huapei veterans, we also tried an appetizer of steamed dumplings. Steamed turnovers might have more aptly described the size of these enormous won tons, deliciously pungent with ginger, bursting with a meaty filling. Six such gargantuan beauties came for $2.50, and they left us wondering how we'd manage with the main course yet to come, a question we had to face squarely when the platter was set before us. Gorgeous it was, and just as gorgeous to the taste buds—tender, lightly breaded pearls of chicken surrounded by a full complement of vegetables and spicy flavors in a sauce so good we went through two bowls of rice sopping it up. And, even with two of us manning the chopsticks on a single portion, some of Huapei's Number 24 went back to the kitchen.

Judging from the procession of equally stunning platters that went by, we'd venture to say that you'll do well no matter what number you pick. But under no circumstances should you order more than one entrée and one appetizer for fewer than three people.

HOURS   Mon.–Fri. 11 am–2 pm; Sat. & Sun. noon–10 pm.

SPECS   401 E. Mount Hope; (517) 484-0846; no cards; no liquor.

DIRECTIONS **Eastbound:** From Exit 95, take I-496 about 7 miles to Larch/Cedar Exit, following signs for S. Cedar St. Go about ¾ mile on Cedar to Mt. Hope. Turn right onto Mt. Hope, and it's on your right. See **Note** after **City Fish Co.** directions (next entry).

Westbound: From Exit 106, take I-496 about 5 miles to the exit for Pennsylvania (stay on 496, not US 127, at the 4-mile point). Turn left onto Pennsylvania (head south) and go about 1 mile to Mt. Hope. Turn right onto Mt. Hope and it's about ½ mile to **Huapei,** on the right, just past the light at Cedar. See **Note** after **City Fish Co.** directions (next entry).

CITY FISH CO., *Exits 95 & 106, Lansing*

If we described this restaurant as fast-food seafood, you'd probably get the wrong impression. Don't think of Long John Silver's or anything like it. True, the seating area and counter service are superficially similar, but down deep where it counts this is an entirely different kettle of fish.

It's a 65-year-old seafood market that could hold its head high on either coast. In central Michigan it constitutes a minor miracle. And the best part of it is that for a few pennies more than the price of the raw fish, you can get it cooked and served on a (plastic) platter.

Two hundred pennies, to be exact, per pound of fish, which means that a ½-pound portion will cost you only a dollar over the market price, and for that dollar you can not only eat the broiled or fried fish but french fries, coleslaw, and a roll as well. What kind of choices do you have? About 40 of them, give or take a few: rainbow trout, walleye pike, small-mouth bass, bluefish, snapper, catfish, smelt, and cod just begin the list. Some of the prices amazed us: $2.29 a pound for catfish, $2.39 for bass, $1.50 for bluefish (whole). The most popular choices (whitefish, scrod, perch, shrimp, and clams, for instance) are already on a menu that obviates the need to stop first at the room-length display case, but we like the idea of seeing our fish glistening on ice before it's sent to the broiler.

Owner Jerry Zimmerman goes to great pains to see that his fish is as fresh as piscinely possible. All of it arrives by air, no more than 24 hours after reaching Boston, Miami, or Seattle by boat. Because of recent contamination problems in the Great

Lakes, Jerry takes no chances, importing freshwater species from northern Canada's frigid, unpolluted waters. Our whitefish was from Great Slave Lake in Saskatchewan. We can't say if it was the point of origin or the free use of butter under the broiler that resulted in its glorious succulence, but we saw little room for improvement.

A few side dishes, ice cream, and homemade cheesecake round out the menu, but the only real reason to come here is a penchant for fresh seafood, simply but competently prepared.

HOURS   Sun.–Thurs. 11 am–10 pm; Fri. & Sat. 11 am–11 pm. Closed Christmas only.

SPECS   3001 E. Saginaw; (517) 351-1936; no cards; beer & wine.

DIRECTIONS   **Eastbound:** Take Exit 95, it's about 8 miles along I-496 to US 127 North (a freeway). Take 127 North for 1 mile to the Saginaw Ave. Exit. Look across Saginaw and you'll see **City Fish**. See **Note** below.

Westbound: Exit 106 puts you on I-496/US 127 North. In about 4 miles, don't bear west with I-496, but continue north on US 127 for another mile and take the Saginaw Ave. Exit. Look across Saginaw and you'll see **City Fish.**

Note: Neither **City Fish Co.** nor **Huapei** is as far out of your way as it might seem, because the I-496 loop through Lansing returns you to I-96 11 miles from where you left it. There will be no lost mileage if you take this loop through Lansing instead of staying on I-96 as it skirts around town. Just be sure not to backtrack after eating; simply return to I-496 and continue in the direction you were already traveling.

TRAVELER'S CLUB, *Exit 110, Okemos*

Decorated in early 20th-century tuba, this former ice cream shop still has the best milk shakes and rhubarb sundaes in town, but much, much more. The tubas (part of restaurant owner Bill White's collection, and played on Sunday nights) are a tip-off that this is no ordinary corner lunchroom. One glance at the Xeroxed menu confirms the hunch.

We came on "Caribbean Month" to find a dinner of *colombo*

de poulet (grilled chicken topped with a curry sauce that included tamarind), *moros y christianos* (black beans steamed with green peppers and bay leaf), *aubergine à la tomate* (eggplants and tomatoes, simmered with bacon, onions, and chiles) and scallion fritters with cornmeal and coconut milk bread. We didn't have to choose between them—we got them all, and the salad bar, for $5.85! Not your ordinary salar bar either, but one that fit the theme: a tropical fruit salad, pickled turnips, mango pickles, sweet-and-sour orange dressing, and pomegranate seeds, among other exotica. The soup was white gazpacho ("no tomatoes makes it authentic," says Bill) and the coffee Jamaican.

That was on a Tuesday. Had we come on Wednesday we would have found rabbit and ground-nut stew with garlic rice, baked paw paw, and banana fritters. And the next month, the menu would change altogether from Caribbean to Indian or Ethiopian or Japanese.

"This is the way I like to eat at home," Bill explained when we asked about his inspiration for such a place. "I'll binge on Mexican food until I'm sick of it, then eat Polish till I'm sick of that." The Lansing area's huge international community has shown no signs of a flagging appetite for what Bill cooks up, and a polyglot crowd can be seen here at almost any time. What do they think of Bill's attempts at their native cuisine? Bill answers proudly: "Just about every month somebody from the featured region will come in in a turban or kemi dress or something, lick the plate clean, and say 'better than Mother's.'"

Well, slight hyperbole perhaps, but we surely didn't send anything back on *our* plates.

In addition to the rotating dinner menu, the Traveler's Club serves breakfasts and lunches that lean heavily toward the vegetarian (but not so heavily as to keep pastrami or buffalo burgers off the menu). Prices are most reasonable, and you can reduce the cost even further if you've any musical talent: Bill offers free coffee for 15 minutes of competent performance on any instrument, a free sundae for 30.

HOURS   Mon.–Sat. 1 am–11 pm; Sun. 9 am–10 pm.

SPECS   2138 Hamilton (corner of Okemos Rd.); (517) 349-1701; no cards; no liquor; children's portions.

DIRECTIONS From Exit 110, turn left if eastbound, right if westbound, onto Okemos Rd. The restaurant is 2¾ miles north of the interchange, at the corner of Hamilton Rd.

AH WOK, *Exit 162, Novi*

You thought Mandarin and Cantonese were out? Try Ah Wok.

The shopping center location is unencouraging, but once inside, it's clear that this is no ordinary moo goo gai pan palace. Glitzy Chinese decorations are naught; in fact, the place is spartanly, though comfortably, furnished with contemporary taste. The menu is *not* printed on billboard-sized cards with spicy dishes in red ink and mild ones in black. But best of all, the flavors are much more than what we've come to expect from "Chinese food."

Take the chicken roll appetizer, for instance ($2.20). It doesn't look like much, but its richly aromatic spices make it a dish to reckon with. A heady amalgam of newfound flavors, a broth called *Yangchow won ton* ($5 for two) redefines the concept of won ton soup. As a dinner entrée, the beef, chicken, and pork of *sam pan wor ba* ($9.75) was deftly sautéed with vegetables and served over sizzling rice that really sizzled. Shredded chicken in Yushan garlic sauce ($7.95) came off with a complex tang, not merely redolent of *Allium sativum*. Lunches are more in line with what we've come to expect of Chinese-American restaurants ($4.50 average) but there, too, the quality is one step ahead of the crowd.

With a 12-year reputation for creativity, Ah Wok has become destination number 1 for diners in Detroit's northwest suburbs with a penchant for the innovative in Oriental cuisine. On at least one occasion, they have called for the chef and tipped him with a standing ovation.

HOURS   Mon.–Thurs. 11 am–9:30 pm; Fri. & Sat. 11 am–11:30 pm; Sun. noon–9:30 pm.

SPECS   Novi Plaza, 41563 Ten Mile Rd. (at Meadowbrook); (313) 349-9260; major cards; full bar.

DIRECTIONS   From Exit 162, head south on Novi Rd. (turn left if westbound, right if eastbound). In 1¼ miles, turn left onto Ten Mile Rd. Go 0.9 mile to Novi Plaza, on the right.

Note: If you are on I-275 take I-96 West after 275 ends, and in 1 mile you'll reach Exit 162. From there, follow directions above.

JUDY'S CAFÉ, *Exit 183, Dearborn*

Judy, Judy, where've you been all our eating lives? We've looked everywhere. At every promising little lunchroom, every simple sandwich shop, every unassuming café, every place that tacked up a HOME COOKING sign and a few calico curtains, we hoped to find you lurking behind the counter, slyly waiting to spring your talents upon our plates. But you weren't there. Where were you?

You were at 15714 W. Warren Ave., that's where, thumbing through your bulging shelf of spattered cookbooks, grinding whole spices into powders, wiping the brow of a weather-weary regular, chasing him out the door to return an overgenerous tip, laughing gustily and confidently behind an apron that says "Never Trust A Skinny Cook."

Now that we know where to find you, we shall return to your 1940s-vintage storefront lunch counter for more of your herbed soups, your fresh pasta dishes, your wok stir-fries, your salmon croquettes and stuffed cabbage and chicken-broccoli strudel, your chocolate cheesecakes, your mixed ethnic menu unabashedly sprinkled with downhome American.

If we lived in the Detroit area, Judy, we'd put ourselves on your mailing list so we could schedule in a few of your $15 reservations-only dinners followed by rounds of Trivial Pursuit or Scrabble (what a great idea!), but since we don't, we'll happily settle for your $3 lunches and your $2 breakfasts next time we're in town. As *soon* as we get into town.

HOURS   Tues.–Thurs. & Sat. 8 am–4 pm; Fri. 8 am–6 pm. Closed Sun., Mon., & holidays.

SPECS   15714 W. Warren Ave., Detroit; (313) 581-8185; no cards; no liquor.

DIRECTIONS   From Exit 183, take the Southfield Freeway (M-39) South about 2½ quick miles to Exit 8/Warren Ave. Turn left onto Warren, and in about ¾ mile, **Judy's** is on your left, between Forrer and Montrose.

CLEMENTINE'S SALOON, *Exit 20, South Haven*

Some bricks, some wood nailed up on the diagonal, a Tiffany-style lamp or two, and a dark, pubby atmosphere make up the clichéd but not unpleasant looks of Clementine's Saloon. The menu runs true to form, from burgers ($2.75), burritos (wet—$4.95), and Reubens ($3.95) to nachos ($2.95), potato skins ($3.95), and spinach salad ($3.50).

We'd heard good things about Clementine's, and we have to admit that while there may not be a lot of originality here, what they do gets done in quite a competent way—a good onion soup for example ($1.95) and a mountain of good commercial tortilla chips dotted with tomatoes and green onions, smothered in acceptable cheddar, and surmounted by a dollop of passable guacamole (the sour cream was the consistency of cream cheese). Nothing to write home about, to be sure, but a good product at a good price. The $2.98 nachos plate would have easily made a happy lunch for two.

HOURS Mon.–Thurs. 11 am–11 pm; Fri. & Sat. 11 am–midnight; Sun. noon–11 pm.

SPECS 418 Phoenix St.; (616) 637-9029; no cards; full bar.

DIRECTIONS From Exit 20 turn right if southbound and left if northbound. Go 1.1 miles on Phoenix St. to the center of town. It's on the left.

THE GOLDEN BROWN BAKERY, *Exit 20, South Haven*

A big, downhome, almost all-American bakery, where the sweet rolls and cookies were only so-so and the Greek pastries were better. Off to one side is a cafeteria that leads to a carpeted and newly beamed dining area.

There was great greasy corned beef hash to accompany our two eggs and toast ($1.50). The malt used in the pancakes and waffles gives them a hearty flavor that seems to make lightness irrevelant.

The lunch menu offers oliveburgers and pastrami sandwiches at $1.79, salmon patties and chicken pot pie in the vicinity of $2.75.

A window on life.

HOURS   Mon.–Sat. 6 am–4:30 pm. Closed Sun. & major holidays.

SPECS   421 Phoenix St.; (616) 637-3418; no cards; no liquor.

DIRECTIONS   Same as for **Clementine's,** above. **Bakery** is right across the street.

THE AUCTION HOUSE RESTAURANT,
Exits 36 & 41, Douglas

Drive 3 blocks from the old highway through Douglas and find good, cheap home cooking where the locals do—in a building that really is old but ends up with the look of a Johnny-come-lately trying to affect the dignity of age. Nothing all that pretentious, however. The net result is just a friendly local restaurant that tries to do simple things and succeeds.

Our ¼-pound hamburger was excellent and set us back a mere $1.50. The homemade vegetable soup was rich, dark, deep, chunky, and delicious (only $1.95 with a sandwich, 75 cents for a cup by itself.) Reubens, clubs, Italian beef, and stuffed croissants run $3.50–$4, but back on the cheap side are dinners from $3.95 (fried chicken) to $6.75 (deep-fried, beer-battered lake perch). A few basic Chinese and Mexican dishes, too ($2.25–$4.50).

The homemade custard pie (95 cents) was delicately seasoned and not too sweet, though the crust was a bit undercooked. If that bothers you, have your principal meal here and go to **Ruthie's Rainbow of Flavors** for an ice cream dessert (see below).

HOURS Sun.–Thurs. 5:30 am–9 pm; Fri. & Sat. 5:30 am–9:30 pm. Closed Christmas.

SPECS 8 Center St.; (616) 857-4292; no cards; no liquor.

DIRECTIONS **Northbound:** From Exit 36 turn right onto Blue Star Highway and go 1.9 miles to a right turn just before the bridge (Main St.). Go 3 blocks on Main to Center. It's on the corner, on the right.

Southbound: From Exit 41 turn right and go 3.2 miles on Blue Star Highway to Main St. just over the bridge. Turn left on Main and go 3 blocks to Center. It's on the corner on the right.

RUTHIE'S RAINBOW OF FLAVORS,
Exits 36 and 41, Douglas

We found a tasty, pleasant, and happy little ice cream parlor with excellent homemade stuff. The ancient ice cream machine churns it out with 16 percent butterfat (which is high), and the product is sure to give you what you need on a hot summer day. A few sandwiches, too—barbecues and Sloppy Joes for about $2.50.

HOURS May–Oct. only: Tues.–Sun. noon–11 pm. Closed Mon.

SPECS 161 Blue Star Highway; (616) 857-2983; no cards; no liquor.

DIRECTIONS **Northbound:** From Exit 36 turn right and go 1.8 miles on Blue Star Highway. It's on the right, just before the bridge.

Southbound: From Exit 41 turn right onto Blue Star Highway and go 3.3 miles across the bridge to **Ruthie's** on the left.

BILLIE'S BOAT HOUSE, *Exits 36 and 41, Saugatuck*

The Kalamazoo River reaches Lake Michigan at Saugatuck, and just by its landscaped shore stands Billie's Boat House. The neighborhood is boutiquey-resorty, and the restaurant is predictably nautical, but neither is overdone. In fact, both are quite pleasant and comfortably understated.

Needless to say, seafood is the specialty. Our walleye pike ($8.50) was broiled so as to leave it firm but tender, and the tartar sauce was not so potent as to overpower the fish's delicate flavor. It was but one of 9 fish dishes that top out at $9.95. The 12 Mexican dishes ($3.25–$5.50) caught our interest, especially since 3 of them were burritos, and the wet burrito ($4.95) is rapidly replacing pizza as the favorite fast food of this part of the world. Perversely, however, we asked for the chimichanga, which arrived good, but not exceptional, marred by gummy "sour cream." Back on the positive side was the cream of mushroom soup—thick but very tasty.

Billie's has a dozen meat dishes to offer ($4.50–$12.95) and 9 salads, including crab, Cobb, steak, Greek, and Mexican ($4.75–$6.25). That's as much variety in this department as we've seen in the Midwest. Sandwiches are $3.25–$6, and you can end your visit with a slice of grasshopper or key lime pie ($1.50).

Not super, but certainly acceptable.

HOURS Summer: Mon.–Thurs. 11:30 am–10:30 pm, Fri.–Sun. 11:30 am–11:30 pm. Winter: Closed at 9 pm and all of Jan. & Feb.

SPECS 449 Water St.; (616) 857-1188; V, MC; full bar.

DIRECTIONS **Northbound:** From Exit 36 turn right onto Blue Star Highway and go 2.2 miles over the bridge to Culver. Turn left onto Culver and go to the end of the street. Then turn right onto Water St., go 3 blocks, and it's on the right.

Southbound: From Exit 41 go 2.9 miles to Culver. Turn right onto Culver and go to the end of the street. Then turn right onto Water St., go 3 blocks, and it's on the right.

LITTLE MEXICO CAFÉ, *Exit 76, Grand Rapids*

The long and short of it is this: superb beans and rice plus good to very good main dishes in an atmosphere guaranteed to give you something to talk about while you wait for your food.

We had just tried a wet burrito in nearby Rockford, so even though the Little Mexico claims to be the home of this Michigan specialty, we wanted to try something less commonly available —a very good vegetarian burrito, for example, that for $3.95 surrounds an avocado stuffing with a good flour tortilla, covers it with green peppers, onions, and celery, douses it in tomato sauce, and then tops the whole works with a layer of melted cheese.

The pork in red chili sauce was good, but not exceptional. At $5.60 it was nearly the most expensive item on the ample menu, but we would not have cared what it cost so long as it came with its accompaniments of rice and beans. As sometimes happens in Mexican restaurants, these humble dishes are so good, so deeply flavored with the good things that lie about in a Mexican kitchen, that we'd have been perfectly happy to sup on them and a bottle of Dos Equis.

You *will* enjoy the food at Little Mexico—we've little doubt of that. Be warned however that as soon as you enter the door you'll find yourself in a long passageway that looks like the entrance to a cave. Follow it a bit and you arrive in a series of rooms that carry out the cave decor by applying stucco so as to hide as many right angles and straight lines as possible. Aztec sculptures (also stucco) and jungle greenery abound. The chairs are made of huge thick chunks of wood as if they were the Tinkertoys of some primitive, Mesoamerican giant.

The pièce de résistance, however, has got to be the wall that explodes in a wildly expressive burst of color to depict an Aztec warrior nearly nude but for a headdress of flowing feathers, offering a bowl of fruit to a god who seems to be either the sun or the eagle who flies above pondering the terrestrial scene.

We were put off at first, but the more we looked, the more we liked. In the end we decided it deserved a place in the restaurant mural hall of fame.

HOURS   Mon.–Thurs. 11 am–2 am; Fri. & Sat. 11 am–2:45 am; Sun. noon–1 am. Closed major holidays.

SPECS   401 Stocking (corner of Stocking & Bridge); (616) 774-8822; major cards; full bar.

DIRECTIONS   **Eastbound:** Take Exit 76 for Lane Ave. At the end of the ramp turn left onto Lane. ■ Go 1 block to the light at Bridge. Turn left onto Bridge and go 0.3 mile to the first light. It's on the left, corner of Bridge and Stocking.

Westbound: Take Exit 76 for Lane Ave. Go 1 block to the stop sign at Lane and turn right onto Lane. Then as above from ■.

SCHNITZELBANK, *Exit 77B, Grand Rapids*

This is the kind of AAA- and Mobil-rated place that we usually skip right by, but we'd heard tales of its prowess before we even left home, so we had to stop.

It *is* a Bavarian wonderland, all right, with all the Prussic bric-a-brac you'd expect, but we did find a few items we hadn't seen in every other Germanic restaurant, particularly the carved wooden statuettes riding all the light fixtures.

Our meal had a questionable start, with day-old pumpernickel and a thrown-together salad, but from there it soared. The tangy hot German potato salad was worth the extra 35 cents charged (though you'd think a place like this could afford to provide it gratis). Wiener schnitzel was excellent, ½ inch thick, lightly breaded, and meltingly tender. If you can catch it as a daily special (every Saturday, and other days less predictably), you'll get a drink and dessert thrown in for the à la carte price of $7.50. Otherwise, most complete dinners run $9–$12; lunch specials like beef roulade or breaded lemon sole are $4.50–$5.75.

HOURS   Mon.–Sat. 11:30 am–8 pm. Closed Sun.

SPECS   342 Jefferson SE (at Wealthy); (616) 459-9527; major cards; full bar.

DIRECTIONS   Exit 77B of I-196 puts you on US 131 South. Go about 1 mile to the Wealthy St. Exit. Turn left, and in ½ mile, at Jefferson, look left and you'll see it.

LITTLE MEXICO CAFÉ, *Exit 85B, Grand Rapids*

See pp. 265–267 for a description of a quite good Mexican restaurant with a decor you won't soon forget.

DIRECTIONS **Southbound:** Take Exit 85B for Pearl St. and turn right at the light at Pearl. ■ Go 4 blocks (around the curve) to Lexington. Turn right and go 5 blocks to Bridge St. It's on the corner, on the left.

Northbound: Take Exit 85B for Pearl St. and turn left at the light at the end of the ramp. Then as above from ■.

VITALE'S PIZZA, *Exit 97, Rockford*

Squire Street is the site of an old mill that has been reconstructed and made the focal point for a number of arty shops and restaurants. Ever in search of a quick meal at bargain prices, we were attracted to Vitale's Pizzeria at the end of the block, partly because of the fine old house that lodges it, and partly because it also advertises Mexican food, submarine sandwiches, a deli operation, and simple pasta dinners. It's cheap, it's fast, and you can get it all to go. If only the food is good, we figured, it would be a perfect highway stop.

We declined to sample the pizza even though the pizza business seems to be the bedrock on which Vitale's was built. And certainly the pizza aroma was good enough to warrant further investigation. But we had heard that the wet burrito rules supreme in this part of Michigan, and this was our first chance to see what the fuss was all about.

Thankfully we ordered only the junior burrito. At $2.50 this enormous flour tortilla stuffed with taco fixings and smothered in a spicy bean sauce would have easily made lunch for two. And it *was* good—good enough in fact to have us gulping down nearly the whole thing when we certainly knew better. If the pizza is half as good, this has got to be one of the best fun-food joints within 100 miles.

In any case, we hope that when the wet burrito fad hits New England, the bean sauce will be imported from Vitale's. Baklava and kosher deli available here too.

HOURS   Mon.–Fri. 11 am–midnight; Sat. 11 am–3 am; Sun. noon– 1 am.

SPECS   Squire & Bridge Sts.; (616) 866-4467; no cards; no liquor.

DIRECTIONS   From Exit 97 turn left if southbound and right if northbound. Go 2.4 miles on Ten Mile Rd. Turn left onto Main St. and go 2 blocks to Bridge St. Turn left onto Bridge, go ½ block, and it's on the left.

THE RED FLANNEL CAFÉ, *Exit 104, Cedar Springs*

* Untried but likely.

We weren't able to check out the Red Flannel Café, but thought you might want to take a chance on a cute little village restaurant with a pink-and-green tile façade and an elongated octagonal window full of rummage-sale teapots. The real attraction, however, is the town, which seems to be the red flannel capital of the world. Presumably some enormously large percentage of the country's red flannel is made here. Why else would almost every store in town have something to do with the stuff, and why else would there be hanging from every lamppost a sign depicting a pair of scarlet long johns waving in the breeze?

This lighthearted spirit seems to have infected just about all of Cedar Springs. Even the radiator repair shop across the street can't resist making jokes. It advertises itself as "a great place to take a leak."

HOURS Mon.–Wed. 5:30 am–7 pm; Thurs. 5:30 am–6 pm; Fri. & Sat. 7 am–3 pm; Sun. 8 am–12:30 pm.

SPECS Main St.; no cards; no liquor.

DIRECTIONS From Exit 104 go east on Route 44 1.3 miles to the light at Main St. Turn left onto Main and go 2 blocks. It's on the left.

THE SHAKER GOOD ROOM,
Spring Lake Exit, Spring Lake

The Shakers were not big on pleasure, what with their vows of celibacy and their insistence on purely functional design. It was a bit of a challenge therefore to guess what a Shaker restaurant would be like. How do you apply the lean principles of functionalist design to cooking? Would Shaker vegetable soup somehow taste the way Shaker furniture looks?

The Good Room really does have the Shaker look, relieved here and there by some candles or dried flowers set out as a bit of un-Shakerly decoration, and by the waitress's flouncy Colonial costumes. So far as the cooking goes, we can tell you only that Shaker vegetable soup, even made with a few canned vegetables, tastes very good, not a deep, rich abundant flavor, but good solid country cooking made from real beef stock. The same general description would apply to all that we tasted here, though we have to note that everything was done just a little bit differently from the usual—parsleyed, buttered new potatoes, for example, instead of the usual baked or fried, and a basket of delicious sweet breads instead of the usual dinner rolls. The smothered chicken was more solid than exciting—three strips of breaded and fried breast meat thoroughly doused with a heavy country gravy. The salad bar was good, studded with pleasant surprises like sweet-and-sour carrots and terrific tarragon and honey-seed dressings.

Prices are reasonable, especially at lunchtime. Soup is $1.10 a bowl; sandwiches are $1.60–$2.60 (half sandwiches for about $1.25); potato slices instead of fries are 75 cents; the bread basket is also 75 cents; and you can work your way through the salad bar for $2.95. Dinners are mostly $6–$8.

Since we later found out that the recipes used here are not true Shaker recipes (though they *are* culled from 19th-century farm journals and cookbooks), our question about functionalist culinary aesthetics was never settled. No matter—you needn't understand it to enjoy it, and everything we tried was good or better.

HOURS   Mon. 11 am–3 pm; Tues.–Sat. 11 am–8 pm; Sun. 9 am–3 pm. Closed major holidays.

SPECS   406 Savidge; (616) 846-4282; no cards (checks okay); no liquor; children's menu.

DIRECTIONS   Southbound: Take the Spring Lake Exit. Turn left at the end of the ramp and go 2 blocks to the stop sign. Follow signs for Spring Lake and Route 104. Go 1 mile, and it's on the right.

Northbound: Take Spring Lake/Route 104 Exit. After crossing the bridge continue 0.8 mile. It's on the right.

CONNIE & DOC'S BARBECUE, *North Muskegon Exit*

We are only partial subscribers to the theory that equates good barbecue with "authentic"-looking barbecue shacks. It is possible to get very good barbecue in fairly dressy restaurants, so you don't really have to go slumming to find excellence. All the same, we've never gotten bad barbecue from a truly shacky-looking barbecue joint, and only once was it less than pretty good.

For these reasons we recommend that the adventurous among you check out Connie & Doc's, as authentic a concrete box of a barbecue shack as there can be, but which, alas, was closed on Sunday.

HOURS   Mon.–Fri. 10 am–7 pm; Sat. 11 am–3 pm. Closed Sun.

SPECS   (616) 728-9403.

DIRECTIONS   From the North Muskegon Exit drive in an enormous loop for 1.3 miles to the first light. Turn left and go 1 block to the access road. Turn right and go 1 block. The shack is on the left.

PEKADILL'S, *Whitehall Exit*

We stumbled onto this lovely and good-tasting ice cream parlor and sandwich shop just 2 easy miles from the road. Katherine and Pete Wessel found themselves in Whitehall from Colorado one day, liked it, and in an effort to figure out how to make a living, bought a dilapidated but charming old building and decided to make it into as spiffy a little eatery as could be found south of Petosky and north of Chicago.

And that it is. All the ice cream is made right here. It's very good, and it comes in a vast variety of forms: Try it in regular cones for 62 cents or in voluminous homemade cones for $1.01; try it in a turtle sundae for $2.79—vanilla ice cream with hot fudge and caramel, sprinkled with pecans and topped by whipped cream and a candy turtle; or try super sundaes ($3.94), puffs, parfaits, malts, sodas, or shakes (including Oreo shakes and Reese's).

There are almost as many ways to get a sandwich at Pekadill's as there are variations on the ice cream theme. Suffice it to say that whole, regular, deli-style sandwiches are $3.17–$3.94, and half-sized versions are $1.68–$2.07. Melts and specialty sandwiches are in the $4–$5 range, with croissants at $3–$4. All come in white, whole-wheat, French, rye, or onion roll, with tortilla and carrot slivers instead of potato chips and a pickle. The meats and cheeses were quite good, and as a whole our sandwich was a winner, even though the white bread was disappointingly soft. Better than usual salads ($1–$3.50), soups, and chili, too.

Even if it weren't great looking, Pekadill's would make a super lunch stop. But a lot of thought went into designing the four separate eating areas this little place offers—a bright, cheerful ice cream parlor out front; a warm, woody, planty, slightly olde-timey room out back (with Franklin stove), and a front porch with a view of Lake Michigan. But what really won our hearts was the wonder of miniaturized landscaping out behind the building. There stone paths wend their brief way between trees and pools. You sit beneath an umbrella-shaded outdoor table and marvel on how relaxed you suddenly feel. You might even believe you've arrived at your vacation instead of hustling to get there.

HOURS   Daily 11:30 am–11 pm. Closed earlier in winter & for major holidays.

SPECS   503 S. Mears Ave.; (616) 894-9551; no cards; no liquor.

DIRECTIONS   Northbound turn left and southbound right at the exit for Whitehall. Go 1.7 miles to the first light in Whitehall (Mears Ave.). Turn left on Mears, go 5 blocks, and it's on the left.

GIBBS' COUNTRY HOUSE, *Ludington Exit*

From Saugatuck northward just about everyone we talked to said that Gibbs' was *the* place for downhome cooking in Ludington. Naturally we expected a homey little in-town restaurant and were shocked to find a huge semiplastic, semiposh, out-on-the-highway place with fancy chandeliers and flocked wallpapers.

Such, we suppose, is the price of success, even when the place has been in the family for some 30 years. People do love it, flocked wallpaper or not.

When the waitress offered us sticky buns, we weren't at all sure we wanted to try them, but the people at the next table enthusiastically urged us on. And good sticky buns they turned out to be—light and not too sticky.

When we took a look at the enormous salad bar, we began to see what Gibbs' was all about. To mention only some of the more unusual items, consider an array of two soups, sunflower seeds, pickled watermelon rinds, blue cheese, canapé sandwiches (ham, tuna, liver, and peanut butter), tabbouli, peas, peanuts, pears, peaches, pasta salad, Jell-O salad, and marshmallows. For just $3.95 you get access to all this, plus another bar of desserts. Even the beverage is included!

We tried the meat-loaf luncheon, however—$5.50 with soup, salad bar, potato, buns, and dessert. The meat loaf turned out to be better than the soup, but not as good as the excellent hash browns. Lots of other lunchtime possibilities at modest prices ($1.75 for a hamburger). Absolutely full dinners are mostly $7–$10 unless you go after steaks and lobsters.

We can't honestly say that we found the food superb or the atmosphere charming, but everything was okay at the least and we doubt you'll do much better hereabouts.

HOURS June–August: Mon.–Sat. 11:30 am–10 pm; Sun. noon–10 pm. Sept.–Dec., April & May: Mon.–Sat. 11:30 am–9 pm; Sun. noon–8 pm. Closed Christmas & Jan.–March.

SPECS 3951 W. US 10; (616) 845-5086; V, MC, AE; full bar.

DIRECTIONS Take the Ludington Exit and turn right onto US 10 at the red flasher. Go 1.8 miles, and it's on the right.

ORGIE'S, *Ludington Exit*

We would have wanted to check out Mr. and Mrs. Organ's restaurant for its name alone, but the six-tone neon rooster in the window clinched our decision to enter. Besides, we wanted an in-town selection for Ludington, a very pleasant-looking town that somehow seemed to typify life in northern Michigan. The genuine tin ceiling was encouraging, and the huge, faded murals were from the days when color photography was a novelty.

Other than these points of interest, we found nothing special to report about Orgie's. But for the lighter-than-usual pancakes, everything was perfectly ordinary, and with it we were entirely content.

Dinners are $3.95–$5.95.

HOURS Summer: Daily 6 am–9 pm, more or less. Winter: Mon.–Thurs. 8 am–8 pm, Fri.–Sun. 5 am–9 pm.

SPECS 118 W. Ludington Ave.; (616) 843-8790; V, MC, AE; no liquor.

DIRECTIONS From the Ludington Exit turn left at the flashing light onto US 10 and go 1.6 miles to town. It's on the right, just past James St. No traffic.

PRINCE, *Touhy Avenue/Golf Road Exits, Des Plaines*

You wouldn't expect really fine Chinese food in a frowsy airport motel, but that's exactly what we found at Prince in the O'Hare-American Inn. Prices aren't bad, and for northbound traffic the restaurant is only 20 seconds from the tollway.

If the Mandarin and Szechuan specialties are even half as good as the hot and sour soup, there's no chance you'll leave unhappy. The garlic chicken was almost as good as the soup, its lack of subtlety more than compensated for by the delicate flavors that found their way into the fried rice; good egg roll, too, made better by superb duck sauce. Everything came in enormous quantities—for $6.50 you can't do better. Prices on the ample menu run from fried rice at $5 to crispy duck at $10, and there's lots to choose from at the low end.

Someone should do a study of Chinese restaurant interiors so that we'd know how to classify a chartreuse-and-plum color scheme and furnishings that are neither bare nor overdone—carpeting and bare tables, a pleasing absence of kitsch. We can complain only about the slightly stale smell that seemed to drift in from the motel. Other than that, Prince is an excellent choice in all respects.

HOURS Mon.–Fri. 11:30 am–10 pm; Sat. 4–11 pm. Closed Sun.

SPECS 2175 Touhy Ave.; (312) 296-9089; major cards; full bar.

DIRECTIONS **Northbound:** Just west of the Touhy Ave. Exit in the O'Hare-American Inn.

Southbound: A schlepp. Exit at Golf Rd. (also called East River Rd. Exit). Turn left at the stop sign, go 1 block, and then turn right at the light onto Golf Rd. (Route 58). Go 0.7 mile to Des Plaines Rd. and turn left. Go 3.2 miles to Touhy. It's on the corner, on the left, in the O'Hare-American Inn.

ROLLIE'S, *Touhy Avenue/Golf Road Exits, Des Plaines*

We had a good, sweetly spiced Italian beef sandwich ($2.15) and excellent Italian ices at this purely Chicago fast-food eatery. It's plain, pleasant, and clean inside. You can get tacos, gyros, Vienna hot dogs, and a good assortment of other quick, cheap eats.

HOURS Mon.–Fri. 6:30 am–8 pm; Sat. 10:30 am–7 pm. Closed Sun.

SPECS 1900 E. Touhy Ave.; (312) 297-7371; no cards; no liquor.

DIRECTIONS **Northbound:** Take the exit for Touhy Ave. and go 4 blocks west at Touhy. It's on the right.

Southbound: A schlepp. Follow southbound directions for **Prince** above. Turn right when you get to Touhy Ave. and go 4 blocks. It's on the right.

PARKWAY VILLAGE INN, *Dixon Exit*

Dixon's current claim to fame is not the neon arch that stretches across Main Street or the wonderful county courthouse with its stubby, bronze dome. It is the fact that Ronald Reagan passed his boyhood here, as you can learn from any number of signs in and around the village.

Dixon will never be famous for its restaurants, but we can report to you that at the Parkway Village Inn, the exterior of which is plasti-stone topped by a sheet-metal mansard roof painted Day-Glo orange, we had a very, very good baked chicken dinner. The chicken was moist and distinctively seasoned, and the rice that came with it was just as good—flecked with pimentos and mushrooms, cooked in a tasty stock, and flavored with pan drippings. The soup, salad, and mashed potatoes, let it be said, were more in line with what you'd expect from the looks of the place, but we are not complaining, especially when we got all this for $4.50 and had a great time chatting with the waitress.

We liked it, and we've no doubt that someone back in that kitchen is really trying. If you go for it, be prepared to put up with red-and-black plastic decor highlighted by cheap wall paneling—looks that are even a bit less pleasant than average for this kind of humble local eatery.

HOURS Sun. & Mon. 6 am–11 pm; Tues.–Thurs. 8 am–2 am; Fri. & Sat. 24 hours.

SPECS 604 Chicago Ave.; (815) 288-1751; no cards; no liquor.

DIRECTIONS From the Dixon Exit (Route 26) head north to Dixon for 1.3 miles to the stop sign at Route 38. Turn right onto Route 38 and go 0.3 mile to the fork. Bear right at the fork. You'll see the inn almost immediately on your right.

THELMA'S DINETTE, *Dixon Exit*

It was too late at night to find out what it was all about, but cluttered, pleasant, and clean little Thelma's Dinette in the middle of town had a sign in the window offering Philippine food for sale. We could detect only 4 items on the menu—empanadas for 60 cents, rice muffins for 50 cents, a pizzaburger at $1.35, and "slopao" for 65 cents.

We guarantee nothing.

HOURS   Mon.–Fri. 6 am–4 pm; Sat. 7 am–4 pm. Closed Sun.

SPECS   105 Galena Ave.

DIRECTIONS   From the Dixon Exit (Route 26) head north to Dixon for 1.7 miles. **Thelma's** is just past the arch over Main St., on the left.

HUB CITY FAMILY RESTAURANT,
Route 251 Exit, Rochelle

Though it's forbidding on the outside, the interior of this friendly local diner is clean and new. There are no surprises on the menu except for an oliveburger and a side dish of sautéed mushrooms. The flavors, too, are about what you'd expect.

The Hub City's greatest virtue, so far as we could tell, was the local people who sat at the counter in May and talked about what to do if stuck out on the prairie in a snowstorm. Answer: Keep three overcoats in the trunk.

The menu is complete and prices are very reasonable.

HOURS   Mon.–Sat. 5 am–8 pm; Sun. 6 am–7 pm.

SPECS   513 Fourth Ave.; (815) 562-6663; no cards; no liquor.

DIRECTIONS   Take the exit for US 51/Route 251/Rochelle. Eastbound turn left and westbound right onto Route 251 toward Rochelle.

Go 1.6 miles to the first right turn after the bridge. Take the right and go 2 blocks. It's on the left.

THE HILLSIDE RESTAURANT, *DeKalb Exits*

The Hillside is the best restaurant we were able to turn up along the East-West Tollway between Chicago and Moline. Not only was our steak done right, the potato moist, and the salad dressing good, The Hillside is a very pleasant place to pass an hour—sort of knotty-pine-woody with little touches of unpretentious formality. The result is cozy, homey, and inviting.

The menu is all solid American stuff, $6.75–$10.75 at dinnertime, with plain and fancy sandwiches at lunchtime between $3 and $4. There are pasta, spinach, and chef's salads at $4–$4.75.

Northern Illinois State University is in DeKalb. We imagine that its students get taken here regularly by visiting parents and suspect it is the presence of those students (and faculty) who are responsible for so nice a restaurant in so small a town.

HOURS   Sun.–Thurs. 11 am–9 pm; Fri. & Sat. 11 am–10 pm.

SPECS   121 N. 2nd St.; (815) 756-4749; no cards; beer & wine.

DIRECTIONS   Eastbound: Take the exit for Annie Glidden Rd. Go straight from the toolbooth to Lincoln Highway. Turn right onto Lincoln Highway and go 1 mile to 2nd St. Park. It's ½ block to the left.

Westbound: Take the exit for DeKalb East Rd. Turn right at the end of the ramp and go 1.4 miles to a stop sign. Turn left and go 1 mile to 2nd St. in the center of town. Park. It's ½ block to the right, on 2nd.

THE DELI AND SANDWICH SHOP,
IL 31 Exit, North Aurora

Here is the perfect quick stop—as fast and as convenient as McDonald's, but as good as a good big-city deli. The menu reads like a balanced ticket in Chicago ward politics: There's a Krakus Polish ham sandwich ($1.85), Jewish pastrami ($1.95), and Italian beef ($2.25), plus hot dogs and turkey sandwiches. All of it is

281

made with the best brands for the nationality in question, and all of it is served with chips or salad and a good kosher pickle on crusty white bread or good hearty rye.

They make their own fruit pies here, and also their own three-bean, potato, and macaroni salads. Service is in clear plastic cups, and you sit at one of eight tiny tables in an environment that is pleasingly barren of all decor.

HOURS   Mon.–Fri. 10 am–9 pm; Sat. 10 am–6 pm; Sun. 11 am–5 pm.

SPECS   215 S. Lincolnway (IL 31); (312) 896-6011; no cards; no liquor.

DIRECTIONS   Immediately north of the exit for IL 31, on the right.

INDEX OF RESTAURANTS
AND TOWNS

[When a restaurant carries two separate page references, the first is the description and the second gives driving directions.]

Index

Index

Our best source of leads to worthwhile restaurants is you, the traveler who cares. Please tell us of any you know that lie close to the road, and we'll check them out for future editions in THE INTERSTATE GOURMET series.

Send your suggestions to:

Summit Books
Code ISG
1230 Avenue of the Americas
New York, NY 10020

Restaurant name_____

Near Highway_____

Exit_____

City_____ State_____

Directions_____

_____

_____

_____

Comments_____

_____

_____

_____

_____

_____